Joseph Thekedathu, THE TROUBLED L   ɔ. ʀANCIS
GARCIA S.J. ARCHBISHOP OF CRANGANORE (1641-59)

Analecta Gregoriana

Cura Pontificiae Universitatis Gregorianae edita

Vol. 187. Series Facultatis Historiae Ecclesiasticae: Sectio B, n. 31

JOSEPH THEKEDATHU S. D. B.

THE TROUBLED DAYS
OF FRANCIS GARCIA S. J.
ARCHBISHOP OF CRANGANORE
(1641 - 59)

UNIVERSITÀ GREGORIANA EDITRICE

ROMA 1972

Francis Garcia S. J.
Archbishop of Cranganore (1641 - 59)

[From a painting kept in the former Jesuit Academy, Paderborn]

JOSEPH THEKEDATHU, S. D. B.

THE TROUBLED DAYS
OF FRANCIS GARCIA S. J.
ARCHBISHOP OF CRANGANORE
(1641 – 59)

Università Gregoriana Editrice

ROMA 1972

Quest'opera di Joseph Thekedathu, *The Troubled Days of Francis Garcia S. J. Archbishop of Cranganore (1641-59)*, è stata pubblicata con l'approvazione ecclesiastica (Vicariato di Roma, 25 maggio 1972) dalla UNIVERSITÀ GREGORIANA EDITRICE, Roma 1972, e stampata dalla TIPOGRAFIA DELLA PONTIFICIA UNIVERSITÀ GREGORIANA

FOREWORD

When the present subject was first proposed to me as a possible theme for a thesis, I was quite unwilling to take it up because of its controversial character. I was by no means eager to gain the ill will of one or the other of the contending parties or, as I feared, of both! What finally induced me to accept it, was the realization that I should be able to give an impartial view, since I do not belong to either of the two great religious families involved in the dispute. It is true that I come from one of the Syrian Christian families of Kerala. But for nearly thirty years I have been away from that region and have been engaged in studying or teaching in other parts of India and in Europe. Hence I believe that while on the one hand I am interested in the history of the St. Thomas Christians, I can also look at things with sufficient detachment and dispassionateness.

This work was originally conceived as something that would complete and, where necessary, correct the picture given by Karl Werth P.S.M. in his "Das Schisma der Thomaschristen unter Erzbischof Franciscus Garzia". Werth had used the documents of the Propaganda Archives only. It was obvious that judgements would become more balanced if the Jesuit Archives which contained another version of the same story, were consulted. In point of fact, however, this work has gone beyond my original intention. As the research in the various archives went ahead, a more satisfactory vision of the whole story emerged.

I wish to place on record my special indebtedness to Fr. Joseph Wicki S.J., the director of this thesis. He has been for me much more than a mere director. Every time that I wanted a favour from him, he was there most willing to oblige. My thanks are due also to Fr. Edmund Lamalle S.J. and Fr. Joseph Metzler O.M.I., the archivists respectively of the Roman Archives of the Jesuits and of the Propaganda Archives, for all the facilities given to me. Another person *to whom I have to be grateful, is Fr. Placid Podipara C.M.I. He was very helpful in clearing up for me a few points of the history of the Church in Malabar. I would like to say a word of thanks also to Fr. Faustino Bufalini O.C.D. who kindly lent me a copy of his unpublished thesis on Sebastiani. Finally I wish to express my sincere gratitude to my superiors who, at the cost of considerable sacrifice, gave me sufficient time to prepare this work.*

Joseph Thekedathu S.D.B.

Rome, 3 July 1970

CONTENTS

ABBREVIATIONS

Acta	—	Acta Sacrae Congregationis pro Gentium Evangelizatione seu de Propaganda Fide.
AHEI	—	Arquivo Histórico do Estado da India (Goa) — The Historical Archives of Goa.
Ajuda	—	Biblioteca da Ajuda.
APF	—	Archivum S. Congregationis pro Gentium Evangelizatione seu de Propaganda Fide (Roma).
ARSI	—	Archivum Romanum Societatis Iesu.
ASV	—	Archivum Secretum Vaticanum.
BNL	—	Biblioteca Nacional, Lisboa.
f., ff.	—	folio, folios.
l. c.	—	loco citato.
LM	—	Livro das Monções.
r	—	recto (right-hand page).
SOCG	—	Scritture originali riferite nelle Congregazioni Generali.
sq.	—	sequentes, sequentia.
v	—	verso (left-hand page).

SOURCES

A. MANUSCRIPT SOURCES IN VARIOUS ARCHIVES

Archivum Romanum Societatis Jesu.
   Goa — vols. 9, 18, 21, 24-II, 25, 27, 28, 29, 34, 47, 49, 50, 53, 56, 68-I,
      68-II.
      N.B. The whole of vol. 68-I and 68-II consists of docu-
      ments and papers pertaining to our subject. So is the
      greater part of vol. 50 and a large part of vol. 49.

*Archivum S. Congregationis de Propaganda Fide (= Pro Gentium
Evangelizatione) (Roma).*
   Acta — (Acta Sacrae Congregationis) vols. 8, 10, 12, 13, 15, 16, 17,
      24, 26.
   SOCG — (Scritture originali riferite nelle Congregazioni Generali)
      vols. 59, 65, 107, 109, 120, 122, 128, 191, 194, 197, 212, 230, 231,
      232, 233, 234, 237, 393.
      N.B. Vols. 232, 233 and 234 deal exclusively with our
      subject. The same is the case with a large part of vol. 191.

Archivum Secretum Vaticanum
   Secr. Brevium, vols. 1359, 1362.
      A number of briefs pertaining to our subject and contained
      in these two volumes have already been published in "Juris
      Pontificii de Propaganda Fide" and in "Bullarium Patronatus
      Portugalliae Regum". Some are, however, still unpublished.

Arquivo Histórico do Estado da India (= Historical Archives of Goa).
   Livro das Monções vols. 23-A, 23-B, 24, 25, 26-B.

Biblioteca da Ajuda 50 - V - 38: a letter of Garcia to the Inquisitors.
   (ff. 240-244).

Biblioteca Nacional, Lisboa.
   Fundo Geral — vol. 34: a note-book containing some jottings on
      Garcia written by Fr. De Magistris S.J. (It has been edited
      by WICKI as an appendix to *O Homem.*).
      vol. 464: Vida do Ill.mo D. Francisco Garcia, arcebispo de
      Cranganor, por Francisco Teixeira.
      This manuscript volume of 117 folios can hardly be called
      a life of Garcia. It is rather an undigested collection of
      various accounts and documents. Much of it is an open

panegyric and apology of Garcia and of the Jesuit missionaries, and an attack on the work of the Carmelites. The author himself tells us (cf. fol. 2) that he was closely bound to Garcia by ties of gratitude. The volume begins with a letter of the author to the city of Cochin, dated 20 December 1659. Apart from some information regarding the work of Garcia as Acting Captain of Cochin in 1658-59, the "vida" contains nothing of importance that is not to be found in the Roman Archives of the Society of Jesus.

B. Printed Sources

BARRETO, FRANCESCO, S.J., *Relatione delle Missioni e Cristianità che appartengono alla Provincia del Malavar della Compagnia di Giesu.* Roma 1645.

Bullarium Patronatus Portugalliae Regum in Ecclesiis Africae, Asiae atque Oceaniae Bullas, Brevia, Epistolas, Decreta, Actaque Sanctae Sedis ab Alexandro III ad hoc usque tempus amplectens. Tomus II (1601-1700). Ed. Paiva Manso. Olisipone 1870.

Juris Pontificii de Propaganda Fide Pars prima complectens Bullas, Brevia, Acta S.S. a Congregationis institutione ad praesens iuxta temporis seriem disposita, Auspice Eminentissimo ac Reverendissimo Domino S.R.E. Cardinali Joanne Simeoni, S.C. d. Propaganda Fide Praefecto, cura ac studio Raphaëlis de Martinis, ejusdem Congreg. Consult. et Missionis Sacerdotis etc. Vol. I Romae 1888; Vol. VII Romae 1897.

PHILIPPUS A SS. TRINITATE, O.C.D., *Itinerarium Orientale.* Lugduni 1649.

PISSURLENCAR, PANDURONGA S. S., *Assentos do Conselho do Estado.* Vol. III (1644-1658). Bastorá (Goa) 1955.

SEBASTIANI, GIUSEPPE DI SANTA MARIA, *Breve racconto della vita, missioni e morte gloriosa del Ven. P.M.F. Francesco Donati Romano dell'Ordine de' Predicatori.* Roma 1669.

——, *Prima Speditione all'Indie Orientali del P.F. Giuseppe di Santa Maria, Carmelitano Scalzo, Delegato Apostolico ne' Regni de' Malavari, ordinata da nostro Signore Alessandro Settimo.* Roma 1666.

——, *Seconda Speditione all'Indie Orientali.* Roma 1672.

VINCENZO MARIA DI S. CATERINA DA SIENA, O.C.D., *Il Viaggio all'Indie Orientali.* Venetia 1678.

WICKI, JOSEPH, S.J., *O Homem das trinta e duas Perfeições e outras Histórias.* (Escritos da Literatura Indiana, traduzidos por Dom Francisco Garcia S.J., publicados e anotados por José Wicki S.J.). Lisboa 1958. (The documents that interest us are found in the two appendices).

BIBLIOGRAPHY

A. Monographs or Articles that deal mainly with the Period under Study

Ambrosius a S. Teresia, O.C.D., *Hierarchia Carmelitana seu series illustrium Praesulum ecclesiasticorum ex Ordine Carmelitarum Discalceatorum*, Fasc. IV, *Ecclesia Verapolitana*. Romae 1939.

Bufalini, Noviglio Sante (= P. Bufalini Faustino, O.C.D.), *"L'Opera Pacificatrice" di Mons. Giuseppe Sebastiani Vescovo Missionario O.C.D. nello scisma dei Cristiani di S. Tommaso Malabar 1653-1663*. Roma 1959. (a thesis presented to the Faculty of Letters of the University of Rome; as yet unpublished).

Eustachio di S. Maria, O.C.D., *Istoria della vita, virtù, doni e fatti illustri del ven. Mons. Fr. Gius. di S. Maria de' Sebastiani*. Roma 1719.

Ferroli, D., S.J., *The Jesuits in Malabar*, 2 vols. Bangalore 1939-1951.

Franco, Antonio, S.J., *Imagem da virtude em o noviciado da Companhia de Jesus do real collegio do Espirito Santo de Evora do Reyno de Portugal*. Lisboa 1714.

Hambye, E. R., S.J., *An Eastern Prelate in India, Mar Aithalaha, 1652-53*, in *Indian Church History Review* 2 (1968) 1-5.

Heras, H., S.J., *The Syrian Christians of Malabar*, in *The Examiner* (Bombay) 89 (1938) 81-82, 91-93, 104-105, 120-121, 135-136, 151-152, 170-171, 187-188, 207, 225-226, 242-243, 258, 278-279, 294.

Kollaparambil, Jacob, *The Archdeacon of All-India*. Rome 1966. (a thesis offered at the Juridical Faculty of the Lateran) (pro manuscriptu).

Werth, Karl, PSM., *Das Schisma der Thomaschristen unter Erzbischof Franciscus Garzia. Dargestellt nach den Akten des Archivs der Sacra Congregatio de Propaganda Fide*. Limburg 1937.

B. General Works

(All the books that deal with the general history of the St. Thomas Christians, naturally speak also of the history of the rebellion of 1653. Some of these general histories, like those of Fr. Bernard T.O.C.D., of W. Germann etc., deal with our subject in considerable detail.)

Assemani, Jos-Simon, *Bibliotheca orientalis Clementino — Vaticana, in qua manuscriptos codices syriacos, arabicos, persicos, turcicos, hebraicos, samaritanos, armenicos, aethiopicos, graecos, aegyptia-cos, ibericos et malabaricos, iussu et munificentia Clementis XI recensuit.* Tomi tertii Pars secunda. Romae 1728.

BELTRAMI, GIUSEPPE, *La Chiesa Caldea nel secolo dell'Unione,* in *Orientalia Christiana vol. XXIX,* n. 83. Roma 1933.

BERNARD OF ST. THOMAS, T.O.C.D., (= The St. Thomas Christians) vol. 2. Mannanam 1921.

Boletim da Filmoteca Ultramarina Portuguesa, nn. 23, 24, 27, Lisboa 1963.

BROWN, L. W., *The Indian Christians of St. Thomas.* Cambridge 1956.

DALGADO, SEBASTIÃO RODOLFO, *Glossário Luso-Asiático,* 2 vols. Coimbra 1919-21.

DE SMEDT, CH., S.J., *Criticism, Historical* in *The Catholic Encyclopedia,* vol. IV, pp. 503-509. New York 1908.

FRANCO, ANTÓNIO, S.J., *Ano Santo da Companhia de Jesus em Portugal. Nas memórias breves e ilustres de muitos homens insignes em virtude, com que Deus a enriqueceu, distribuídas pelos meses e dias de todo o ano. Ia edição. Prefaciada e anotada por Francisco Rodrigues.* Pôrto 1931.

GAUCHAT, PATRITIUS, O.M.Conv., *Hierarchia Catholica medii et recentioris Aevi,* vol. 4. Monasterii 1935.

GEDDES, MICHAEL, *The History of the Church of Malabar, from the Time of its being first discovered by the Portuguezes in the year 1501.* London 1694.

GERMANN, W., *Die Kirche der Thomaschristen. Ein Beitrag zur Geschichte der orientalischen Kirchen.* Gütersloh 1877.

GIAMIL, SAMUEL, *Genuinae Relationes inter Sedem Apostolicam et Assyriorum Orientalium seu Chaldaeorum Ecclesiam.* Romae 1902.

GOETSTOUWERS, J. B., S.J., *Synopsis Historiae Societatis Jesu.* Lovanii 1950.

GOUVEA (DE), A., *Jornada do Arcebispo de Goa Dom Frey Aleixo de Menezes Primas da India Oriental religioso da Ordem de S. Agostino . . .* Coimbra 1606.

HOUGH, J., *The History of Christianity in India,* 2 vols. London 1839.

HUONDER, ANTON, S.J., *Der einheimische Klerus in den Heidenländern.* Freiburg i. Br. 1909.

JANN, ADELHELM, O.Min.Cap., *Die Katholischen Missionen in Indien, China, und Japan. Ihre Organisation und das portugiesische Patronat von 15. bis ins 18. Jahrhundert.* Paderborn 1915.

KOWALSKY, NICOLA, O.M.I., *Serie dei Cardinali Prefetti e dei Segretari della Sacra Congregazione "de Propaganda Fide".* Romae 1962.

MACKENZIE, G. T., *Christianity in Travancore,* in *Travancore State Manual,* vol. II, pp. 135-223. Trivandrum 1906.

MEERSMAN, ACHILLES, OFM, *A few Notes Concerning Archbishop Francesco Antonio Frascella O.F.M. Conv. in Goa (1640-1653),* in *Miscellanea Francescana* 59 (1959) 346-351.

MENON, ACHYUTA, C.,*The Cochin State Manual.* Ernakulam 1911.

MÜLLBAUER, MAXIMILIAN, *Geschichte der Katholischen Missionen in Indien von der Zeit Vasco da Gamas bis zur Mitte des 18. Jahrhunderts.* Freiburg i.B. 1852.

MUNDADAN, A. M., C.M.I., *The St. Thomas Christians of Malabar under Mar Jacob* (1498-1552). Bangalore 1967.

PANIKKAR, K. M., *Malabar and the Portuguese (1500-1663)*. Bombay 1929.

PANJIKARAN, JOSEPH C., *Christianity in Malabar with special reference to the St. Thomas Christians of the Syro-Malabar Rite,* in *Orientalia Christiana,* Vol. VI, n. 23, Roma 1926, pp. 93-136.

———, *The Syrian Church in Malabar.* Trichinopoly 1914.

PAULINUS A S. BARTHOLOMAEO, *India Orientalis Christiana Continens fundationes ecclesiarum, seriem episcoporum, missiones, schismata, persecutiones, reges, viros illustres.* Romae 1794.

PHILIPOSE, E. M., *The Indian Church of St. Thomas,* 1907. (second edition in Malayalam by Mathew E.P., Kottayam 1951).

PLACIDUS A ST. JOSEPH T.O.C.D., *A Short History of the Malabar Church.* Rome 1965. (typewritten).

PODIPARA, J. PLACID, C.M.I., *Die Thomas-Christen.* Würzburg 1966.

RAE, G. MILNE, *The Syrian Church in India.* Edinburgh - London 1892.

RAULIN, J. F., *Historia Ecclesiae Malabaricae cum Diamperitana Synodo.* Romae 1745.

RODRIGUES, FRANCISCO, *A Companhia de Jesus em Portugal e nas Missões.* Pôrto 1935.

SALDANHA, M. J. GABRIEL DE, *História de Goa, vol. I - História Política.* Nova-Goa 1925 (2nd edition).

SCHURHAMMER, GEORGE, S.J., *The Malabar Church and Rome during the Early Portuguese Period and Before.* Trichinopoly 1934.

THALIATH, JONAS, T.O.C.D., *The Synod of Diamper* (Orientalia Christiana Analecta, 152). Rome 1958.

THEVARAMANNIL, C., *Mar Abraham.* Rome 1965. (a thesis offered at the Gregorian University, Rome; as yet unpublished).

TISSERANT, EUGÈNE, Cardinal, *Eastern Christianity in India, A History of the Syro-Malabar Church from the earliest time to the present day,* (Authorized adaptation from the French by E. R. HAMBYE S.J.) Bombay, Calcutta, Madras 1957.

VEYSSIÈRE DE LA CROZE, MATHURIN, *Histoire du Christianisme des Indes.* La Haye 1758.

WICKI, JOSEF, S.J., *Lettere familiari del P. Roberto Nobili S.J.* (1609-1649), in *Archivum Historicum Societatis Jesu* 38 (1969) 313-325.

(I)

AN INTRODUCTORY CHAPTER

1. A HIGHLY CONTROVERSIAL SUBJECT

It is no exaggeration to say that the subject that is going to be studied, viz the history of the St. Thomas Christians of Malabar under Archbishop Francis Garcia S.J., is one of the most controverted points of the history of the Church in India. Writers who perhaps felt that they had at all costs to defend the honour of their religious families or of their churches, have tended to take sides rather than make an objective judgement on the rather complicated events of the period. Hence one does not need to be surprised if the judgement of these historians on the government of Archbishop Garcia is very divergent.

For Antonio Franco, a Portuguese Jesuit writer of the first decades of the 18th century, Garcia was nothing less than a saintly prelate who administered his diocese perfectly.[1] According to him the Apostolic Commissaries (Carmelites) worked in such a way as to deprive the Jesuits of their mission and to make themselves masters of it.[2] On the other hand Fr. Vincent Mary of St. Catherine O.C.D. (the companion and secretary of the first Apostolic Commissary, Sebastiani) repeatedly affirms that the Christians of St. Thomas did not want to hear of Garcia and that they were in no way disposed to return to his obedience and to that of the Jesuits.[3]

One would be making a mistake if one imagined that such sharp differences of opinion on our subject were a thing of bygone centuries only. Unfortunately there have

---

[1] "... homem entre nòs de grande exemplo na santidade dos seus costumes. E na administraçam da sua Igreja Prelado consummado em tudo"; FRANCO, *Imagem ... de Évora*, p. 439-440.

[2] FRANCO, *Ano Santo*, p. 505.

[3] *Il viaggio all'Indie Orientali*, pp. 188-189, 219-220, 223, 229.

been too many instances in our own days to prove the contrary. Thus in 1938 the articles on "The Syrian Christians of Malabar" published by Fr. Heras S.J. in "The Examiner" of Bombay, in which inter alia he tried to glorify the character of Garcia and belittle the work of Sebastiani, evoked a very sharp "letter to the editor" from Fr. Victorino O.C.D. of Ernakulam.[4] The letter called into question not merely the impartiality but even the authenticity of the documents on which Fr. Heras relied! Similarly the views expressed by Fr. Ferroli S.J. in the second volume of "The Jesuits in Malabar" (1951), regarding the relative merits of Garcia and Sebastiani, were indignantly and elaborately rejected by Fr. Faustino Bufalini O.C.D. in 1959 in a dissertation which he presented to the Faculty of Letters of the University of Rome.

Passion and partiality have by no means been lacking in the works of many other writers as well, whether Protestants, Jacobites, Catholics or others.

2. A CRITICAL LOOK AT THE PREVIOUS WORKS

Leaving aside the writings of the contemporaries of Garcia, which will be discussed in the next section on the sources, I intend now to say something about the rest, whether they be monographs or articles that deal mainly with the period under study, or general histories of the St. Thomas Christians. As I pointed out in the previous section, it can be said in general about most of them that they give a one-side view of the facts. Besides, many of the writers had no access to a large part of the sources and therefore had to rely on a cautious evaluation of the few published sources and on second or third hand information. The comparatively few that have taken the trouble of going through the original sources, have been on the whole content with consulting the sources of one party or the other. The only exception, as far as I know, is Jacob Kollaparambil, whose unpublished dissertation on "The Archdeacon of All-India" (1966) is based on a painstaking examination of all the pertinent sources of our period.

----

[4] *The Examiner* (May 14, 1958) p. 294.

The first person to carry his researches beyond the published works and to study the period in question directly from the archives was Karl Werth PSM. The fruit of his patient work in the Propaganda Archives was a book published in 1937: "Das Schisma der Thomaschristen unter Erzbischof Franciscus Garzia". Unfortunately he did not consult the Roman Archives of the Society of Jesus and the Historical Archives of Goa, both of which, but more especially the former, contain much material on his subject. This omission has led him at times into errors. For instance, on pp. 49-50 and 64-65 he mistakenly maintains that Archbishop Atallah, the intruder from the Middle East, was burned at the stake in Goa. Again, on p. 62 he wrongly asserts that Garcia was guilty of not fulfilling his pastoral obligation of visiting his diocese. In this chapter itself when we shall come to the question of the sources, I shall have an opportunity to show that this accusation was nothing but a calumny. Yet it must be admitted that on many points Werth has succeeded in giving us a rather unbiassed picture. Not being an interested party, he did not feel himself obliged either to defend or to denigrate any one. This disinterestedness also enabled him often to form judgements independently of the more extreme and evidently suspect statements contained in some of the papers in the Propaganda Archives. There is no doubt, however, that his judgements and conclusions would have been still more dependable, had he perused the papers of the Jesuit Archives as well. There is one mistake into which he has fallen because of his ignorance of the country and of the people about whom he wrote. An attentive reading of p. 6 and a comparison of it with pp. 82 and 94-95 leaves one with the impression that he has at times confused the St. Thomas Christians living in the southern parts of the Archdiocese of Cranganore with the "Southists".[5]

_____

[5] The St. Thomas Christians of Malabar are divided into two communities called the "Northists" (Vadakkumbhagakkar, in Malayalam) and the "Southists" (Thekkumbhagakkar). The members of these two communities do not as a rule intermarry. There is no agreement among historians as to the origin of this distinction. The names Northists and Southists have little reference to the localities in which the two communities have been living now for cen-

A year after the publication of Werth's book, Fr. Heras
S.J. published a series of articles in "The Examiner" of
Bombay on "The Syrian Christians of Malabar". For the
description of the rebellion of 1653 and of the other events
connected with it, he relied exclusively on a few of the documents of the Jesuit Archives, in particular, on the narration that Fr. Bras de Azevedo S.J. had made in 1666.[6]   The
articles of Fr. Heras can hardly escape the accusation of
partiality. When discussing, for instance, the causes of the
rebellion (p. 207), he censures Archbishop Alexis de Menezes of Goa, the Archdeacon, the Portuguese, — in short,
every one except his own confreres! Yet it is obvious to
any impartial person that the Jesuit archbishops and missionaries of Malabar have to bear their share of the blame.
On p. 226 Fr. Heras brands the directions sent to Garcia
by Dom Bras de Castro, the governor of Portuguese India,
as "interference of the civil authorities in purely religious
affairs", quite forgetting that these authorities interfered
because Garcia had written to them asking for their help![7]
In spite of these and other defects, the articles of Fr. Heras
served the useful purpose of making people realise that
regarding the events connected with the rebellion of 1653
there existed a version very different from the usual one.

Fr. Ferroli S.J.[8] in the second volume of his work "The
Jesuits in Malabar" (1951), followed more or less the same
methods as Fr. Heras; but he treated the whole question in
greater detail. His researches in the Jesuit Archives were
more extensive, and probably he made use of some of the
documents of the Historical Archives of Goa as well. Also
the printed work of Fr. Vincent Mary of St. Catherine O.C.D.,
"Il Viaggio all'Indie Orientali", was consulted to a limited
extent. But the Propaganda Archives were practically left
untouched. Looking at the results achieved, it must be
admitted that some of the conclusions of Fr. Ferroli have

---

turies. Thus Northist communities may be found in the north, cen-
tre or south and viceversa.

[6] ARSI, *Goa 49*, ff. 178-209: "Carta da Missão da Serra dos Christãos de São Thomè".

[7] AHEI, *LM 23-B*, ff. 377-78: letter of Garcia to the Viceroy on
30.6.1653, requesting help.

[8] He was a professor of physical science and seems to have taken
up the writing of history only as a hobby.

contributed to a better understanding of the period under study. Thus for instance, on pp. 29-31 he proves satisfactorily that the archbishops and the Jesuit missionaries were not to be blamed for the diminution and the irregularity of payment of the allowances of the Cattanars,[9] about which the latter had been complaining bitterly. While acknowledging that on some points Fr. Ferroli has made a contribution to a better understanding of our period, I must hasten to add that by no means can his work (I mean, that part of his work which deals with our subject; it is not my intention to say anything about the rest) be considered impartial. The account of the quarrel between the Archbishop and the Archdeacon is too one-sided to be true. Much of it is a mere translation or summary of the descriptions left behind by Garcia and his closest associates. Further, it must be added that in his eagerness to defend Garcia from every possible angle, Fr. Ferroli falls time and again into errors and inaccuracies. For instance, on p. 37 he denies rather emphatically that Garcia ever suggested to the authorities of Goa that the customs rights of the ruler of Cochin should be touched in order to force the latter to help Garcia. I shall quote the exact words of Fr. Ferroli: "It seems natural to suppose that this underhand stroke had been suggested by the Archbishop, but one of the Archbishop's entourage denies that touching the revenues of the Raja of Cochin ever entered into the plans of Don Garcia, as a means to influence the return of the rebels. This had probably been suggested by meddlesome persons in Cochin." Yet it is absolutely certain that Garcia himself made the suggestion in his letter to the Viceroy on June 30, 1653.[10] What is still more amazing is that Ferroli makes mention of this letter on p. 36 of his book. It is obvious that he has not read through it! I do not know from where Fr. Ferroli obtained the information regarding the denial made by "one of the Archbishop's entourage". Since Fr. Ferroli hardly ever cites his sources except in a very general way as a kind of bibliography at

---

[9] Cattanar is a word used also nowadays to indicate the priests of the St. Thomas Christians. The Portuguese often used to spell it as Cassanar or Caçanar. The etymology of the word is disputed.

[10] AHEI, *LM 23-B*, ff. 377-378. It is the original, written by an amanuensis and signed by Garcia. *The suggestion regarding the customs rights is found on f. 377v.*

the beginning of the chapters, it is often not possible to
check his statements. If "one of the Archbishop's entourage" really made such a denial, it would only show how
cautiously one should proceed in accepting the statements
of such persons. Yet one gets the impression that Fr. Ferroli is inclined to accept uncritically all what they say.
Again, on p. 49 Fr. Ferroli affirms that Garcia "had lived
long in Malabar before being made a bishop. He had given
many missions in the Serra.[11] He knew the people and the
Cassanars. Don Garcia was not the man to break them by
his rigour". As usual we are not told the source from which
Fr. Ferroli obtained all this information. From the old
catalogues of the Jesuit Provinces of Goa and Cochin we
learn that Garcia taught philosophy in the Jesuit College of
Cochin between 1607 and 1610.[12] Earlier from 1603 he had
been in the same college as a student of theology.[13] This
more or less agrees with what Garcia himself says about his
having spent five years in Cochin.[14] Now to teach philosophy
or to learn theology in the College of Cochin is not the same
as getting to know the Christians and the Cattanars of the
Serra. In fact when Archbishop Stephen Britto came to
know that the Jesuit authorities had chosen Garcia to be his
successor, he remarked that Garcia lacked experience of the
people of the Serra. These are his words: "I would have been
happier had he been younger, so as to be able to learn the
language and *to acquire some experience of this people* so
different from the rest . . ." [15] Further, on p. 87 Fr. Ferroli
says that Bishop Chandy's "rule over the Serra was little
less than a disaster". Nothing which Fr. Ferroli has adduced
in his book justifies such a harsh remark. What is known
of Bishop Chandy from elsewhere would seem to prove the
contrary. Omitting others, let me cite the testimony of Fr.
Bras de Azevedo S.J. who cannot be suspected of undue partiality towards Bishop Chandy. He wrote on July 28, 1666

---

[11] Serra is the name most often used by the Portuguese to indicate the hilly regions where the majority of the St. Thomas Christians lived. Serra in Portuguese means a mountain range.

[12] Cf. ARSI, *Goa 24-II*, ff. 428v, 443; *Goa 27*, f. 9v; *Goa 29*, f. 5v.

[13] Cf. ARSI, *Goa 24-II*, ff. 326, 327.

[14] Cf. ARSI, *Goa 68-II*, f. 442.

[15] ARSI, *Goa 18*, f. 139: letter of Britto to the Jesuit General on
1.1.1633.

that Archdeacon Thomas de Campo sent an embassy to the Jesuit fathers at Ambalakkad regarding his submission to the Church, because he saw that *many were submitting to Bishop Chandy*.[16]

From Fr. Ferroli's book I pass to the yet unpublished dissertation of his critic Fr. Faustino Bufalini O.C.D. The work is entitled: "L'Opera Pacificatrice di Mons. Giuseppe Sebastiani Vescovo Missionario O.C.D. nello scisma dei Cristiani di S. Tommaso Malabar 1653-1663." While I admit that many of the conclusions that Fr. Bufalini arrives at are correct, it is but fair to point out that he seems to take too uncritically whatever has been written by his confreres (Sebastiani and Vincent Mary). Time and again he cites the accusations against the Archbishop and the Jesuit fathers which are to be found in Sebastiani's letters, general accounts or books, as so many unquestionable statements of fact. When discussing the problem of the reliability of the sources, I shall have occasion to show that not everything that Sebastiani adduces can be so uncritically accepted. It would also appear that Fr. Bufalini accepts without sufficient circumspection all what he sees in the Propaganda Archives in favour of his thesis, even when the very tone of the writing should warn him to proceed more warily. For example, on p. 216 he quotes a certain Theatine, Fr. Antony Poma, who wrote that Archbishop Garcia used to say that the king of Portugal had given him a black wife (the Church of the Serra) and that he did not care if she perished. I too came across these papers in the archives,[17] but I did not consider the story worthy of credit, especially since it is in open contradiction to the statements of other respectable people like the Rector of the Franciscan College of Granganore who declared that Garcia used to be moved to tears if the conversation happened to touch the rebellion of the Serra. Garcia often told him, continues the witness, that he would willingly suffer the loss of his right hand if he could thereby bring about the conversion of his Christians.[18] It is to be noted that Fr. Antony Poma was never in Malabar.

---

[16] ARSI, *Goa 49*, f. 204: "Carta da Missão da Serra dos Christãos de São Thomè".

[17] APF, *SOCG 233*, ff. 174-175.

[18] ARSI, *Goa 68-II*, f. 565: an authenticated Italian copy of the document.

Hence the information that he furnished must have been to a large extent based on rumours. On the other hand the Rector of the Franciscan College lived in the town where Garcia too stayed. So he is likely to be better informed. Another criticism that has to be made against Fr. Bufalini is that he has based his work almost exclusively on the documents of one party. He has not consulted the numerous papers to be found in the Roman Archives of the Society of Jesus. Thus in several cases he has been unable to see what the other side in the dispute has to say about certain papers and testimonies that he has made use of in his work.

The survey given above is sufficient to show that there does not yet exist a fully documented and impartial study of the troubled days of Archbishop Garcia.

3. THE SOURCES: THEIR RELIABILITY

The original documents concerning our period are distributed very unevenly. Those that pertain to the years before the general rebellion of 1653 are comparatively few and are to be found for the most part in the Roman Archives of the Jesuits. But also in some of the documents of the Propaganda Archives, especially in the testimonies of some witnesses, there are occasional references to the conditions that existed before 1653. Regarding the chief events of the rebellion itself there is a certain abundance of material in both the above mentioned archives. For the years between 1653 and 1657 there is once again comparative dearth of material. The Historical Archives of Goa supply some interesting documents pertaining to these years. But the documents become really abundant after the arrival of the Apostolic Commissaries in India, and they fill entire volumes both in the Propaganda Archives and in that of the Jesuits. It may be noted, by the way, that only a negligible number of the documents of the archives have been published so far.

Besides the material found in the archives, the "Prima Speditione ..." and the "Seconda Speditione ..." by Bishop Sebastiani and the "Viaggio all'Indie Orientali" by Fr. Vincent Mary of St. Catherine O.C.D. are contemporary publications of great value for the history of our period. It is of course to be noted that they give us only the Carmelite point of view. Other books published in the same period, e.g. "Relatione delle Missioni ... del Malabar ..." by Fr. Francis Barreto S.J. and "Itinerarium Orientale" by Philippus a S. Trinitate O.C.D., though useful, are less important.

Passing on to examine the reliability of the sources, I am inclined to agree with L.W. Brown who says in his book, "The Indian Christians of St. Thomas", that neither the Jesuits nor the Carmelites wrote impartially. It is not at all my intention to accuse the members of these revered religious families of having deliberately made false statements. On this point De Smedt S.J. in his article "Criticism, Historical" says: "it is not enough to be satisfied that the witness did not wish to utter a deliberate lie; if it could be reasonably shown that he had a personal interest in warping the truth, grave suspicions would be raised as to the veracity of all his statements ... Frequently prejudice or passion secretly pervert the natural sincerity of a man who really respects himself and esteems the respect of others. It is possible, and that with a certain good faith, to deceive both one's self and others." [19]

Coming down to particulars, we find that even before the heated polemics between the Apostolic Commissaries and Garcia started, the latter was already at loggerheads with the Archdeacon, the Recollects of Edapally and with the Goan Inquisition and its commissary in Cochin. Then came the Carmelites and we have a flood of documents and papers prepared by the two sides to justify their respective positions. Under these circumstances it is impossible that these papers contain merely an impartial exposition of facts. We know that in 1658 Garcia forwarded to Fr. Simon Teixeira S.J., the procurator of the Portuguese Assistance in the Jesuit Curia, two sets of documents: one to defend his case against his rebellious subjects and the Apostolic Commissaries before the Propaganda, the other to defend himself before the Cardinals of the Inquisition against the rebels, the Goan Inquisitors and their commissaries.[20] These documents make up a considerable portion of the contents of the

---

[19] *The Catholic Encyclopedia*, vol. IV, p. 505.
[20] ARSI *Goa 68-I*, f. 187: Letter of Garcia to Fr. Simon Teixeira S.J. on 13.7.1658.

volume, Goa 68, of the Jesuit Archives. A number of the other documents regarding our subject, found in the same archives were drawn up on similar occasions. Thus at the end of 1645 when the Archdeacon and his friends intended to petition Dom Philip Mascarenhas, the newly appointed Viceroy of Portuguese India, against Garcia, the latter got a number of documents ready, to defend himself and to accuse in turn the Archdeacon and his allies. It is obvious that collections of documents made on such occasions would contain only what is favourable to the collector and his case. In fact there are indications that prove my contention. Garcia stated once that Sebastiani wrote to him 25 letters in all.[21] Yet in the collection we find only a few which serve his purpose.

We find also that many of the accounts depicting the achievements of the Jesuit missionaries contain obvious exaggerations. For instance, we read more than once that before the Jesuits began to work among the St. Thomas Christians the very name of Rome was held in horror among them;[22] that before their arrival there was not even one person in the whole of that Church that acknowledged the authority of the Apostolic See etc.[23] No one who has made a study of the history of the Church in Malabar in the 16th century, would dare to make such statements today.

Moreover there are some documents in the Propaganda Archives that call in question the reliability of several of the testimonies and certificates obtained by Archbishop Garcia and the Jesuit Fathers in their favour. Thus Dom Gaspar de Lima, a senator of Cochin, in his sworn declaration of 6 November 1659 deposed that he and two other public officials of Cochin refused, in spite of the request of the Jesuit Fathers, to sign the statements drawn up against the Apostolic Commissary since they contained much that was false. He adds that they were later signed by some other individuals in the name of the City.[24] The same thing is asserted by Canon Joseph de Rego of Cochin.[25] A certain

---

[21] ARSI, *Goa 68-II*, f. 439v.

[22] *Ibid.* f. 508v: Letter of Fr. Francis Barreto S.J. (provincial) to Fr. Matthew of St. Joseph O.C.D. (1658).

[23] *Ibid.* f. 532v. See also f. 582.

[24] APF, *SOCG 232*, f. 358.

[25] *Ibid.* f. 356. It is useful to note, however, that Canon Joseph de Rego was the brother-in-law of Dom Gaspar de Lima.

deacon called Varghese who had been the Malayalam language secretary of Archbishop Garcia, declared on September 20, 1659 that the Jesuit Fathers had fabricated several documents against the Commissaries and induced many Cattanars to sign them, even though the latter did not know their contents. The Cattanars, continues the witness, were induced partly by fear.[26] Fr. Carlo Ferrari, a Theatine working in Goa, wrote on April 13, 1661 that after Sebastiani had left India with many documents, the Jesuit Fathers managed with bribes and with force to get the very same people to declare that they had signed the papers for Sebastiani without knowing their contents since they could not understand Sebastiani's way of speaking. He says also that the rumour which the Jesuits spread in Cochin about the nomination of Fr. Barreto S.J. as bishop of that city, helped very much their drive for certificates in their favour. Though the Cathedral Chapter of Cochin as a body could not be induced to contradict its earlier testimony, some of the canons and dignitaries individually gave them the desired certificates.[27]

I have adduced the above statements not because I regard them as proved, but merely to show that it would be very imprudent uncritically to accept all what is contained in the Jesuit Archives or elsewhere in favour of Garcia and the Jesuit missionaries.

The documents of Carmelite origin come in next for examination. The relations between the Papal Commissaries (Carmelites) on the one hand and Archbishop Garcia and the Jesuits on the other became tense not very long after the arrival of the former in Malabar. This tension was bound to have its influence on the documents composed by the Commissaries and their helpers. We should be imagining them to be superhuman beings if we expect that in those circumstances they would be completely impartial. It was also to be expected that if any one went to offer them information unfavourable to Garcia and the Jesuits, they would not waste much time to sift that evidence. As a matter of fact we find that among the accusations against

---

[26] *Ibid.* f. 355.
[27] APF, *SOCG 234*, f. 182.

Garcia forwarded to Rome by Sebastiani,[28] there are some that are demonstrably false. For example, we are told that Garcia never visited the Archdiocese except once when he visited three or four churches![29] But it is certain that Garcia made several pastoral visits in different parts of his vast archdiocese. When he was still only coadjutor to Archbishop Britto, he made one such visitation. The Annual Letter of the Jesuit Province of Malabar for the year 1640 [30] describes that visitation and says that Garcia managed to reach also those places which had never been visited by his predecessors. Fr. Bras de Azevedo S.J. too affirms the same thing, adding that this visit covered the southern parts of the Archdiocese, and that Garcia reached as far south as the city and court of Travancore where there was the southern-most church of the Serra.[31] On December 20, 1658 eight Cattanars and one deacon led by George Bengur (one of the foremost Cattanars) declared on oath that during the years prior to the rebellion Garcia used to visit his archdiocese, going even to the farthest ends of it, reaching places which no predecessor of his had ever reached. They went on to affirm that he used to spend several months on these visits.[32] Garcia himself wrote to Fr. Hyacinth of St. Vincent O.C.D. (the 2nd Papal Commissary) on August 22, 1658 that he had several times visited his archdiocese, from Quilon in the south to Palur in the north. Once he had gone as far as Cape Comorin. To the east he had gone to the farthest churches of Trugure, Muthalakkodam and Mailakombu.[33] In a report which Garcia sent in 1645 to the Jesuit authorities in Rome we read that ever since he became archbishop he was making the visitation of his archdiocese every year, spending two to four months for the purpose each time. He added that in the previous year (1644) he had made a thorough visitation of the northern parts.[34] In the bio-

---

[28] "Punti dei quali vengono tassati Mons. Arcivescovo della Serra ed i Padri della Compagnia di quella Missione". APF, *SOCG 233*, ff. 151-156.

[29] *Ibid.* f. 151.

[30] ARSI, *Goa 56*, f. 489: The letter was written on 17.1.1641.

[31] ARSI, *Goa 49*, f. 195v: "Carta da Missão da Serra dos Christãos de São Thomè".

[32] ARSI, *Goa 68-II*, f. 687.

[33] ARSI, *Goa 68-I*, f. 182v.

[34] ARSI, *Goa 68-II*, f. 526v-527.

graphical notes on Archbishop Garcia composed by his secretary, Fr. Hyacinth De Magistris S.J., we read that Garcia visited his archdiocese several times.[35] The same thing is affirmed by several other persons.[36] Thus we see that there are too many witnesses each of whom is independent of the rest, that testify to the fact of Garcia's making these visitations. There is no good reason to question the veracity of their statements. This is especially true of the Annual Letter of 1640, written at a time when there were no major quarrels in the Archdiocese of Cranganore. Another false charge made against Garcia in the same document ("Punti dei quali vengono tassati Mons. Arcivescovo...") was that he had never conferred the sacrament of Confirmation, and that that sacrament was quite unknown in the Serra for at least 40 years.[37] The Annual Letter of 1640 when describing the visitation that Garcia made in the stead of the aged Britto, explicitly mentions that wherever he went the people were confirmed. Nay it goes on to describe the disturbance that a certain disaffected Cattanar stirred up in an out of the way church. He urged the Christians of the place not to receive Garcia since the latter had slapped the people in the churches he had visited earlier, evidently alluding to the light slap given during the sacramental rite.[38] The sworn statement of Cattanar George Bengur and others, referred to a while ago, also affirms that during the visits to the churches Garcia always confirmed those who had not yet received that sacrament.[39] A third accusation against Garcia was that he knew very little Malayalam and no Syriac. Also in this case, anyone who has carefully gone through all the existing original records will have no hesitation to dismiss it as sheer calumny. Fr. De Magistris S.J. gives a list of the languages that Garcia knew. Malayalam and Syriac are mentioned in the list.[40] Garcia himself says something to the point in his letters, when try-

---

[35] WICKI, *O Homem das trinta e duas Perfeições...*, p. 326 (2nd appendix).
[36] ARSI, *Goa 68-I*, ff. 54-55; *Goa 68-II*, f. 549, 580.
[37] APF, *SOCG 233*, f. 151.
[38] ARSI, *Goa 56*, f. 489.
[39] ARSI, *Goa 68-II*, f. 687.
[40] WICKI, *O Homem...*, p. 326 (2nd appendix).

ing to prove to the Governor of Portuguese India and to
Sebastiani that he was a man of learning, experience and
prudence. To Sebastiani he says that he knows Malayalam
so well that he has composed a Malayalam-Portuguese and
a Portuguese-Malayalam dictionary. He knows also Syriac,
both the Chaldean dialect and the Maronitic one. He claims
also to be able to read two different Malayalam scripts and
two Syriac scripts.[41] In his letter to Dom Bras de Castro,
the governor of Portuguese India, he wrote that he had translated the book, Flos Sanctorum, from Tamil to Malayalam
for the use of his flock. He knew Syriac so well that he
could open any book in that language and translate it
straightaway into Latin or Portuguese.[42] It is to be noted
that in these letters Garcia was not refuting any charge that
he did not know these languages. He was adducing his
thorough knowledge of these languages and his theological,
philosophical and juridical learning and the high offices
that he had held in the Society of Jesus, as a proof of his
learning, experience and prudence. Also Fr. Bras de Azevedo
S.J. says that Garcia got the "Flos Sanctorum" translated
into Malayalam, and that part of the translation was done
by Garcia himself.[43] I think enough has been said to show
that some of the charges against Garcia forwarded to Rome
by Sebastiani were baseless. Going through these lists of
accusations, one gets the impression that Sebastiani (or his
companions) took down everything that was said against
the Archbishop without checking their veracity.

It is, however, more disconcerting to note that at times
Sebastiani has presented contradictory information regarding the very same persons. In a report which he made to
Pope Alexander VII in 1659 after his first return from
Malabar he affirms that the refusal of the rebellious Christians to submit once again to the government of the Jesuits
is very unreasonable and unjust, "since the virtue of these
fathers deserves all affection and love."[44] But during those
same months he submitted to the Congregation of the

---

[41] ARSI, *Goa 68-II*, ff. 441v-442. Cf. also *Goa 68-I*, f. 61v.
[42] ARSI, *Goa 50*, f. 98.
[43] ARSI, *Goa 49*, f. 196: "Carta da Missão da Serra...".
[44] APF, *SOCG 233*, f. 505: "...è odio irragionevole, da barbari, et
ingiustissimo, *essendo la virtù de medesimi Padri meritevole d'ogni
affeto e devotione.*"

Propaganda a report in which he affirmed exactly the opposite about the Jesuit missionaries! "The Jesuits in those parts are very different from those here. They are different in their dress, manners and religious observance." [45]

It is necessary to point out also that in the Jesuit Archives there are some writings that dispute the reliability of many of the testimonies obtained by the Apostolic Commissaries in their favour and against the Jesuits. Fr. Bras De Azevedo S.J., for instance, alleges that Sebastiani was able to obtain from the Cathedral Chapter of Cochin several certificates to his satisfaction, since the Chapter left the issuing of these certificates to the vicar general who happened to be a priest dismissed from the Society of Jesus. [46] The Jesuit provincial of Cochin, Fr. Francis Barreto, wrote to the Jesuit General that it was enough for two Christians to say something against the Jesuits, especially that they did not want them in the Serra, and immediately the Commissaries would have that declaration taken down by the notaries. They would then publish everywhere that no one wanted the Jesuits. It was, he wrote, the habit of the Commissaries to exaggerate and to attribute to all what had been said only by one or two. [47] In a charge-sheet drawn up by the Jesuits of Cochin against the Apostolic Commissaries we read that Sebastiani made some Cattanars who had submitted to Garcia, sign a paper without telling them its contents. The Cattanars strongly suspected that the paper contained some accusation against the Society of Jesus, since its contents were so carefully withheld from those friendly to the Society. [48]

I would like to make it clear that I cite these charges of unfairness, not because I consider them to be proved, but merely to show that one has to be very circumspect in the use of contemporary writings, whether they are of Carmelite or of Jesuit origin.

---

[45] APF, *SOCG 233*, f. 481: "... i Religiosi della Compagnia in quelle parti, *sono diferentissimi* da questi nostri nell'habito, *nei costumi e nell'osservanza.*"

[46] ARSI, *Goa 49*, f. 188r: "Carta da Missão da Serra ..."

[47] ARSI, *Goa 68-I*, f. 150: Letter dated 12.11.1658.

[48] ARSI, *Goa 68-II*, f. 521v: "Notitia rerum, quas contra PP. Societatis Coccinensis Provinciae gesserunt PP. Carmelitani discalceati, Summi Pontificis Commissarii."

4. The Method and Division of this Work

The present work is intended to be an independent and fresh study of the troubled days of Archbishop Garcia in Malabar. It is based almost exclusively on a direct examination of the contemporary writings. But what has been said in the previous section on the sources, amply illustrates the difficulty of such a work. I shall now try to indicate what I consider to be the only method of work that is likely to yield satisfactory results.

In controverted cases (the great majority of the events of our period are controverted at least under some aspect) reliable conclusions can be reached only by a careful confrontation of the various accounts coming from the contending sides, taking especially into consideration what third parties, if available, may have to say. Even the tiniest bit of information from third parties may prove to be most useful. If in spite of every care no moral certainty can be reached, the historian should honestly admit the fact, and resist the temptation of presenting as certain what is only probable. It is on these lines that I hope to proceed.

Fortunately there are also a few points that are not disputed. In these it would be enough, I think, simply to narrate the facts as found in the sources, comparing all the available accounts in order to exclude errors arising from inadvertence or carelessness on the part of the original writer.

This introductory chapter will be followed by another, dealing mainly with the events from the beginning of Garcia's government to the general rebellion of 1653. The rebellion itself will be treated next. Then there will follow a description of the fruitless efforts made by the various authorities in India to win back the rebels. The fifth and the longest chapter will narrate the intervention of the Papal Commissaries and the misunderstandings and quarrels between them and Garcia. These quarrels were at their height when Garcia died. To end this study abruptly with the death of Garcia would be rather unnatural, since the main event that took place during his government, viz the rebellion of his flock, was in no way settled at the moment of his death. That is why I considered it proper to add another chapter that treats briefly of the events up to the consecration of Bishop Chandy. The book ends with a critical estimate of Archbishop Garcia.

(II)

THE PERIOD OF RELATIVE CALM

Though the life of Francis Garcia prior to his becoming the archbishop of Cranganore does not, strictly speaking, form part of our subject, it would not be out of place to preface the detailed enquiry of his activity as archbishop with a summary account of his early life.

1. A BRIEF SKETCH OF THE LIFE OF GARCIA UP TO HIS ACCESSION TO THE ARCHBISHOPRIC (1641)

Francis Garcia was born around the middle of the year 1580 at Alter do Chão in the diocese of Elvas in Portugal.[1] His parents, John Garcia and Catherine Gomes, belonged to the noblest families of the locality. He entered the Society of Jesus at Évora on 12 June 1598. He was still a student of theology when he left for India in 1602 in the company of about sixty other Jesuits. The expedition to the East was led by Fr. Albert Laercio, an Italian Jesuit, who was then procurator of the vice-province of Malabar.[2] The Jesuits were distributed in different ships, and Garcia himself with 17 others voyaged in the ship São Roque.[3] He continued his theological studies in India. In January 1604 he was still only a cleric. But the catalogue of December 1605 speaks of him as a priest who was doing the fourth

---

[1] ARSI, *Goa 24-II*, f. 331v. According to this ancient catalogue of the Jesuit vice-province of Cochin, Garcia was 25½ years old in December 1605. So he must have been born around the middle of the year 1580. Cf. also FRANCO, *Imagem... de Évora*, p. 412; WICKI, *O Homem...*, p. 325 (2nd Appendix).

[2] WICKI, l.c.; FRANCO, l.c.; ARSI, *Goa 28*, ff. 14v-16.

[3] ARSI, *Goa 28*, f. 15.

year of theology. The reports of these years praise his intelligence and his progress in the study of theology.[4]

In 1606 we find him working in the mission of Punnaikayal on the Fishery Coast. He was there nearly two years when he was called to the college of Cochin to teach philosophy. He must have been quite a successful teacher since the report of the year 1608 describes him as a person suited for the activities of the Society, especially teaching.[5] In 1610 he was sent from Cochin to the College of St. Paul in Goa as professor of theology. He continued to teach there also in the following year. But in 1612 we find him at the college of Salsete, near Goa, in the capacity of professor of moral cases. In the two succeeding years he was superior and procurator at Bandra and Thana.[6] On 8 November 1615 he made the solemn vows.[7] In the following year we find him once again in the College of St. Paul. This time he was not merely professor of theology but also consultor. In 1618 he was vicar at Margão. Two years later he was at the college of Rachol[8]. The catalogue of January 1627 describes him as a 46 year old priest who has lived 29 years in the Society and who has taught philosophy for 3 years and theology for 5, and who has spent 12 years in various mission stations. His intelligence, prudence and proficiency in various languages are specially stressed. He is described as suited for all the ministries of the Society.[9] The report of 1633 says that he was then among the Christians of Salsete. But earlier he had been rector of the colleges of Bassein and of St. Paul, superior of the Professed House in Goa and vice-provincial. According to the information furnished by Fr. De Magistris[10], Garcia had occupied also the posts of visitor and provincial before he was appointed bishop.[11]

---

[4] ARSI, *Goa 24-II*, ff. 326, 327, 331v, 339v.

[5] *Ibid.*, ff. 359v, 428v, 435, 443.

[6] ARSI, *Goa 27*, ff. 9v, 15v, 20, 25v, 30v; *Goa 25*; f. 5v; *Goa 29*, f. 5v.

[7] ARSI, *Goa 25*, ff. 33, 55v.

[8] *Goa 27*, ff. 32, 37v, 41v; *Goa 25*, f. 28v.

[9] *Goa 25*, ff. 33, 41.

[10] Fr. Hyacinth De Magistris S.J. was born in 1606 in the diocese of Cremona in Italy. In 1626 he entered the Society of Jesus. Several years later he left for India. He was the constant companion, secretary and confessor of Garcia for many years until the latter's death. From 1654 to 1657 he was away in Portugal and in Rome to plead Garcia's case. After Garcia's death he returned to Rome

It was in the year 1632 that the Jesuit superiors decided to recommend Fr. Francis Garcia as coadjutor and future successor to Archbishop Stephen Britto. From a letter of the latter to the Jesuit General, Fr. Vitelleschi, on 1 January 1633 we learn that Britto was not very happy about the choice. He acknowledged that Garcia had many qualities. But he gave Fr. Vitelleschi clearly to understand that he would have preferred some one else who was younger.[12]

The official presentation of Garcia as the king's nominee took place on 17 February 1635. Pope Urban VIII issued the brief "Romanus Pontifex" on 23 June 1636, appointing Garcia titular bishop of Ascalon and coadjutor and future successor to the Archbishop of Cranganore or Angamaly.[13] Garcia was in Bassein when the news of the nomination by the king reached him. He immediately began to study Syriac. When the brief of the Pope arrived, he arranged for his episcopal consecration which took place in 1637 on the feast of All Saints in the church of the Jesuit Professed House in Goa. Soon he left for Cranganore. He stayed there at the Jesuit college, continuing to lead the life of an exemplary religious.[14]

Since Britto could not any longer visit his flock because of his advanced age and sickness, Garcia offered to visit the archdiocese in his place. This visitation which covered the southern parts, took place in the year 1640. Garcia made it in the company of Fr. De Magistris. They visited also places which had never been previously seen by prelates, confirming the faithful, settling quarrels and punishing the evil-doers. The fines that were imposed, were not taken by the bishop for himself, but used for the ornamentation and improvement of the churches and for the marriage of orphan girls. The bishop was not accompanied by the arch-

---

as procurator of the Province of Malabar. In 1662 he was chosen as visitor of the Jesuits in Brazil. But before he could exercise his office, he was deposed. Finally he returned to India and died in Goa on 11 Novembre 1668. Cf. WICKI, *O Homem* ..., p. XVIII, note 1; Ibid. p. 329.

[11] ARSI, *Goa 25*, f. 55v; WICKI, *O Homem* ..., p. 326 (2nd Appendix).

[12] ARSI, *Goa 18*, f. 139.

[13] ARSI, *Goa 68-II*, ff. 649-650: copy of the papal brief; *Hierarchia Catholica medii et recentioris Aevi*, vol. 4, pp. 96, 167.

[14] ARSI, *Goa 49*, f. 195v; FRANCO, *Imagem ... de Evora*, p. 413.

deacon on this journey and this stirred up some trouble in some places. But on the whole the visitation was a success.[15]

Archbishop Britto died of apoplexy in the night between 2 and 3 December 1641. Garcia immediately succeeded to the archbishopric.[16]

2. The Troubles with the Archdeacon and Others until the General Rebellion of 1653

The eleven or twelve years between the accession of Garcia and the general rebellion of 1653 were marked by an almost continuous tug of war between the Archbishop and the Archdeacon. Other combatants too, often entered the scene, but always merely in the capacity of auxiliaries and not as principals. The two main contenders were convinced that they had very good reasons for the unyielding positions that they assumed. Garcia was determined to govern his archdiocese personally and not to yield to the demands of the Archdeacon that he should do as Britto had done in the later years of his government, viz exercise all important acts of jurisdiction only with the consent of the Archdeacon. In rejecting these demands Garcia could in all sincerity appeal to the accepted practice and the canon law of the Western Church, where the bishops really ruled their dioceses. Apparently he did not realise that since he was called upon to govern a church which had century old traditions of its own based on the canon law of the Chaldean Church,[1] he should make an effort to adapt himself to its traditions. Nay he was convinced, and these are his very words, that he would be guilty of sin if he gave in to the demands of the Archdeacon,[2] and hence he felt that he was bound to defend his jurisdiction even at the cost of his blood and of his life.[3] The Archdeacon, Thomas Parampil,[4]

---

[15] ARSI, *Goa 56*, f. 489: The annual letter of the Jesuit Province of Malabar, written on 17.1.1641; *Goa 49*, f. 195v.

[16] *Goa 49*, f. 196; Franco, *Imagem ... de Évora*, p. 414.

[1] Cf. Kollaparambil, *The Archdeacon of All-India*, p. 71 for a list of the honours and powers of the archdeacon in the Chaldean Church.

[2] ARSI, *Goa 68-I*, f. 181v; f. 228.

[3] *Ibid.*, f. 29.

[4] Thomas Parampil, alias Thomas de Campo, was appointed

on the other hand, was equally determined to maintain the
traditional status of the archdeacon in the Church of the
St. Thomas Christians.   He himself as well as very large
sections of the Cattanars and Christians considered the
status of the archdeacon intimately bound up with their
national honour. He knew very well that under the Chaldean bishops the archdeacons had in fact governed the
Malabar Church and that it was only the new regime of the
Jesuit bishops that had reduced the archdeacon to a very
subordinate position.[5] He knew also that his uncle had
fought hard for his lost powers and privileges and had succeeded in wresting from Archbishop Britto a document
according to which the latter agreed not to confer sacred
orders, dispose of parishes, impose excommunications or
suspensions, in short, not to do anything of importance
without the consent of the archdeacon.[6] After his uncle's
death he himself had exercised these powers until the death
of Britto and he did not see any reason why a change of
archbishop should bring about any change in his status and
powers.

Since the two started from such diametrically opposed
principles, it was inevitable that they should come to a

---

archdeacon by Archbishop Britto in succession to Thomas's uncle,
Archdeacon George of the Cross, who died on 25 July 1640 (cf. KOL-
LAPARAMPIL, op. cit., pp. 160, 163). Thomas hailed from Kuravilangad
(APF, SOCG 233, f. 459). He was not yet thirty years old when he
was made archdeacon (ARSI, Goa 50, f. 218). It does not seem that
Thomas possessed any of the virtues of his uncle. In fact, several
witnesses of the processes instituted against him in 1657 and 1662
deposed under oath that Thomas was given to drinking. Some of
them declared that when a seminarian, he was not pious and that
he was not above suspicion in the matter of chastity. He was, they
added, quite an ignorant priest. The only thing that he knew was
a certain amount of Syriac. (APF, SOCG 232, ff. 115-145; SOCG 234,
f. 323). It is to be noted, however, that these witnesses were all
angry with him because of his persistence in schism and his repeated breach of promises.

[5] Cf. ARSI, Goa 68-II, ff. 739, 741: portions of the "Ecclesiae Cranganorensis Christianorum S. Thomae Apostoli Calamitates et Remedia" written by Fr. De Magistris S.J.

[6] ARSI, Goa 68-I, f. 90; Goa 50, f. 218v: "Breve informação da
Christandade dos Christãos de S. Thomé que chamão da Serra, e
dos seus ultimos Arcebispos e Arcediagos", probably written by
Garcia himself. Goa 50, f. 188; Goa 68-I, ff. 28, 97: other descriptions
by Garcia.

clash. The fierceness of the clash, however, was determined by the character of the combatants. That Archbishop Garcia, in spite of being personally virtuous, was harsh with others, vindictive and hard headed, is affirmed by a number of persons like Sebastiani,[7] Vincent Mary of St. Catherine,[8] four vicars of the diocese of Cochin [9] etc. These persons were all more or less opposed to Garcia and hence one has to be vary cautious in accepting their views about him. But the harshness of Garcia's character is confirmed by no less a witness than his immediate predecessor, Archbishop Britto S.J. In a letter to Fr. Vitelleschi, the general of the Jesuits, dated 29 December 1639 Britto expressed his serious anxiety about what might happen in the Serra after his death. He tells the General that in such elections he should give the first preference to those who have much experience of the people. "In the Serra things are not as elsewhere. Elsewhere any one would do. Here one needs to have much patience and gentleness. We are very anxious about what might happen in the future when I shall no longer be there by the side of my successor, seeing that he has a harsh temperament".[10] Garcia himself seems to admit to a certain extent this trait in his character. Complaining to the Jesuit General about the behaviour of Bishop Michael Rangel O.P. of Cochin and about the favour which the latter was showing the rebels, Garcia confessed that he was not by nature long-suffering.[11] As regards the character of Arch-

---

[7] APF, *SOCG 233*, ff. 471v, 469.

[8] *Il Viaggio...*, p. 162. Vincent Mary is milder than the others. He speaks merely of a certain amount of harshness which he further qualifies as well intentioned.

[9] APF, *SOCG 232*, f. 96: Copia d'una lettera di 4 Parrocchiani scritta al R.P. F. Giuseppe di S. Maria Commissario Apostolico. The four vicars were: Fr. Andrea di Pigno, Fr. Emmanuel Vaz, Fr. Christopher Miranda and Fr. Dominiic Mendes.

[10] "...se requere muita paciencia e muita brandura, o que nos tem posto a muitos em largos cuidados do que poderâ soceder ao diante faltandolhe eu, *pela aspera natureza do successor*". ARSI, *Goa 68-I*, f. 361v.

[11] "Creiame V.P. que *com eu ser na natureza mal sofrido* que tenho sofrido a este Prelado cousas assi por palavra como por escrito por nos não ouvirem que os mesmos P.es nossos e seculares estam pasmados de como lhe sofro tanto: mas assi he necessario por amor de escandalo: com tudo elle cada dia faz hua arreceio que hum

deacon Thomas, something has already been said in foot-
note no. 4. Here it may be added that his tergiversations,
breach of promises and the repeated forgeries to which he
had recourse in order to keep the episcopal dignity which
he sacrilegiously usurped, show him to be a thoroughly
unscrupulous individual. Between the harsh and intransigent Garcia and the unscrupulous and resolute Thomas
there was hardly any possibility for a reasonable and lasting
compromise.

Already at the very moment of the accession of Garcia
to the archbishopric there was trouble between the two.
Thomas demanded that in return for his recognition of
Garcia as archbishop the latter should affix his signature to
the famous document that Britto had given to his uncle.[12]
But Garcia resisted. Hence Thomas and his friends held
aloof for about 30 days. In the end Fr. De Magistris succeeded in persuading Thomas to go to Cranganore and to
make his submission.[13] As may be easily imagined, it was
only a tactical move on the part of Thomas and not by
any means a definite abandonment of his claims. Perhaps
he wanted to see if he could gain the good will of Garcia by
a show of submission and in this way obtain more easily
what he wanted. He was, however, disappointed. Garcia
showed no inclination whatever to share his powers with
the Archdeacon. He settled matters personally, and merely
consulted the Archdeacon when he happened to be present.
When the latter was not at hand, he acted on his own
initiative.[14]

Thomas was naturally angry at this and so within a
month after his submission he went and persuaded the kings
of Cochin and Kaduthuruthy (Vadakkankur) to issue orders
forbidding the Archbishop to enter their kingdoms and forbidding the Christians and Cattanars of their kingdoms to
go to see the Archbishop. The kings issued the order because they were told that Garcia had inherited fifty thousand
gold coins from his predecessor and that they could legitim-

---

dia perca a paciencia e lhe responda como elle merece". ARSI, *Goa
68-II*, f. 478.

[12] ARSI, *Goa 68-I*, ff. 28, 97; *Goa 50*, f. 188: Narration by Garcia.

[13] *Goa 50*, f. 219v; *Goa 68-I*; f. 91v; *Goa 49*, f. 196: Narrations by
Garcia and by Fr. Bras de Azevedo S.J.

[14] *Goa 50*, f. 218; *Goa 68-I*, f. 90: Narrations by Garcia.

ately claim a part of this sum as inheritance tax. Unfortunately for Thomas, the king of Cochin soon found himself in need of Garcia's intervention to get the Portuguese fleet to stay ten days longer in the waters of Cochin, to ward off an invasion by the Zamorin of Calicut. Some time after this in an interview which he had with the king of Kaduthuruthy, Garcia managed with the help of the Christians of the place to convince also that king that there was no truth in the incredible tales told by the Archdeacon. Garcia did not of course forget to increase the persuasive force of his arguments with a suitable bribe. Thomas instead was unable to give the king the bribe he had promised and so found himself shut out from that kingdom by royal order.[15]

The relations between Garcia and Thomas continued more or less in this way during the first three or four years of Garcia's government. In 1643 Thomas joined hands with the Recollects of Edapally and Angamaly [16] who were then at odds with some of the Christians of the latter place. By bribing the local king he managed to have access to the treasury of the former Cathedral Church of Angamaly and appropriated the contents, in spite of the resistance of those who were favourable to the Archbishop. In 1644 he convened a meeting of the Cattanars at Edapally for the purpose of presenting a joint demand to Garcia that the latter should respect the traditional status and powers of the archdeacon. The meeting, however, broke up without results since only ten or twelve priests from the southern parts went to attend it. Thomas therefore went to Cochin and entered into talks with the Archbishop and a sort of peace was once again arranged.[17]

Mutual recriminations, however, started very soon after this. The Archdeacon complained that the Archbishop was paying no heed to him and that important appointments and decisions were being made without his concurrence.

---

[15] ARSI, *Goa 68-II*, f. 525; *Goa 68-I*, ff. 6, 23: Narrations by Garcia.

[16] This is the name given to the members of a local congregation of religious founded by Archbishop Britto at the instance of the former Archdeacon.

[17] ARSI, *Goa 68-I*, ff. 6, 23; *Goa 68-II*, f. 525-526: Narrations by Garcia. *Goa 21*, f. 18: Letter of Garcia to the General of the Jesuits on 14 November 1644.

Garcia retorted that he made these appointments and decisions during his tours of the archdiocese. It was not his
fault if the Archdeacon did not want to accompany him
during his pastoral visits. Another complaint of the Archdeacon was that he was not being given his share of the
money realised from the fines that Garcia imposed on
offenders. Garcia justified himself saying that in the first
two years he paid him about two-fifths of these fines. After
that he did not consider it necessary to continue the payment since Thomas, far from helping him, was rather ob-
structing him in every possible way.[18] From defence Garcia
passed now to a vigorous counter-attack. He accused
Thomas of favouring those excommunicated or suspended
by him, with the result that these Cattanars did not any
longer care for the censures of Garcia and administered
many sacraments invalidly.[19] The situation was evidently
becoming more complicated.

It was at this moment that news reached Malabar that
in December of that year (1645) Dom Philip Mascarenhas,
the newly appointed viceroy of Portuguese India, would be
stopping for some days at Cochin on his way to Goa from
the island of Ceylon where he had till then been governor.
The announcement of the visit was the signal for a spurt of
feverish activity on both sides. The Archdeacon knew that
the Dutch were advancing with ever greater determination
and success towards Ceylon and the Malabar Coast. The
Portuguese authorities in the East did not have sufficient
means at their disposal to stem this advance. Because of
the war with Spain there was also not much hope of obtaining any reinforcements from Europe. Any prudent viceroy
would then be keen on obtaining the whole-hearted support
of all possible local allies. The help of the warlike Christians of the Serra would be invaluable when it came to a
trial of strength between the Portuguese and the Dutch for
the possession of Cochin.[20] The Archdeacon could therefore
be fairly sure to obtain a sympathetic hearing from the

---

[18] ARSI, *Goa 68-II*, f. 526v: Narrations by Garcia.

[19] *Goa 68-I*, ff. 6, 23: Narration by Garcia.

[20] Cf. AHEI, *LM 22-B*, ff. 373-374: copy of a letter of the captain
of Cochin, Antony da Silva de Meneses, to the governors of Portuguese India. The letter is probably of the year 1652. But the problem was more or less the same also in 1645.

Viceroy. Thomas had still with him the precious document given to his uncle by Archbishop Britto. He would show the Viceroy that the ancient privileges of the archdeacon, ratified also by this document, were not being respected by the Archbishop.[21] Garcia on the other hand decided that it was high time to put an end to the repeated acts of insubordination on the part of the Archdeacon and his constant complaints to higher authorities. In the presence of the Viceroy the Archdeacon could be more easily bullied into signing away his ancient privileges. The presence of the Dominican bishop of Cochin was likely to cause some embarrassment over the question of the admission of the other religious in the Serra. In fact, for some years past the bishop of Cochin had been insisting that, in accordance with the brief of Pope Urban VIII dated 22 February 1633 and the instructions issued on 14 April 1636 by Cardinal Barberini (the Prefect of Propaganda), the Serra should be open to the other religious as well, and not kept by the Jesuits as their exclusive domain.[22] But Garcia could effectively counter his arguments by pointing out to the Viceroy that the King had decided the question once and for all in favour of the Jesuits. The clearly expressed mind of the King would certainly not be disgregarded by his Vicegerent in the East. If by any chance (though it was most unlikely) the Viceroy should have any scruple about going against the express orders of the Pope, it could easily be removed by arguing that the brief was obtained surreptitiously and that it had not passed through the Chancellery of Lisbon.[23] Though the presence of Bishop Rangel could be embarrassing for this question, he was likely to be most helpful in resisting the claims of the Archdeacon

[21] Cf. ARSI, *Goa 50*, f. 218: "Breve informação da Christandade da Serra..."

[22] Cf. AHEI, *LM 25*, f. 118: copy of the letter of Bishop Michael Rangel, O.P., of Cochin to the Portuguese king on January 28, 1646; APF, *Acta 12*, f. 67; *Acta 13*, f. 28. — Cf. ARSI, *Goa 50*, f. 102; *Goa 68-II*, ff. 477-478: letter of Garcia. — Cf. APF, *SOCG 109*, f. 116, 127: Letter of Bishop Rangel to Propaganda.

[23] Cf. ARSI, *Goa 68-I*, ff. 11, 22-23: a paper prepared by Garcia or by his close associates for the perusal of the Viceroy. — Cf. also AHEI, *LM 25*, f. 118: the letter of Bishop Rangel to the king of Portugal on 28 January 1646.

for autonomy,[24] since the Bishop would not fail to see that the example of the Serra could become contagious in his own diocese! A great patriot like Archbishop Garcia who went to the extent of repairing at his own expense the fortifications of Cranganore and of personally patrolling that fortress in the night in times of danger and who at the age of eighty did not hesitate to take over the command of the City of Cochin,[25] could not have failed to consider the question of the help which the martial Christians of the Serra could render the Portuguese forces in case the Dutch attacked Cochin. But he probably calculated that the loyalty of the St. Thomas Christians would be surer if they were to be brought more directly under his authority than if they were left under that of the unreliable Archdeacon.

Whatever the calculations of the two main contenders, they went about actively canvassing for allies and documents in view of the proximate visit of the Viceroy. It was the Archdeacon that made the first move. He had now the whole-hearted support of the Recollects of Edapally who were thoroughly annoyed with Garcia because he had refused to give the tonsure to several of the young men presented by them. Together, therefore, they went and bribed the King of Kaduthuruthy[26] who promptly issued orders forbidding the Archbishop to appoint or to remove vicars in his kingdom and directing that these things be done by the Archdeacon. The king's proclamation referred also to a document which the Archdeacon had prepared for the maintenance of the traditions and customs of the Christian community, which were being damaged by the unreasonable attitude of the Archbishop. The king said that he had been informed by the Archdeacon that some of the Christians had refused to sign it. These were now ordered to sign under pain of exile. If the Archbishop failed to make peace with the Archdeacon, the king would not allow him and the Jesuits to enter his kingdom. In the meantime no letters of

---

[24] Cf. ARSI, *Goa 68-I*, f. 61v: "Sommaria Relatione della Christianità della Serra".

[25] WICKI, *O Homem...*, p. 327-328 (2nd Appendix).

[26] ARSI, *Goa 68-I*, f. 22; another copy on ff. 10v-11: an account regarding the Recollects of Edapally sent by Garcia in 1645 to the Jesuit authorities in Rome.

the Archbishop were to be read in the churches of the kingdom.[27]

Archdeacon Thomas wrote also to the other churches of the Serra denouncing the Archbishop as one who failed to observe earlier agreements. The refusal to ordain the young men of Edapally was prominently mentioned among the offences of the Archbishop. The Cattanars and the people were, therefore, asked not to receive the vicars appointed by Garcia and not to allow the Jesuits to enter their churches, in case they came. The Viceroy was already on his way to Cochin. The Cattanars were invited to accompany the Archdeacon when he would go to speak with the Viceroy.[28] The Archdeacon approached also the king of Cochin who issued a proclamation in his favour on 21 November, even though a few days previously, at the request of one of the Jesuits, he had issued another in favour of Garcia! A week after the proclamation of the king, Thomas sent a circular to all the churches of the kingdom of Cochin telling the Cattanars and the Christians of the failure of Garcia to keep the promises made by Archbishop Menezes at the time of the Synod of Diamper and those made by Archbishop Britto regarding the powers and prerogatives of the archdeacon. The Cattanars and Christians were therefore invited to sign a document which was to be presented to the Viceroy and which had already been signed by those of the kingdom of Kaduthuruthy.[29] This paper contained a long list of complaints. The most important of these referred to the refusal of Garcia and the Jesuits to allow other religious to work in the Serra, to the desire of the Christians to be ruled by a Syrian prelate or at least by a non-Jesuit, to the improper management by the Jesuits of the Seminary of Vaipicotta and their failure to teach theology to the seminarians. The Archbishop is accused of appropriating part of the allowances of the Cattanars, of intercepting their complaints to the Pope and to the king of Portugal, of trying

---

[27] Goa 53, f. 218: Ola (palm leaf document) of the king of Kaduthuruthy. Another slightly different translation of the same ola is to be found in Goa 68-I, f. 10. — Cf also Goa 68-I, ff. 32v, 114, 142.

[28] ARSI, Goa 50, f. 111v: Translation of the ola of the Archdeacon to the vicar, priests and people of Agaparambu.

[29] Goa 53, f. 218: Translation of the olas of the king of Cochin and of the Archdeacon.

to destroy the Recollects of Edapally and of harassing the Cattanars with fines.[30]

The Archbishop and the Jesuit missionaries too were active all the while. They made two elaborate judicial enquiries regarding the rebellious conduct of Archdeacon Thomas and his allies (especially the superior and procurator of the Recollects of Edapally). The first enquiry took place within the limits of the Archdiocese of Cranganore between 2 October and 3 November 1645. No less than 22 priests, many of whom were vicars, were questioned on 18 articles. These articles referred especially to the almost continuous rebellion of the Archdeacon ever since Garcia became archbishop, to the efforts that he made to set the local kings at variance with Garcia and to his favouring those punished by Garcia. Other articles accused the Archdeacon of misappropriating public funds. The Recollects were accused of helping the Archdeacon in his rebellion and of not living like religious. Finally there were other articles that praised the government of Garcia, the apostolic zeal of the Jesuit missionaries and their management of the seminary of Vaipicotta. None of the witnesses denied any point. In some cases they merely said that they were not sufficiently informed so as to be able to give their view. On most of the points, however, they were in agreement.[31] The second enquiry was made by a lay judge of Cochin (John Furtado Cavaleiro) from 11 to 16 November.[32] Sixteen persons were questioned on eight articles which dealt in general with the rebellious behaviour of the Archdeacon, his inciting others to rebellion and the support that he

---

[30] *Goa 68-I*, ff. 12-16 and 18-21. Some of these accusations are not as fanciful as one might imagine. The accusation against Garcia regarding the intercepting of communications to and from higher authorities is confirmed by Canon Joseph de Rego of Cochin (a Portuguese) who declared under oath that a relative of his who had been for some time captain of Cranganore, had to put up with the enmity of Garcia because of his refusal to hand over to Garcia a letter which the Viceroy had sent to the Archdeacon. APF, *SOCG 232*, f. 355v.

[31] ARSI, *Goa 50*, ff. 142-172: the original; ff. 114-140; a copy.

[32] In a letter to the king of Portugal on January 28, 1646 the bishop of Cochin bitterly complained about this action of Garcia. Cf. AHEI, *LM 25*, ff. 118v.

received from the Recollects of Edapally.[33]   Besides getting
these judicial enquiries made, Garcia and the missionaries
prepared a reply to the accusations contained in the paper
of the Archdeacon.[34]   Other memoranda too were prepared
to influence the Viceroy in their favour.[35]

It may be noted by the way, that while Garcia and the
Jesuit missionaries obtained many witnesses to testify to
their good government, and to accuse the Archdeacon, the
Recollects and their allies, of insubordination, rebellion etc.,
the Bishop of Cochin accused Garcia and the Jesuit missionaries of oppressing the Christians of the Serra, who, he
declared, were neither schismatics nor disobedient, but
obedient children of Holy Church.[36]

When the Viceroy reached Cochin, the Archdeacon, accompanied by many Cattanars, went to make his complaints
against Garcia.   After hearing both sides the Viceroy induced them to make a compromise.   But the document that
was prepared by Garcia on 12 December 1645 can hardly be
called a compromise.   It was rather a document that intended to set the seal on the extinction of the traditional prerogatives of the archdiaconate.   None of its clauses compromis-
ed in the least the authority and jurisdiction of the archbishop.   The most important clauses may be summarised
thus:

1.   When the archdeacon is at hand, the archbishop
will *consult* him regarding the affairs of the Christians.   But
if he is away, the archbishop will decide by himself.

2.   When the archbishop intends to confer orders, he
will inform the archdeacon about it and obtain from him
information regarding the life and conduct of the candida-
tes.   But if the archdeacon cannot be found, the archbishop
will proceed by himself.

3.   Before the archbishop hands over to the vicars the
papers of their appointment, these papers will be passed to
the archdeacon who will *without demur affix his signature!*
But even if he refuses to sign these papers, the vicars will

---

[33] ARSI, *Goa 50*, ff. 32-63.

[34] ARSI, *Goa 68-I*, ff. 12-16; 18-21.

[35] *Ibid.*, ff. 11; 22-23.

[36] AHEI, *LM 25*, ff. 118-119: copy of the letter of Bishop Rangel
to the Portuguese king on 28 January 1646. See especially f. 119. —
Cf. also ARSI, *Goa 50*, f. 102; *Goa 68-II*, ff. 477-478.

all the same take possession of their parishes and govern them!

4. When the archbishop holds a synod for the good of the archdiocese as a whole, he will invite the archdeacon, so that he together with the rest of the Cattanars may help the archbishop to make decisions. When the archbishop holds other less important meetings of the Christians, he will inform the archdeacon, so that he can attend it if he wishes. But these meetings will carry on even if he does not wish to attend.

5. When the archbishop makes his visits to the churches, he will inform the archdeacon of it, and the latter will accompany him unless legitimately impeded.

There follow four other clauses regarding the Recollects of Edapally, the churches of Vaipicotta and Angicaimal and the question of the allowances of the vicars and of wine for masses. The conclusion contains an exhortation to the Archdeacon and the Cattanars to regard these as special favours granted to them by the Archbishop and to be accordingly grateful! All previous agreements with former archbishops regarding these questions are declared to have no more validity. The paper was signed by the Viceroy, the Archbishop, the Archdeacon and four Jesuits.[37]

What is to be thought of this document? Reading it carefully, one gets the impression that the shrewd lawyer in Garcia managed to find such words that would give a superficial reader the impression that much was being granted to the Archdeacon, even though in reality nothing substantial was being granted. The first article, for instance, professes to speak of "what pertains to the jurisdiction of the archdeacon" ("Que no que toca a iurisdição do Arcediago da Serra ..."). One would imagine that something substantial is coming. But when one has carefully read through the rather confusing wording of that first article, one is disillusioned to note that all that pompous talk about the jurisdiction of the archdeacon boils down to his right of being consulted by the archbishop in the affairs (civil suits) of the Christians! In fact, Garcia says elsewhere that *none of the concessions* that he made to the Archdeacon in the

---

[37] ARSI, *Goa 50*, ff. 64-66: authenticated copy; *Goa 68-I*, ff. 8-9: another copy; APF, *SOCG 191*, f. 579: Italian translation.

presence of Dom Philip Mascarenhas, *spoke of matters that*
pertained to jurisdiction! [38]   The line that separates such
conduct from outright deception is very thin indeed.   Again,
the third article speaks of the archbishop passing to the
archdeacon the papers of the appointment of the vicars.
The archdeacon is expected to affix his signature without
questioning.   If the archdeacon has no say whatever in the
matter, why then this empty ceremony and why pretend that
all that was a special concession and privilege ("ouverão
todos por particular favor"), as we are told in the conclusion
of the document?   This, of course, does not mean that Archdeacon Thomas did well when he changed altogether the
tenor of the document in his letters to the churches.

The day after the agreement was signed, Garcia, imagining that he had effectively and for ever stifled the pretensions of the Archdeacon, paid him his allowance and appointed five vicars according to his recommendation.   But on
the same day Thomas sent from Mattancherry a thoroughly
altered text of the agreement to all the churches.[39]   The
version of Thomas contained only five articles.   The last
of them was the most important and it summarised and
deformed beyond recognition the first five articles of the
genuine document: "When it is a question of conferring
orders or appointing vicars or doing any other business, it
has been agreed that *nothing can be done unless the Archbi-*
shop and I get together to treat of them."   The other articles too were altered in his favour.[40]   As soon as Garcia
came to know of this, he sent copies of the Archdeacon's
version to the Viceroy and asked him to write to the kings
of Cochin and Kaduthuruthy to favour him.   But the Viceroy declined to do so, pointing out that the conditions of
Portuguese India were such that he could not afford to
alienate these kings.   He suggested, instead, that Garcia
should bribe the Archdeacon.   But Garcia rejected the suggestion, saying that it would be tantamount to furnishing
his enemy with arms.[41]

---

[38] ARSI, *Goa 50*, f. 218; *Goa 68-I*, f. 90: narration by Garcia.
[39] *Goa 68-I*, f. 28v: narration by Garcia.
[40] *Ibid.*, ff. 45-46: authenticated copy of the Portuguese translation; ff. 8-9: another copy; *Goa 50*, f. 76: another authenticated copy;
APF, *SOCG 191*, f. 588: Italian translation.
[41] ARSI, *Goa 68-I*, f. 28v: narration by Garcia.

Thomas now wrote to the Cattanars accusing the Archbishop of not keeping the terms of the agreement made before the Viceroy and of going back to his old ways of doing everything by himself. Thomas, therefore, asked the Cattanars not to receive the Jesuits in their churches until the Archbishop would change his ways.[42]

Several months passed. In July 1646 the Archdeacon met Christopher Telles, the captain of Palliporto and a professed knight of the Order of Christ, and told him of his desire to make peace with the Archbishop. He alleged that in the past he had rebelled against the Archbishop because of the evil counsels given him by others. But now he had resolved to live in peace and obedience. When Christopher Telles informed Garcia of this, the latter imposed two conditions: the Archdeacon would have to surrender the paper granted to his uncle by Dom Britto, and send to the churches, with the signatures of the Archbishop and the Archdeacon, the proper translation of the agreement made before the Viceroy. The Archdeacon agreed to the terms. A meeting between Garcia and Thomas was accordingly arranged at the seminary of Vaipicotta. Garcia went there accompanied by the Rector of the Jesuit college of Cranganore and other Jesuits. The Archdeacon had a number of Cattanars with him. Christopher Telles who was present in the capacity of mediator, asked the Archdeacon to hand over the paper of Dom Britto. Thomas now pretended that he had no such paper with him! To prevent a break-down of the negotiations, it was suggested that he should sign a document saying that the famous paper of Archbishop Britto was no longer in his possession and that in case he ever discovered it, he would not make use of it. But he refused to do this and he would not also sign the Malayalam translation of the agreement made before the Viceroy, saying that if he did so before settling the other problems to be discussed, the Archbishop might not yield him anything. Christopher Telles and the Rector of the college of Cranganore (Fr. Diogo Cardoso S.J.), then, offered to stand security for the Archbishop. Thomas, however, could not be induced to

---

[42] *Ibid.*, f. 295v; *Goa 50*, f. 110v: ola of the Archdeacon.

change his stand and the meeting served only to widen the breach.[43]

Thomas now went off to the south, visited some churches and made an agreement with a number of Cattanars that the vicars appointed by Garcia should not be recognized, but that all the Cattanars belonging to a church would be authorised to perform the functions of the vicar, dividing equally among themselves the income of the church. After this he returned to the northern parts. At Narame (Tripoonithura) he had some Cattanars and Christians who favoured Garcia, arrested with the help of the king of Cochin. He won over also the king of Kottayam who ordered the Cattanars and Christians of his territory to follow their traditions and not to receive any vicars without the written authorization of the Archdeacon. All the priests belonging to each church were to perform jointly the functions of the vicar. They were forbidden to accept or to read in the churches papers sent by the Archbishop. It seemed as though Thomas would triumph. But in the end everything fizzled out since he lost the support of the king of Cochin and of the other kings because of his failure to give them the money that they expected. On top of this, there arose also a quarrel between him and his chief supporters, with the result that Thomas thought that it might be worth while to send once again feelers of peace to the Archbishop. But Garcia stood firm by his former conditions, adding to them one or two new ones. The negotiations, therefore, proceeded no further.[44]

Probably it was at about this time that Garcia appointed Fr. Jerome Furtado, a Portuguese priest, as his vicar-general. We do not know exactly when this appointment took place. But from December 1647 onwards we see him issuing decrees in that capacity.[45] Previously he used to sign as "viga-

----

[43] ARSI, *Goa 50*, ff. 78v-79v: authenticated copy of the sworn statement made by Christopher Telles on 5 September 1646; *Goa 68-I*, f. 30: another copy; *Goa 50*, ff. 84-88: declarations of three Jesuits who were present at the meeting: *Goa 68-I*, ff. 28v, 218v: narrations by Garcia.

[44] ARSI, *Goa 68-I*, ff. 28v-29; *Goa 50*, f. 218v-219: narrations by Garcia. *Goa 50*, ff. 110v-111: olas of the king of Kottayam to the churches of Kottayam; ola of the Archdeacon to the king of Kottayam.

[45] *Goa 50*, ff. 112, 111v, 110.

rio de Vara (a sort of Forane-Vicar).[46] Under the former
archbishops the archdeacon used to be also vicar-general.
Hence this new move on the part of Archbishop Garcia was
certainly not going to contribute to a reconciliation between
him and the Archdeacon. Most probably Garcia had by
now made up his mind to humiliate and to break the Archdeacon, since he found it impossible to bend him to his
will. In a document of 1657 we find the demotion of the
archdeacon listed prominently among the injuries done by
Garcia to the Christians of the Serra.[47]

Garcia was very annoyed to note that the support given
to the Archdeacon by the Dominicans and by the Carmelites,
stood in the way of his plans to humiliate him and to break
his resistance. In the report that he made in 1647, Garcia
complained bitterly of both the Dominicans and the Carmelites. The Dominicans were blamed for supporting not only
the Archdeacon but also the Recollects of Edapally whom
Garcia did not hesitate to call "a spark sent from hell (scintilla infernal) in order to destroy this Church!" According
to Garcia, these Recollects succeeded under the cloak of
sanctity to deceive others, including the Portuguese. The
Recollects are accused of not observing their rules. But
what brought on them the indignation of Garcia in a special
way was the support that they gave to the Archdeacon. A
certain Carmelite priest called Fr. Diogo de Jesus is also
blamed by Garcia for backing the Archdeacon. This Carmelite paid Thomas a visit and offered to plead his case
before the Pope and before the king of Portugal. He tried
also to see if he could personally bring about a reconciliation between Garcia and Thomas. But Garcia insisted on
his former conditions and Thomas did not consider it worth
while to go any further.[48]

Some years earlier another Carmelite priest called Fr.
Joseph Alexis of Jesus and Mary had established himself
for some time at Kuravilangad and had succeeded, in spite
of the opposition of the Archbishop, to start there the Con-
fraternity of Our Lady of Mount Carmel. Nearly five thous-

---

[46] *Ibid.*, ff. 110, 114.

[47] APF, *SOCG 232*, f. 96: "Copia d'una elttera di 4 Parrocchiani
scritta al R.P.F. Gioseppe di S. Maria Commissario Apostolico".

[48] ARSI, *Goa 68-I*, f. 29: narration by Garcia. (Other copies in
ff. 97-98 and *Goa 50*, ff. 188-190).

and persons, including the Archdeacon and several Cattanars, received the scapular. An yearly feast also was being
celebrated there in honour of the Virgin of Carmel. Through
the good offices of this priest the Archdeacon now sent two
letters, one addressed to the Pope and the other addressed
to the cardinals of the Propaganda, in which he complained
that the Jesuits were not allowing him to exercise his jurisdiction, and asked that the Carmelites be admitted in the
Serra. He accused the Jesuits of "wanting to be sole masters
wherever they go" and of having prevented the execution
of the papal brief which allowed also other religious to work
in the Serra.[49] These letters were probably accompanied by
another letter in Syriac, written on 8 December 1647, in
which the Archdeacon told the Holy Father that the three
Carmelite fathers, Joseph Alexis of Our Lady, John Baptist
and Louis Alvarez, would inform him in detail of the op-
pressions of the Archbishop and the Jesuits.[50] Two years
later, with a more formal document the Archdeacon authorized these three Carmelites and the Prior of the monastery
of Santa Maria della Scala (in Rome) to act as his procurators in Goa, Portugal and Rome.[51]

The ever increasing bitterness of the quarrel between
the Archbishop and the Archdeacon was beginning to cause
serious concern to the Viceroy. He rightly feared that
something disastrous might happen if the quarrel was not
settled in time. In a letter of 15 January 1648 he reminded
the king of Portugal that the people of the Serra were solidly
behind the Archdeacon who was one of them and who by
long tradition enjoyed great prestige and authority among
them. He expressed his fear that the Serra might be lost

---

[49] APF, *SOCG 191*, ff. 535, 537: letters (originals) of the Archdeacon to the Holy Father and to the cardinals of the Propaganda. The
letters are not dated. But they were written certainly after 14 September 1646, since they speak of Bishop Rangel "of holy memory".
It is most likely that they were written together with a syriac letter
dated 8 December 1647. — VINCENZO MARIA, *Il Viaggio* ..., p. 172. —
ARSI, *Goa 68-II*, f. 451. According to the Jesuits, Fr. Joseph Alexis
was a fugitive from his monastery. He won the good will of Fr.
Chandy Parampil (the vicar of Kuravilangad and future bishop)
by absolving some Christians excommunicated by the Archbishop.
(cf. *Goa 50*, ff. 184-185).

[50] APF, *SOCG 191*, f. 539v. An Italian translation is found in f. 540.

[51] *Ibid.*, f. 559: the original document, dated 9 December 1649.

if things went ahead that way.[52]. From a certain distance
the Viceroy was probably able to see the situation more
clearly than Garcia and Fr. De Magistris who were there
right in the middle of the quarrels. Both of them reported
to the Jesuit General towards the end of 1649 that the Serra had never been so quiet as then. They indeed admitted
that the Archdeacon was still in rebellion and that he continued his efforts to cause trouble with the help of the local
kings. But he was not able to do much because he had no
following.[53]

It seems most likely that it was during these years
(1648 and 1649) that the Archdeacon took the fatal step of
writing secretly to the Coptic Patriarch of Alexandria, to
the Jacobite Patriarch of Antioch and to the Nestorian Patriarch of Babylon, giving them exaggerated reports of the
state of abandonment in which the St. Thomas Christians
found themselves because of the alleged absence of a bishop,
and asking them to be so kind as to remedy the situation.[54]
It has been mentioned earlier that the Archdeacon sent his
complaints and petitions to Rome at the end of 1647 through
the good offices of certain Carmelite priests. On the same
occasion and also two years later he appointed these same
priests his procurators in Rome, Lisbon and Goa. In spite
of all this, it would seem that he did not have much hope
of any prompt action on the part of Rome. Past experience
showed him that his adversaries were far too powerful for
him in Rome and still more in Portugal.[55] Even if the Pope
were to issue another brief allowing also other religious
to work in the Serra, it was not likely to receive any better
treatment than the brief of 1633 which remained a dead
letter because of the opposition of the Archbishop who argued that the king of Portugal had been granted the privilege of providing for the Serra and that the king had clearly

---

[52] Cfr. FERROLI, *The Jesuits in Malabar*, vol. 2, p. 31.

[53] ARSI, *Goa 9-I*, f. 182: letter of Fr. De Magistris. *Goa 68-I*, f. 30:
letter of Garcia.

[54] APF, *SOCG 191*, f. 658: letter of Fr. Elzeario di Sansay, a Capuchin missionary in Cairo, to the Propaganda on 5 October 1649. Other
copies of the same letter are to be found in *SOCG 212*, ff. 207-8; 247.
— VINCENZO MARIA, *Il Viaggio...*, p. 162; SEBASTIANI, *Prima Spediz.*,
p. 3. ARSI, *Goa 68-I*, f. 62: "Sommaria Relatione della Christianità..."

[55] APF, *SOCG 191*, f. 119.

declared his intention of not allowing others to go there.[56]
It must have been, then, the feeling that there was no way
out of the situation, that drove the Archdeacon to write secretly to the Eastern Patriarchs not in communion with
Rome.

It has already been mentioned that Archbishop Garcia
and Fr. De Magistris wrote to the Jesuit General at the end
of 1649 that the Archdeacon had at that time almost no following. Garcia therefore came to the conclusion that it was
the most favourable moment to proceed juridically against
the Archdeacon. The latter furnished Garcia an additional reason by going and joining the Recollects of Edapally
without his permission and taking possession of their churches of Edapally and Angamaly.[57] On 14 January 1650 Archbishop Garcia solemnly laid an interdict on the two churches of Edapally as long as the Archdeacon would remain
there. The juridical steps that preceded the decision were
the following. From 30 December 1645 onwards until 9
January 1650 on various occasions and in various places
Garcia obtained the sworn testimonies of seven witnesses
regarding the culpability of the Archdeacon on nine points.
The substance of the accusations was that the Archdeacon
usurped the jurisdiction of the Archbishop and impeded
the latter from exercising his jurisdiction. He published a
falsified version of the agreement made before the Viceroy
and also asserted in some churches and before the civil authorities that he had lately discovered from a book that the
Archbishop could only confirm and ordain and that the
whole of the jurisdiction of the Serra pertained to the Archdeacon. Finally, he joined the Recollects of Edapally in an
irregular way and then took possession of their house with
the help of the local king. On 30 December 1649 from Diamper Garcia formally cited the Archdeacon to appear before
him within eight days to answer the charges. Needless to
say, the Archdeacon refused to take any notice of the cita-
tion. The Promoter of Justice of the archdiocese of Cranganore now suggested that Garcia should declare Archdeacon Thomas to have incurred the excommunication of the

[56] ARSI, *Goa 50*, f. 102; *Goa 68-II*, ff. 477-478: report of Garcia to
the General of the Jesuits.
[57] *Goa 50*, ff. 219; *Goa 68-I*, f. 91: narration by Garcia.

bull "In coena Domini", for taking away his jurisdiction.
But Garcia concluded the process, saying that, though the
Archdeacon had incurred the excommunication of the bull
"In coena Domini," he was not declaring it for the time
being, but merely placing under interdict the two churches
of Edapally, which the Archdeacon had taken possession
of with the help of the king.[58] Thomas paid no attention
whatsoever to the interdict. He and his partisans continued
to say mass and do everything else as before in those churches.[59]

In 1652 the Captain of Cochin, Antony da Silva de Menezes, made one last effort to re-establish peace between the
Archbishop and the Archdeacon. But while both professed
to desire peace, neither was willing to yield anything! Garcia
insisted on the observance of the agreement of 1645. Thomas did not want even to hear of it. Hence the breach continued.[60]

3. THE GENERAL CONDITIONS OF THE ST. THOMAS CHRISTIANS
     AT THIS TIME AND THE WORK OF THE JESUIT MISSIONARIES
                    AMONG THEM

Our sources are very much at variance regarding the
total number of the St. Thomas Christians at this time.
Some accounts give figures as high as two hundred thousand
or even three hundred thousand,[1] while others insist that

---

[58] *Goa 50*, ff. 104-109: authenticated copy of the process.

[59] *Ibid.*, f. 219: narration by Garcia.

[60] *Ibid.*, f. 70: authenticated copy of a letter of the captain to
the Archdeacon on 31 March 1652. — *Ibid.*, f. 71: authenticated copy
of a certificate issued by the captain on 25 November 1652.

[1] In the instructions issued in 1655 by the Propaganda to Fr.
Hyacinth of St. Vincent O.C.D. it is said that the Archdeacon has led
with him into revolt 150,000 Christians and 300 priests (ARSI, *Goa
68-I*, f. 295v). — This number was given to the Propaganda by Fr. De
Magistris S.J. At the same time Fr. De Magistris claimed that when
he left India, about 50,000 Christians were obeying the Archbishop.
So the total comes to 200,000. But Fr. Bras de Azevedo S.J. in his
"Carta da Missão da Serra..." accuses Fr. De Magistris of having
presented exaggerated reports in Rome. (Cf. *Goa 49*, ff. 178-209;
APF, *SOCG 191*, f. 581). — Archdeacon Thomas in his letters to the
Holy Father and to the cardinals of the Propaganda gives the num-
ber of the Christians as more than 200,000. (APF, *SOCG 191*, ff. 535,

the St. Thomas Christians were no more than seventy or eighty thousand.[2] They were divided in about ninety parishes,[3] spread over the territories of about twenty rajahs and a multitude of petty chieftains. About half of the parishes, however, lay within the three kingdoms of Cochin, Kaduthuruthy and Kottayam.[4]

These Christians were held in great esteem by the pagan kings in whose territories they dwelt. They were regarded as belonging to the nobility. The majority of them were traders or soldiers.[5] They would not baptize those of low castes lest they should lose their social position! They used, instead, to send them to the Portuguese for baptism, and after baptism they would not admit them to their churches, and would not have any relations with them. They washed themselves in case they happened to touch some one of a lower caste.[6] Their ecclesiastical head had exclusive jurisdiction over them in all spiritual matters and in civil cases. From the sworn statement made by four vicars of the diocese of Cochin on 10 December 1657 we learn that during the time of the quarrels between the Archbishop and the

---

537). Sebastiani too gives the same number. He adds that the "Southists" were only about 5,000. (APF, *SOCG 233*, ff. 457v-458). — BARRETTO, on p. 20 of his *Relatione delle Missioni...*, says that the St. Thomas Christians reach the number 150,000.

[2] A report of 1644 regarding the missions looked after by the Jesuit Province of Malabar (*Goa 56*, f. 527), the Annual Letters of 1648 and 1654 from the Malabar Province (*Goa 56*, ff. 538, 554), as also the "Carta da Missão da Serra..." written by Bras de Azevedo S.J. in 1666 (*Goa 49*, ff. 178-209) give the number of the St. Thomas Christians as 80,000.

FRANCO in his *Imagem... de Évora*, p. 428 insists that the Christians were only "seventy thousand and not 150,000 as the commissaries said in Rome".

[3] The annual letter of 1643 says that the parishes of the Serra were 93. (ARSI, *Goa 56*, f. 506v).

The report of 1644 gives the number of churches as 92. (*Ibid.* f. 527). BARRETTO's, *Relatione delle Missioni...*, p. 20 says that the St. Thomas Christians lived in 95 parishes.

According to Sebastiani, the Christians of the Serra were divided in 85 parishes. (APF, *SOCG 233*, ff. 457v-458).

[4] ARSI, *Goa 68-I*, ff. 29v, 64-65.

[5] BARRETTO, *Relatione delle Missioni...*, p. 20.

[6] APF, *SOCG 233*, f. 472: "Breve Racconto di tutto l'operato dal P.F. Gioseppe di S. Maria...".

Archdeacon, the kings intruded into the field of the exclusive jurisdiction of the Archbishop.[7]

The children did not generally make their confession and communion until their marriage which, however, took place as soon as the boys and girls reached the threshold of puberty. The Christians had very many days of fast, but the fast was reduced to a very rigorous abstinence. On the days of fast they would eat only rice and vegetables. According to Sebastiani, the Christians practised simony, usury[8] and divination. They had with them books of magic and they observed superstitious practices[9] on occasions like marriage. They were poorly instructed in the faith.[10] The people as well as the priests, in general, had a salutary fear of ecclesiastical censures.[11] From what the Archdeacon wrote to the Pope and to the cardinals of the Propaganda in 1647 about the people's admiration for the Carmelites because of their "ascetic lives, fastings and because they refrained from eating meat, taking instead only fish all their lives",[12] we can gather that the people were inclined to ascetic lives, or at least that it was an ideal that they looked up to with respect.

The students to the priesthood studied at the seminary of Vaipicotta. Throughout the time of the government of Archbishop Garcia the rector of the semnary was a certain Fr. Salvador Machado S.J. He taught the seminarians Syriac and Malayalam. It does not seem that there were other fathers attached to the seminary. Once the seminarians received the tonsure, they considered it a question of honour not to turn back from the road chosen. This was so from times immemorial. The king of Portugal bore the expenses of the seminary, at least in theory.[13]

---

[7] *SOCG 232*, f. 96.

[8] Lending money even at normal rates of interest was then considered "usury". Cf. the article on "Usury" found on pp. 235-238 of vol. XV of *The Catholic Encyclopedia*, New York 1912.

[9] It would be helpful to remember that many European missionaries of the time were inclined to see superstition where there was none. Just think of the famous "Chinese rites"!

[10] APF, *SOCG 233*, f. 472: Breve Racconto di tutto l'operato dal P.F. Gioseppe di S. Maria... — ARSI, *Goa 56*, f. 507v: Annual letter of 1643.

[11] BARRETTO, *Relatione delle Missioni...*, p. 26.

[12] APF, *SOCG 191*, ff. 535v, 537.

[13] Cf. BARRETTO, *Relatione delle Missioni...*, p. 25. — ARSI, *Goa*

The picture that one gets about the general level of learning among the Cattanars is really shocking. Testimonies from all sides seem to confirm the fact, though they give very different explanations of the causes of this ignorance. Fr. Vincent Mary O.C.D. in his letter of 2 April 1657 to the Cardinal Prefect of the Propaganda wrote of the great ignorance of the ecclesiastics of the Serra. They knew just enough Syriac to celebrate mass and to recite the divine office. Their ignorance in the matter of jurisdiction was such that they dispensed and absolved in all cases without scruple.[14] The Jesuit who wrote a rejoinder to this letter accepted the fact as true, but sought to free the Jesuit teachers of the seminary and the archbishops from all blame, throwing the whole of it on the seminarians who had, according to him, no desire to learn anything. They stayed at the seminary unwillingly. They made use of a thousand excuses to go to their homes whenever possible. Then they would return to the seminary a few weeks before the ordinations. The Archbishop had to put up with all this, and in order to avoid greater evils he used to ordain them when they learned enough Syriac to understand the psalms, the gospels and the missal.[15] Garcia too said more or less the same things in a report which he wrote in his defence in 1645. He added that theology could not be taught in the seminary because the pupils did not know and did not want to learn Latin.[16] On the other hand the Archdeacon and his friends attributed this ignorance to the unwillingness of the Jesuits to teach the seminarians anything worth while. He wrote to the Holy Father in 1647 that the Jesuits had not taught any one in the Serra Latin and Portuguese, though they had been working there for over 40 years and though these languages were taught in all the other churches. According to the Archdeacon, the Jesuits did not want to teach these languages because they did not want that there should be any one in the Serra who should be able to claim and maintain their legitimate rights.[17] It is interesting to note that

---

49, f. 189; *Goa 29*, f. 93v; *Goa 56*, f. 506v. — APF, *SOCG 232*, f. 127; *SOCG 233*, f. 472.

[14] ARSI, *Goa 68-II*, f. 448.

[15] *Ibid.*, f. 452.

[16] *Ibid.*, ff. 527v-528.

[17] APF, *SOCG 191*, ff. 535, 537. — Cf. also the complaints made to the Viceroy in December 1645. (ARSI, *Goa 68-I*, ff. 18v-19).

the annual letter of 1644 of the Malabar Province, when speaking of the seminary of Vaipicotta, says that the seminarians corresponded to the care of the Jesuit superiors by learning their lessons etc. There is no hint nor any complaint whatever of their not wanting to study.[18] This makes it rather difficult to accept the later explanations given by Garcia and others under the stress of accusations made against them. It is true that in October-November 1645 several witnesses gave explanations similar to those given above by Garcia.[19] But this does not solve the problem since we see that in 1657 other witnesses said the contrary.[20]

The ecclesiastics were very much respected even by the Hindus, nay even by the kings. The Christians made sure that they were given this respect. The king of Portugal paid an yearly allowance to all the vicars, or parish priests. The distribution of this money was made by the archbishop who made use of it as a means to keep the vicars obedient to him. As a rule the vicars were changed every three years. The other priests and the clerics were very generously ("con assai pia liberalità") maintained by the Christians.[21]

The greatest solemnity among the St. Thomas Christians was the first mass of a priest. The mass would last as much as three or four hours. A sumptuous meal would follow the mass, and then the people would return to the church to make their gifts to the new priest who would sit on a chair with a table in front. The offerings used to be so abundant as to constitute the priest's patrimony.[22]

A great annual feast was that of Our Lady of Edapally, attended not only by the St. Thomas Christians but also by the inhabitants of the city of Cochin. It was celebrated on the day of the new moon of February. The feast was preceded by a three day's fast. Out of the offerings made by the faithful, a large quantity of rice and vegetables used to be cooked and distributed to thousands of the fasting people. The archbishop vested in pontificals blessed this rice before distribution. Many people used to preserve this rice, regarding it as miraculous, and eat it when sick. The

---

[18] *Goa 56*, f. 522.
[19] *Goa 50*, ff. 142-176. See the replies to the 16th article.
[20] APF, *SOCG 232*, ff. 115-145.
[21] BARRETTO, *Relatione delle Missioni ...*, pp. 29, 26.
[22] *Ibid.*, pp. 26-27.

people used to pass the three nights singing and dancing. In the morning there used to be always numerous confessions and communions.[23] Another very largely attended feast was that of "Moonu Noyambu" (the three days' fast of Jonas) in the church of Kuravilangadu, which was the chief church of the southern parts.[24] During the government of Archbishop Garcia many churches were renewed. He insisted very much on the churches being kept clean. Sacred vessels and vestments were at times presented to the churches by him. At other times he ordered that these be bought with the income of the churces themselves.[25]

The Recollects of Edapally and Angamaly, founded as a local religious congregation in 1626 by Archbishop Britto at the instance of the archdeacon, Cattanars and people, continued to exist also during the time of Archbishop Garcia. The Recollects had never been very numerous because their life was a very secluded one and the rules were extremely severe.[26] A certain Audepe (Joseph) Cattanar of Kaduthuruthy declared during the elaborate investigations made by Garcia against the Archdeacon and his allies in October-November 1645, that the total number of the Recollects (including the dead) was not more than ten or twelve. In 1645 they numbered only eight. But only two stayed at Edapally and one at Angamaly. The rest lived in their own homes because of molestations by the local king and because of disagreement with the rest of the religious. Hence they could not any longer have a choir. An effort to revitalise the group by accepting some young men who would eventually become priests and Recollects, did not meet with the favour of Garcia.[27] In fact, for various reasons the archbishops and the missionaries had become suspicious of them and of their close relations with the archdeacons. The glowing reports that the Jesuit missionaries used to give in the earlier years[28] soon gave way to outright condemna-

---

[23] *Ibid.*, pp. 27-28.

[24] ARSI, *Goa 56*, f. 507; *Goa 50*, f. 114.

[25] BARRETTO, *Relatione delle Missioni...*, pp. 24-25. — WICKI, *O Homem...*, p. 326 (2nd Appendix).

[26] ARSI, *Goa 34*, ff. 1-2; *Goa 68-I*, ff. 20v-21.

[27] *Goa 50*, ff. 116, 194-195; *Goa 68-I*, ff. 19, 20v-21, 22.

[28] "Vivono in questa cristianità due comunità, che vivono ... *con grande edificatione, esempio e virtù*". BARRETTO, *Relatione delle Missioni...*, p. 28.

tions. In various reports Garcia accused them of faithlessness to their rules. But in the eyes of Garcia their chief crime was the support that they gave to Archdeacon Thomas. It is to be noted, however, that Bishop Rangel of Cochin and the Dominicans warmly espoused the cause of the Recollects. So whatever their faults may have been, they could not have been the blackguards ("scintilla infernal") that Garcia would have us believe. If they had been so scandalous as described by Garcia, the good friars of St. Dominic would not have given them such unconditional support. Garcia, however, was determined that the Recollects should not receive from Rome approbation as a religious congregation. Hence he wrote to the Jesuit General, imploring him to see to it that the approbation would not be given.[29] One of the chief accusations made by the Cattanars and Christians against Garcia after the general rebellion of 1653 was that he had destroyed the Congregation of the Recollects.[30]

The Jesuit missionaries who worked among the St. Thomas Christians, were attached to the Jesuit college of Cranganore. From the "De Statu et necessitate Provinciae Malabaricae" written by Fr. De Magistris in 1661 we learn that there existed two endowments of the king of Portugal: one was for the maintenance of the archbishop of the Serra and the other for that of fourteen missionaries who would work in the Serra.[31] It must have been probably due to the diminished income from these endowments that during the years of the government of Garcia the number of the missionaries actually working in the Serra was always very much less than fourteen. From the annual letters of these years it is clear that besides Fr. Salvador Machado who looked after the seminary of Vaipicotta and Fr. De Magistris who stayed with the Archbishop, there were only two or at the most three other Jesuits who worked in the Serra. There were a few more fathers at the college of Cranganore; but these were busy with their duties in the college itself.[32]

---

[29] ARSI, *Goa 50*, f. 102; *Goa 68-I*, f. 29v.

[30] APF, *SOCG 233*, f. 472; *SOCG 232*, f. 127.

[31] ARSI, *Goa 49*, f. 245.

[32] *Goa 56*, ff. 491, 506v, 521, 537v: annual letters of 1642, 1643, 1644 and 1648. — *Goa 21*, f. 18: Garcia's letter to the Jesuit General. — *Goa 68-I*, f. 20v: information given by Garcia on 19 October 1651. —

Several of the annual letters and other reports briefly describe the zealous activity of the missionaries during their tours of the Serra. On reaching a church, the missionaries would teach the children catechism, hear the confessions of the people, distribute holy communion and the indulgences which they had from the Pope. Often enough, people who had not been to confession for many years, made their confession to the missionaries. At times invalid marriages and scandalous lives were set right. At other times the missionaries succeeded to settle long-standing and serious litigations between powerful families, to bring about peace between the Christians and their kings or between the Christians and the Hindus. If they reached a church at the time of some important feast, they helped to add to the solemnity by staging sacred plays with the help of the children of the locality. At times these dramas would last the whole night! On feast days the missionaries preached to the people several times. These tours lasted several months. Needless to say, they were quite strenuous and demanded much spirit of sacrifice from the missionary. Often he had to go barefooted. Generally he had with him no other companions than a cleric in minor orders, a boy to serve mass and a young man to carry the baggage.[33]

The zeal and the spirit of sacrifice of the Jesuit missionaries of the Serra is affirmed by a number of witnesses. Another point about which there can be no doubt, is their exemplary observance of chastity. As some of the witnesses point out, though the Christians rebelled against them en masse and were very angry with them because of real and imaginary grievances, no one of the rebels dared to say a word impugning the purity of their lives.[34]

On other points, however, there were complaints and accusations. Thus they were accused of excluding the other religious families from the Serra; of not publishing the papal brief that allowed the other religious to work there; of destroying the local congregation of the Recollects be-

---

Cf. also what the viceroy wrote to the king of Portugal on 15 January 1648. (FERROLI, op. cit., p. 31).

[33] Goa 56, ff. 507-508, 521, 527; Goa 68-I, ff. 20v, 42, 70; Goa 68-II, ff. 605-606.

[34] Goa 68-I, ff. 161, 171v-173, 213, 273. — Goa 68-II, ff. 549v, 551-552, 561-562, 582, 588, 675, 730.

cause of the fear of being supplanted by them; of looking down upon the Cattanars and the people, never allowing them to sit in their presence, even though the Portuguese were always invited to sit; of not wanting to teach philosophy or theology or sacred scripture to the seminarians of Vaipicotta; of defrauding the archdeacon and the Cattanars of a part of their allowances; of making the seminarians pay for their upkeep though the king of Portugal was paying for it; of dealing with the Cattanars in a high-handed way when they visited the churches; finally, of exacting some money from the Cattanars and the Christians who went to see the Archbishop on some business, though the king of Portugal was paying for the maintenance of the Jesuits and of the Archbishop.[35]   Some of these accusations, however, are expressly denied by other witnesses.[36]   I do not intend to examine this question now in detail, since it will be discussed at sufficient length in the third chapter.

All what remains now is to see briefly the relations between Archbishop Garcia and the Jesuit missionaries and their local superiors. At the beginning of the government of Garcia the relations were excellent. The annual letter of 1642 says that Garcia paid what was just to the Jesuits of the colleges of Cochin and Cranganore for any help which they gave him. At the time of Britto they used to be given nothing.[37] We see also Garcia writing to the Jesuit General on 14 November 1644 to say that he was very satisfied with the three helpers he had, viz Fr. Hyacinth De Magistris, Fr. George da Fonseca and Fr. Louis Vieira.[38] The relations, however, deteriorated very much by 1649. In the letter which Garcia wrote in his own hand to the Jesuit General on 1 December of that year, he complained rather bitterly against several of the Jesuit missionaries and their local superiors. He said that things were very different from what they used to be once. When the Jesuits began working in the Serra and for many years after that, the fathers used to help the Christians even in their difficulties with the local kings and chieftains. Besides, they used to attend the first masses and the weddings of the more influential

[35] APF, *SOCG 232*, ff. 115-145; cf. also f. 96.
[36] ARSI, *Goa 50*, ff. 142-176; *Goa 68-II*, ff. 561-562.
[37] *Goa 49*, f. 493v.
[38] *Goa 21*, f. 18; cf. also *Goa 68-II*, f. 477v.

families, thus gaining their good will, and also making use of these occasions to administer the sacraments of confession and communion to many people. The expenses of the fathers used to be met by the college of Cranganore. But of late the superiors decided that the expenses should be borne by those who invited them. They decided also that the difficulties which the Christians might have with the kings, should be seen to by Garcia and not by the fathers, even when the latter happened to be on the spot. The fathers claimed that they went to the churches merely to preach and to hear confessions. Hence, if on reaching a church they found that the Christians were divided and quarrelling because of the allegiance of some to Garcia and of others to the Archdeacon, they promptly left the place, saying that they had not gone to look for trouble. They claimed also that they were visiting the churches as exempt priests of the Society and that therefore they did not at all depend on the Archbishop. They complained that Garcia made them cut a bad figure by making them the executors of his decisions against the Cattanars and the Christians. But Garcia explained to the General that it was not true and that the complaints arose from an improper understanding of the situation. He then went on to refute with indignation the pretension of the provincial of Cochin and of the rector of Cranganore that Garcia should pay the missionaries more for their work. He concluded the letter saying that when he was in the Society he had to obey only the superiors, but now almost everyone expected him to act according to his wishes! [39] This letter shows that at this time Garcia's relations with some of the Jesuit missionaries and their superiors was none too cordial. But Fr. De Magistris was always most faithful to him. In fact, he wrote to the General on 20 November 1649, praising the zeal of the Archbishop and attributing to this zeal any difficulty which he may have with the local superiors. [40]

---

[39] *Goa 21*, ff. 20-21.
[40] *Goa 9-I*, f. 182.

THE OUTBREAK OF THE STORM

1. THE GENERAL REBELLION OF THE ST. THOMAS CHRISTIANS AGAINST GARCIA AND THE JESUITS

In March 1652 an oriental prelate called Atallah [1] (=Adeodatus) made his appearance at Surat. He had set out from Cairo and gone to India in response to the letter that Archdeacon Thomas had sent to the Coptic Patriarch of Alexandria.[2] Atallah's intention to reach the St. Thomas Christians became known and there were several people that tried to prevent it. Fr. Luigi della Concezione, the prefect of the mission of Pegu, was one such. In his letter of 24 January 1653 he informed the Propaganda that in the middle of March 1652 he had seen in Surat "a schismatic bishop sent from Aleppo by his patriarch". Fr. Luigi wanted to speak to the bishop and to protest in the name of the Catholic Church and in the name of the king of Portugal. But he did not succeed, since the bishop could not be found any more. Hence he informed the Archbishop of Goa and the Inquisition.[3] Fr. Vincent Mary O.C.D. tells us that the Capuchin missionaries of Surat, too, informed the officials of the Goan Inquisition about the movements of Atallah.[4]

---

[1] I do not enter now into the question of the orthodoxy or heterodoxy of Atallah, nor give any details about his life. The third section of this chapter will be entirely dedicated to a discussion of these points.

[2] ARSI, *Goa 68-I*, ff. 82v-83: "Relação da Christiandade da Serra...". *Ibid.*, f. 42: a statement of the Portuguese officials of Cochin. APF, *SOCG 191*, f. 658: letter of Fr. Elzeario di Sansay O.F.M. (Cap.) from Cairo to the Propaganda on 5 October 1649.

[3] APF, *Acta 26*, pp. 230-231.

[4] VINCENZO MARIA, *Il Viaggio...*, pp. 162-163.

In August of the same year Attallah reached San Thomé (Mylapore).[5] It is probable that he first went to the English fort of Madras where he met two Capuchin fathers called Ephrem and Zeno. On 25 August he appeared at the church of Mãe de Deus in Mylapore, with a letter from Fr. Ephrem. Two of the Jesuit fathers led him to Fr. Marçal de Leiva, the rector of their college. Atallah was very afraid by now, since he imagined that the Jesuits intended to arrest him. But Fr. Marçal assured him that no harm would be done to him. He offered him a fine room at the college and Atallah was very satisfied with the treatment received.[6]

Fr. Ephrem, Fr. Zeno, as well as the Jesuit fathers were quite suspicious of the orthodoxy of Atallah. According to the author of the "Summaria relação da Cristandade da Serra", Atallah's "errors were notorious" and so the local commissary of the Inquisition, Fr. Louis Fragoso O.P., intervened. The Jesuits were asked to guard him carefully and to deliver him to the officials of the Inquisition in Goa.[7]

---

[5] Our sources do not agree about the date of the arrival of Atallah in Mylapore. The latin translation of the letter that Atallah sent from Mylapore to the St. Thomas Christians, says that he reached Mylapore on 2 August 1652. (APF, SOCG 232, f. 2). The author of the "Relação da Christandade da Serra, seus Principios, progressos e revoluções ate o anno de 1656" (ARSI, Goa 68-I, ff. 77-89) says that Adeodatus (= Atallah) reached Mylapore on a Dutch ship on 25 August 1652. The rector of the Jesuit college of San Thomé, Fr. Marçal de Leiva wrote to Archbishop Garcia on 1 September 1652 that Atallah reached the church of Mãe de Deus in Mylapore on 25 August 1652, with a letter from a certain Capuchin father called Ephrem who resided at the English fort near San Thomé. (ARSI, Goa 21, f. 23). Now, it is possible that Atallah was reckoning dates according to the Julian Calendar. But this hypothesis would not account for a difference of 23 days. Probably Atallah reached Madras-Mylapore earlier than 25 August. The letter of Fr. Marçal not only does not exclude that possibility, but seems even to favour it. He says that on that day Atallah appeared at the church of Mãe de Deus with the letter of Fr. Ephrem. So Atallah should have reached the locality earlier, so that he had time to meet Fr. Ephrem etc. The author of the "Relação..." who did not have any direct relations with Atallah, had naturally to depend on others for informations like this. It is even possible that he took the date from Fr. Marçal.

[6] ARSI, Goa 21, f. 23: letter of Fr. Marçal Leiva S.J. to Garcia on 1 September 1652.

[7] ARSI, Goa 68-I, ff. 102, 182. — Cf. WICKI, Lettere Familiari del

In July 1652 (hence, before the events described above) three seminarians and one layman from Malabar had reached Mylapore as pilgrims to the shrine of St. Thomas. Since the Jesuit fathers of Mylapore did not, at least at the beginning, impose many restrictions on the freedom of Atallah, these seminarians were able to talk to him freely. In fact, we learn from the letter of Fr. Marçal de Leiva S.J. to Archbishop Garcia that one of the seminarians called Zacharias Cherian Unni of Ambalakkad talked a great deal with Atallah.[8]

When the pilgrims returned to Malabar, they carried with them a letter of Atallah, addressed to the St. Thomas Christians and their heads, in which he declared himself to be "Ignatius, Patriarch of the whole of India and China", who had received all powers from the Pope. He requested that they should send as soon as possible 2 priests and 40 laymen to obtain his release and to conduct him safely to Malabar.[9]

Archdeacon Thomas and his close friends were quick to exploit the situation fully. They published in all parts of the Serra the news that a Syrian patriarch sent to them by the pope in answer to their numerous petitions, had been unjustly imprisoned in Mylapore by the Jesuit Fathers. Everywhere there was the wildest excitement. It was decided that a general meeting of the St. Thomas Christians should be held at Udayamperur (Diamper) to discuss about the best way to liberate the Patriarch. The Archdeacon wrote to the captain of Cochin, to the civil authorities of the City, and to the Cathedral Chapter, complaining of the injustice that was being done by the Jesuits in preventing Mar Atallah from proceeding to Malabar, seeing that he had been sent by the Pope himself. The excited people, of course, had no clear idea as to how to accommodate the

---

P. Roberto Nobili S.I., in Archivum Hist. Soc. Jesu 38 (1969), 322 for some information regarding Fr. Louis Fragoso O.P.

[8] ARSI, Goa 21, f. 23.

[9] APF, SOCG 232, f. 2: latin translation of the letter of Atallah. SOCG 234, f. 355: Syriac copy of Atallah's letter. On 24 June 1662 Cattanar George Bengur (one of the foremost members of the Malabar clergy) attested under oath that it was a faithful copy of the letter sent by Atallah in 1652, and which he himself had read at that time.

claims of Atallah with those of Garcia. Some of them were of the opinion that Garcia was now too old and hence should lead a retired life at Cranganore, and Mar Atallah should actually rule the archdiocese. Others instead were of the opinion that Atallah should take over the government only after the death of Garcia.[10]

When the proposed general meeting of the St. Thomas Christians took place at Udayamperur, it was decided that they should send a letter to the Archbishop, requesting him to take Mar Atallah to Malabar. They wrote to Garcia that for many years they had not sent any letters to Babylon or elsewhere. The only one to whom they had sent their complaints was the Pope. If Atallah came from Babylon, they would have nothing to do with him. But if he was sent by the Pope, he should not be molested. To obviate the possibility of suspicions and disturbances in the future, the best thing to do would be to take the Patriarch to Cochin and to examine his claims, so that the people would be satisfied that no injustice was being done. To hold a general consultation on the whole problem, they would request Garcia to go to one of the churches of the Serra. But Garcia replied them that even if Atallah's claim to have been sent by the Pope were true, he would not allow him to enter the Serra, since he came without the permission of the king of Portugal.[11] This reply could not but irritate those present. Before dispersing, they decided that as many as possible should assemble at Mattancherry, when Mar Atallah would be in Cochin on his way from Mylapore to Goa.[12]

Ibid., f. 361: Italian translation of the letter.

[10] ARSI, *Goa 50*, ff. 219-220; *Goa 68-I*, f. 91: narration by Garcia. *Ibid.*, f. 102: "Sommaria Relação da Christandade da Serra".

[11] APF, *SOCG 232*, f. 117: the sworn declaration of a witness examined by Sebastiani in 1657. Similar statements were made by six other witnesses also. (See ff. 115-145). The witnesses add that Garcia replied on a very small piece of paper, in order to show his contempt. — *SOCG 234*, f. 338: the sworn declaration of Cattanar George Bengur on 20 June 1662. He was very loyal to Garcia except for a short while at the beginning of the rebellion; Hence his testimony on this point should be most weighty. He says that he too saw and read the reply of the Archbishop in this sense. — *SOCG 233*, ff. 285 sq.: letter of the Archdeacon to the Inquisitors of Goa in 1656.

[12] APF, *SOCG 232*, f. 116v: statement of witnesses examined by Sebastiani.

In an effort to gain the sympathy of as many as possible, the Archdeacon wrote a letter to the Dominicans of Cochin, complaining to them that the Jesuits treated the St. Thomas Christians worse than if they were their slaves. The Jesuits were able to do all that, because the St. Thomas Christians did not have any one as their protector and defender. God had in the end pity on them and sent them a Syrian archbishop. But the Jesuits, intent on destroying the Church of St. Thomas, arrested him at San Thomé. The Christians then wrote to the Archbishop, but he did not approve their proposal. The letter concluded with the remark: "Let them, (the Jesuits) do as they want. We too shall do the same!".[13]

In the meantime the people rose up in rebellion in several places, declaring the Jesuits to be schismatics and heretics, in as much as they held in prison a holy patriarch sent to them by the Pope. The Christians of Parur are said to have gone so far as to station armed boats in the rivers, in order to kill any Jesuits whom they should chance to meet. The Christians of Vaipicotta went armed to the church and to the seminary. They closed the door which led from the seminary to the church and told the rector of the seminary, who was also the vicar of the church, never again to set foot in the church. The seminarians were then invited to leave the seminary. All of them did so except two who continued to remain there in spite of threats and insults.[14]

When the news finally arrived that the fleet sailing from Mylapore was approaching Cochin, the Archdeacon accompanied by a large number of Cattanars and thousands of armed men,[15] moved towards Mattancherry. Their leaders

---

[13] ARSI, *Goa 68-I*, ff. 350-351: authenticated Italian translation of the letter of the Archdeacon to the prior and to the other religious of the Dominican monastery of Cochin. Cf. also f. 326. *Goa 50*, ff. 83-84: another authenticated copy. Cf. also f. 220.

[14] ARSI, *Goa 49*, ff. 179v-180: narration by Fr. Bras de Azevedo S.J.

[15] Our sources do not agree regarding the number of the people that assembled at Mattancherry. Some accounts say that the Archdeacon was accompanied by 25,000 armed men. FRANCO in his *Imagem ... de Évora*, p. 420 speaks of 16,000 men. One of the eye witnesses who testified before Sebastiani in 1657 says that there were about 5,000 men with the Archdeacon. (APF, *SOCG 232*, f. 120v). Cf. *Ibid.*, ff. 115-145.

spoke to the captain of Cochin, the civil authorities, the
cathedral chapter and the superiors of the various religious
orders, asking that Atallah be taken before them so that
they could examine his credentials. They declared that they
were ready to punish him if he would be found to be an
impostor. They sought also the intervention of the queen
of Cochin, promising her 150,000 fanams if she would obtain the landing of Mar Atallah in Cochin. The queen tried
her best to induce the captain and the other authorities of
the city to satisfy the request of the Christians.[16]

On the whole, the opinion of the civil and religious
authorities of Cochin was in favour of allowing the Archdeacon and a few Cattanars to meet and to question Mar
Atallah in the presence of the commissary of the Holy Office
(=Inquisition) and some religious of the city. In fact, Fr.
Francis of St. Andrew, the commissary of the Holy Office
and the prior of the Augustinian monastery in Cochin, sent
word to the Archdeacon that if the latter so desired, such
a meeting could be arranged. But both the Archbishop and
the Archdeacon opposed a meeting of that kind. The Archdeacon insisted that Atallah should be produced before the
whole crowd and examined by all of them! The Archbishop,
on the other hand, insisted that no one at all should be
allowed to meet and examine Atallah![17] When the Commissary of the Holy Office demanded that, in order to know
the truth and to calm the Christians, Atallah should be
brought to the city, Garcia opposed the move by accusing
the Commissary of being partial to the Archdeacon because
of gifts which he had received from the latter.[18] Whether

---

[16] ARSI, *Goa 49*, f. 180: narration by Fr. Bras de Azevedo S.J. —
APF, *SOCG 234*, f. 337v: sworn statement of Cattanar George Bengur. — *SOCG 232*, f. 116v et sq.: sworn statements of several witnesses.

[17] ARSI, *Goa 18*, ff. 169-170: authenticated copy of the letter of
Fr. Francis of St. Andrew to Lopo Vaz Perez. — APF, *SOCG 232*,
f. 120v: sworn statement made by a witness in 1657. ARSI, *Goa 68-I*,
f. 37: letter of Garcia to Tristão da Silveira de Meneses, general of
the land and sea forces of the South, on 30 December 1652.

[18] APF, *SOCG 232*, f. 349: sworn statement of Hyacinth Franquo,
a painter. The witness declared that he came to know all this, because on that occasion he had been sent by the Archdeacon as his
messenger to the Commissary of the Holy Office, to the captain of
Cochin and to the religious superiors of the city.

this last point be true or not, it cannot be denied that the
Commissary and the Archdeacon were having a friendly
exchange of letters at about this time. Some of these letters
as well as the sworn declarations of some witnesses prove
the willingness of the Commissary to advise the Archdeacon
as to whether and how to write the letters of protest to the
captain of Cochin, to the city, to the cathedral chapter
etc.[19] According to a statement made by 4 vicars of the diocese of Cochin in 1657, also two Jesuits, Fr. Bruno (an ex-
provincial) and Fr. Salvador Machado (the rector of the seminary of Vaipicotta), advised the Archbishop to let Atallah
land in Cochin; but their advice was not accepted.[20]

Since Garcia was afraid that, in spite of his opposition,
the captain of Cochin and others might insist that a meeting
between Atallah and a few Cattanars would be the best way
out of an ugly situation, he wrote a letter on 30 December
1652 to Tristão da Silveira de Meneses, the general of the
land and sea forces of the South. After describing the
difficult situation in which he and the Jesuit missionaries
found themselves, Garcia went on: "The one who should
put a remedy to these disorders is the captain of the city.
But I know for certain that he has decided to send some Cattanars chosen by the Archdeacon, together with some member of the cathedral chapter and some religious of the city
to the Armenian,[21] to ask him who he is, whether he has with
him bulls from the Pope, or whether he has been sent by
some schismatic. To make these enquiries is no business
of these people. It is rather the concern of the viceroy
who represents the king, without whose permission no prelate may come to these parts. It is the concern also of the
Inquisitors, since this man is a schismatic and a heretic
like *all the rest* of his countrymen! Besides, these people

---

[19] ARSI, *Goa 18*, ff. 167-173: authenticated copies of the letters
of the commissary (Fr. Francis of St. Andrew) to Lopo Vaz Perez
who acted as interpreter and messenger between the Commissary
and the Archdeacon. — *Goa 68-II*, ff. 491-494: sworn declarations of
6 witnesses in June 1653.

[20] APF, *SOCG 232*, f. 97v. They claim to have heard this several
times from Fr. Salvador Machado himself. — Cf. also *SOCG 233*,
f. 456 where Sebastiani repeats the same thing.

[21] The name "Armenian" was often employed by the Portuguese
of the time, to indicate any Christian of the Middle East.

do not realize that the intention of the Archdeacon and of
his followers is to cause confusion. When they go to meet
him, we can be certain that they will tell him in Syriac
(which our ecclesiastics who accompany them do not understand) to declare that he has been sent by the Pope and
that the Jesuits took from him his letters of appointment
and burned them. With this declaration these people will
become even more convinced that he has been sent by the
Pope. They will also make him say that he gives all his
powers to the Archdeacon. In fact, they already say that
in his letter from San Thomé he has written so to the Archdeacon. Hence I request and demand of you in the name
of the King, of the Viceroy and of the Inquisitors, not to
give your consent to that meeting, since no good can come
out of it. Instead, I ask you to take him to Goa, to be
questioned by the Viceroy and by the Inquisitors, to whom
belong enquiries about him".[22] It seems that also a certain
Michael Feira de Almeida, a person in the service of the Inquisition, warned the commander of the fleet that if Atallah
made his escape, the commander would have to pay for it
with his life.[23]

Considering all these warnings, the commander of the
fleet decided that the ships should not even enter the chan-
nel of Cochin, but should remain outside the bar. After
only two days of stay, the fleet set sail for Goa. The authorities of Cochin offered their excuses to the queen of Cochin
for not getting Atallah to land in the city, saying that they
had no power over the commander of the fleet.[24]

Before describing the frenzied reaction of the disappointed crowds, I would like to stop for a moment to consider the motives of the Archdeacon and of the Archbishop
in rejecting the proposal for a meeting between Atallah and
a restricted group of Cattanars in the presence of some of
the religious authorities of Cochin. The Archdeacon opposed the move, probably because he feared that a calm examination of the claims of Atallah by a small group of Cattanars (from which group he could evidently not exclude such
prominent and sincere men like Cattanar Chandy Parampil

[22] ARSI, *Goa 68-I*, f. 37. The original.

[23] *Ibid.*, ff. 181v-183: reply of Garcia on 22 August 1658 to Fr.
Hyacinth of St. Vincent O.C.D.

[24] ARSI, *Goa 49*, f. 180: narration by Fr. Bras de Azevedo S.J.

and Cattanar George Bengur) might perhaps bring to light
his treasonable correspondence with the Patriarch of Alexandria and other Eastern Patriarchs not in communion with
Rome.   Instead, in a meeting of Atallah with the whole of
the assembled crowds, there would be no question of any
calm and serious examination.   If necessary, there would
even be the possibility of using force to take Atallah to the
interior of the Serra.   If on the other hand, his insistence
that Atallah should be produced before the whole crowd
would make the Portuguese authorities intransigent, Thomas
was not worried.   He had his plans ready for that even-
tuality.

As for the motives of Garcia, there is no need to make
any conjectures.   His letter to Tristão da Silveira, cited
above, tells us clearly why he objected to the meeting.   What
I would like to point out now is that the dangerous possibili-
ties feared by Garcia, could have been easily prevented by
taking a few reasonable precautions.   Garcia was afraid
that the delegation of the Cattanars could suggest to Atallah
in Syriac what replies he should give, since the Portuguese
ecclesiastics who would accompany them did not know that
language.   But this difficulty could have been overcome by
sending also a Jesuit father along with them.   Besides, it
must be pointed out that the fear of Garcia was based on
the supposition that in a delegation made up of the most
prominent Cattanars there would be none that would rebel
against such dishonest behaviour.   Such fears and supposi-
tions were quite gratuitous and unrealistic, as proved by
later events.   In fact, as we shall see later, Cattanars like
Bengur George, Chandy Parampil etc. had no hesitation to
abandon the Archdeacon as soon as they were really sure
that they had been deceived by the Archdeacon and Cattanar Ittithommen.[25]   It would be useful to cite here the sta-

---

[25] In all the contemporary accounts that have come down to us,
Cattanar Ittithommen is described as a very wicked person.   We are
told that he was a most cunning impostor and that he had the bad
fame of being a concubinary and a magician.   At the time of Archbishop Britto he was punished for incest.   Even on feast days he
often neglected to say mass or to hear it.   He rarely recited the
divine office.   He became an enemy of Garcia when the latter
refused to appoint one of his pupils as vicar in his parish (the Southist parish of Kallicherry).   He knew Syriac exceptionally well.   It
was he that forged the supposed papal briefs and the supposed second

tement of Cattanar Bengur George: "Surely, if the Patriarch had been shown to us and if we had found him to be without the papal brief, so many evils would never have befallen us, and the Archdeacon would never have been able to intrude as archbishop." [26] It is to be remembered that this Cattanar remained very loyal to Garcia all the time except for a short while at the beginning of the general rebellion. Archbishop Garcia as well as Fr. Barretto and Fr. De Magistris showered praises on him.[27] Hence there is no reason to suspect that his judgements would be unfair to Garcia.

Let us now return to see the reaction of the crowd. When they saw that the ships set sail for Goa, all their hopes of having Atallah as their prelate disappeared. In an excited meeting that was held at Mattancherry, some of the calmer spirits still managed to persuade the rest to write once again to the Archbishop. The letter said that they felt very upset, since the Jesuits had sent the Patriarch away without giving them a chance to meet him and to examine him. They would therefore request the Archbishop to go and console them. He could take with him the retinue he wanted, but not any one of the Society of Jesus. If he refused to listen to their petition within 24 hours, they would no longer consider themselves his flock, but would choose another prelate to rule the archdiocese.[28] Needless to say, Garcia considered it too dangerous to go to meet the angry and excited crowd in Mattancherry. Also the authorities of the city of Cochin advised him not to venture out. About five years later, in his letter to Fr. Hyacinth of St. Vincent O.C.D. (the second Apostolic Commissary), Garcia adduced one more reason. He said that he refused to go to attend the meeting

---

and third letters of Atallah, which were used by the Archdeacon in order to deceive the people. He was eighty years old in 1666.

Cf. APF, *SOCG 234*, f. 324: sworn statement of the vicar of Muttam on 31 March 1662. — *Ibid.*, f. 337v: sworn statement of Cattanar George Bengur on 20 June 1662. — *Ibid.*, f. 355: sworn statement of Cattanar George de Campos on 3 February 1663. He was one of the clerics that had met Atallah. — *Ibid.*, ff. 342-365: Syriac copies of the fictitious and genuine letters of Atallah, of the fictitious papal briefs to Thomas de Campo, and their Italian translations.

Cf. also ARSI, *Goa 49*, f. 192.

[26] APF, *SOCG 234*, f. 338.

[27] ARSI, *Goa 68-I*, f. 116v; *Goa 68-II*, ff. 440, 719v-720, 743.

[28] APF, *SOCG 232*, f. 120v et sq. *SOCG 234*, f. 338v.

at Mattancherry "because the meeting was illegitimate. The members should not govern the head." [29]

Seeing that Garcia did not go to meet them nor send them any reply, the Cattanars and the Christians became even more enraged. They entered the church of Our Lady ("Nossa Senhora de Vida") at Mattancherry and in front of a crucifix with lighted candles they solemnly swore over the holy gospels that they would not any longer obey Garcia nor have anything to do with the Jesuits, but would recognise Archdeacon Thomas as the governor of their church.[30] It was further decided that those who would not obey the Archdeacon as their prelate, would forfeit their caste. Before dispersing to their villages and market-towns, they agreed that they would meet again at Edapally for the festivities of "Munnu Noyambu" (the three days' fast in honour of Jonas).[31] These regrettable events took place on Friday, 3 January 1653.

---

[29] ARSI, *Goa 68-I*, ff. 181v-183. Another copy in ff. 228-230.

[30] This oath is known in Malabar tradition as the "Coonan Cross Oath". According to this tradition, a rope was tied to the open air cross that stands in front of the church of Mattancherry, so that all could touch at least that rope when the oath was being made.

Now it is curious that not even one of the extant contemporary accounts speaks of this! They all describe, instead, the oath made inside the church, in front of a crucifix with lighted candles. Cf. APF, *SOCG 232*, ff. 120v-121: sworn statement of an eye-witness in 1657.

ARSI, *Goa 68-II*, ff. 491-494: sworn statement of six witnesses in June 1653. — *Ibid.*, f. 373v: Garcia's reply to the Inquisitors of Goa in 1656. — *Goa 68-I*, f. 102: "Sommaria Relação da Christandade da Serra". — SEBASTIANI, *Prima Speditione*, p. 4.

Nevertheless I believe that the documentary evidence cited above and the traditional account can be made to agree. The Cattanars and the more important lay leaders made their oath inside the church before the crucifix and over the holy gospels as described by the documents. As many of the others as possible pressed into the church. But the crowd was far too large for the church, and hence the majority who had to be content with their places in front of the church and around the Coonan Cross, might have indulged in some spectacular display of the kind described by the traditional account. The very unusual character of this oath made in the open, must have helped to impress it in the memory of the participants and of all those who heard of it, with the result that people later on spoke only of that, and not of the more prosaic oath made inside the church.

[31] ARSI, *Goa 68-I*, f. 102. — APF, *SOCG 232*, f. 121.

It is to be observed that the St. Thomas Christians, while rejecting Archbishop Garcia and the Jesuits, did not in any way intend to throw off their allegiance to the Pope. On the contrary, they issued a manifesto and exposed it in public places, stating that they rejected Garcia and the Jesuits, *because* the latter disobeyed the Pope and removed from them the patriarch sent by the pope.[32] This point is clear also from a letter which the Cattanars and the people wrote to the captain of Cochin a short while after the rebellion against Garcia. They beg the captain to do his best to restore to them the patriarch whom the Jesuits removed from them. In case the Jesuits have already murdered him, let any one belonging to "any of the four religious orders",[33] who knows Syriac and who is able to help them in their functions, go to them *according to the order of the Pope* and they will certainly obey him. But they declare that they do not want any Jesuit, since they are their enemies and "the enemies of the Roman Church." [34]

The "Munnu Noyambu" celebrations of 1653 at Edapally took place a few weeks later. There was a larger crowd of Cattanars and Christians attending the feast that year, since the rumour had gone round that a letter brought by Atallah from the Pope would be read during the feast. The crowd was estimated to number between five and eight thousand. Wednesday, 5 February, was the last and the most solemn day of the feast. That evening the letter was read and explained in Malayalam by Cattanar Chandy Kadavil ("Caro") of Kaduthuruthy. Also Cattanar George Bengur helped to give the necessary explanations. The people were told that the letter had been sent to the Archdeacon by Mar Atallah. In reality, however, it was nothing but a forgery made by Cattanar Ittithommen. He managed to get the seminarian George Campos who had met Atallah at Mylapore and who had brought the genuine letter of Atallah, to say that he had brought also this other letter.[35] According to it, Arch-

---

[32] ARSI, *Goa 68-I*, f. 102: "Sommaria Relação da Christandade da Serra". See also what Garcia wrote to Fr. Hyacinth of St. Vincent (*Goa 68-I*, f. 225). — Cf. also AHEI, *LM 25*, f. 120; *Goa 68-II*, ff. 451v-452.

[33] The Dominicans, the Franciscans, the Carmelites and the Augustinians.

[34] AHEI, *LM 25*, f. 121: the original.

[35] The other two seminarians, viz Zacharias Itti of Chengannur

deacon Thomas was granted all the powers of the Archbishop with regard to matrimonial dispensations and absolu-
tions from censures. The people were told also that the
Archdeacon had with him another letter of Atallah which
was to be read after lent, and which conferred on him powers
to ordain and to bless the holy oils. The enthusiastic crowds
acclaimed Thomas as the governor of the archdiocese, with
four of the most prominent Cattanars as his councillors.[36]
The four Cattanars were: Parampil Chandy of Kuravilangad,
Bengur George of Agaparambu, Kadavil Chandy of Kaduthuruthy and Anjilimootil Ittithommen of Kallicherry.

At Edapally it was decided that after lent they should
meet again, but this time at Alangad (Mangat). The meeting actually took place on 22 May 1653. Cattanar Ittithommen had by now forged another "letter of the Patriarch",
which authorised the episcopal consecration of the Archdeacon by twelve simple priests. Some of the more instructed Cattanars like George Bengur had their scruples on
the matter, since they had with them a Syriac book brought
to Malabar by Mar Abraham,[37] which said that no one may
be consecrated bishop without three episcopal consecrators.
But the general atmosphere of enthusiasm at Alangad was
such that in the end they too agreed with the rest. After
the invalid consecration ceremony, they wrote to all the
churches of the St. Thomas Christians, asking them to recognise Thomas Parampil as their legitimate archbishop.
All did so except the Southist churches of Kaduthuruthy and
Udayamperur. But we know from the testimony of the

---

and Zacharias Cherian Unni of Ambalakkad (*Goa 21*, f. 23), always
denied that Atallah gave them more than one letter. But George
Campos (a relative of the Archdeacon) deceived all by affirming
that he had secretly received from Atallah also other letters. But
later he was struck by remorse and he fled to the Archbishop and
confessed the truth. (APF, *SOCG 234*, f. 324). On f. 355 is to be
found the sworn statement that Cattanar George made on 3 February
1663, saying that he brought from Mylapore only one letter and that
the other letters said to have been brought by him were fabricated
by Cattanar Ittithommen.

[36] ARSI, *Goa 68-II*, ff. 496-499 and ff. 503-506: the sworn statements
made by eight witnesses in February 1653. — *Ibid.*, ff. 373v-374:
narration by Garcia. — APF, *SOCG 232*, f. 121: sworn statement of
a witness.

[37] He ruled the St. Thomas Christians immediately before the
Synod of Diamper.

vicar of Udayamperur that even in those churches some of the people stood for the Archdeacon.[38]   Before the end of 1653 the Southist church of Kottayam and perhaps also some other church of theirs decided not to recognise the Archdeacon as archbishop.[39]   Besides, it seems certain that some of those who withdrew from the obedience of Garcia, remained independent, without adhering to either party.   The former cathedral church of Angamaly belonged to this group.[40]

It is not possible to establish with certainty the number of those that remained faithful to Garcia.   The accounts vary.   Some of them speak of 200 laymen and 15 to 25 Cattanars.   Others say that there were about 1000 laymen and 15 Cattanars.   In any case, it is clear that they were but an insignificant minority.[41]

It would seem that the declarations and actions of two or three ignorant Portuguese friars of Cochin, who were moved by their jealousy for the Jesuits, helped to confirm the Cattanars and the Christians of the Serra still further in their belief that the Archdeacon had been consecrated legitimately by order of the Pope.   One of these friars was a certain Franciscan called Antony of the Mother of God.   He is accused by the Jesuits of having declared that in the absence of bishops, simple priests could consecrate a bishop, and that therefore the Archdeacon was as much a bishop as any one else.   He is blamed also for having gone to meet the Archdeacon at Edapally after his rebellion and for having declared that a brief in Syriac which was shown to him and which he did not understand, bore the seal of Pope Urban VIII.[42]

---

[38] APF, *SOCG 234*, f. 338v: sworn statement of Cattanar Bengur George on 20 June 1662. — *Ibid.*, f. 335: sworn statement of the vicar of Udayamperur on 29 April 1662. — *SOCG 232*, ff. 115-145: statements of several sworn witnesses in 1657.

[39] ARSI, *Goa 50*; f. 97v: the refutation by Garcia or by one of his associates, of the accusations contained in the letter of the viceroy, dated 21 October 1653.

[40] APF, *SOCG 232*, f. 319: letter of Garcia to the Propaganda on 25 July 1659. — *SOCG 233*, f. 66: letter of the Cattanars and Christians of the former cathedral church of Angamaly to the Pope on 25 July 1659.

[41] Cf. APF, *SOCG 232*, ff. 115-145.

[42] ARSI, *Goa 50*, f. 196: sworn testimony of Francisco Simões

Soon after his "consecration" the Archdeacon began to exercise all episcopal functions, including the conferring of holy orders. According to a number of accounts, he laid down that he was to be paid 150 fanams for the minor orders, 64 for the subdiaconate and 150 for the priesthood.[43] This together with the amounts that he realised for the granting of matrimonial dispensations, formed the main source of his income.

2. The Causes of the Rebellion

In the second chapter as well as in the first section of this third chapter I analysed the actions and the events that led to the rebellion of the St. Thomas Christians against Archbishop Garcia and the Jesuits. These actions and events constituted merely the proximate causes of that rebellion whose roots can be traced farther back in history. Here I shall examine also these more remote and fundamental causes and give a complete view of the whole.

The beginnings of the discontent which finally exploded in 1653, can be easily traced back at least up to the Synod of Diamper, held under the presidency of Archbishop Alexis de Menezes of Goa. Cardinal Tisserant in his "Eastern Christianity in India" (p. 65, foot-note 2) cites the following remark that C. De Clerq makes in "Conciles des Orientaux Catholiques": "All the causes of subsequent dissensions ... are provoked by Menezes' excessive reforms and also by doing away with the hierarchy of the rite". This does not of course mean that everything done by Archbishop Menezes and the Synod of Diamper deserves to be condemned. On the contrary, "it is undoubtedly to the credit of the Synod that it clearly defined the Catholic doctrine at a time when this was most needed and that it tried to reform, although with a Latin bias, some abuses that had crept into church discipline".[1] Had Menezes and the synod controlled by him

---

and Fr. Manoel Ferreira in July 1653. — *Ibid.*, f. 96v: Reply of Garcia to the Viceroy's letter of 21 October 1653. — *Goa 68-II*, ff. 491-494: testimonies by several persons. — *Ibid.*, ff. 611, 742: accounts written by some Jesuits.

[43] APF, *SOCG 232*, ff. 115-145. See especially ff. 117v-118.

[1] THALIATH, *The Synod of Diamper*, pp. 2-3.

stopped there, they would have fully deserved the gratitude of succeeding generations. But unfortunately Menezes went further and sought to destroy at one blow what he considered the root-cause of all the shortcomings that he found in the church of Malabar. By means of threats, bribes and force he succeeded in severing the longstanding connection of the Malabar Church with the Patriarchate of Chaldea, even though the Patriarch in question (Simon Denha) was fully in communion with Rome. The next step was to entrust that Church to a Latin prelate and to bring it under the patronage of the Portuguese crown. Several of the ceremonies and rites in the celebration of holy Mass and the administration of the sacraments, were hastily and unnecessarily changed in order to bring them more in line with Latin usages. All this inevitably provoked an amount of discontent.

That the St. Thomas Christians always remained very attached to the bishops of their own rite and merely tolerated the government of the Latin bishops, is clear from the many petitions that they wrote from time to time to the various authorities, in which they pleaded for Syrian bishops.[2] Garcia himself noted this with utter disappointment. He gloomily wrote in the last months of 1652: "It is astonishing to see how attached these Cattanars and Christians are to the bishops from Babylon. Some young men who went on a pilgrimage to the tomb of St. Thomas, in spite of the fact that they are at present studying in the college of Vaipicotta and are treated with so much tenderness by the Jesuit fathers, no sooner they see this schismatic (Atallah) at the tomb of St. Thomas, than they run back post-haste to announce the news to the Archdeacon, narrating also the many 'miracles' performed by the schismatic".[3]

The changes that were made in the ceremonies of the Mass and of the sacraments, went against the natural spirit of conservatism so characteristic of the Indian, especially the Indian of those days. The stricter rules of discipline and pastoral care imposed on the Cattanars and the more vigilant supervision to which they were now subjected, were bound

---

[2] Cf.e.g. the complaints presented by the Archdeacon and the Cattanars and Christians to the viceroy in December 1645. (ARSI, *Goa 68-I*, f. 18v).

[3] ARSI, *Goa 50*, f. 219; another copy in *Goa 68-I*, f. 91.

to be regarded as galling by the more easy-going among them. From their point of view, the only thing that might compensate in some slight way the many disadvantages of the new system, was the monthly allowance promised by the king of Portugal to the vicars of the churches and for the maintenance of the seminarians of Vaipicotta. But in course of time, even this one redeeming feature tended to become less and less meaningful. With the decline of the Portuguese power in India and elsewhere, the allowances of the Cattanars and of the seminarians were reduced, and the payment became irregular and unreliable.[4]

It was but natural that most of the odium of the new and unwanted arrangements should fall on the Jesuits and their archbishops. They had acted as the right hand of Archbishop Menezes at the synod itself. But more than anything else, they were the ones that took the place of the ousted Syrian bishops. Under such circumstances, any imprudence on their part would aggravate the situation and make them still more unpopular. Such acts of imprudence were unfortunately not lacking.

The first and, as events proved, the most disastrous of these was the attempt of the Jesuit archbishop to eliminate the authority and the special position that the archdeacons held for centuries in the Church of Malabar. In a memorandum entitled "Ecclesiae Cranganorensis Christianorum S. Thomae Apostoli Calamitates et Remedia" submitted to the Propaganda, Fr. De Magistris S.J. admits that before the Jesuit prelates took over the administration of the Serra, the archdeacon practically ruled it. "The archdeacon was held in such honour and wielded so much power that he easily surpassed the bishop in power and influence". The reason for this, he says, was that the bishops had always been foreigners and needed the help of the archdeacon to maintain themselves in their see and to act as their interpreters with the people.[5] The fundamental mistake that the

---

[4] ARSI, *Goa 68-I*, f. 19v-20: complaints made by the Archdeacon and his friends to the viceroy in December 1645, and the reply of Garcia. — APF, *SOCG 233*, f. 235v: "Brevis et succincta relatio...". See the remarks made by the Cattanars present at the meeting of the church of Muttuchira (Muttiere) in 1658. — *SOCG 234*, f. 134v: Letter of Sebastiani to the Propaganda on 3 September 1660.

[5] ARSI, *Goa 68-II*, f. 739. (The document is found also in APF, *SOCG 233*, ff. 333-353).

Jesuit archbishops made was to imagine that since they knew well the language of the people and enjoyed a certain prestige with them because of their zeal and because of their influence with the Portuguese authorities, they could dispense with the services of the archdeacon and rule the archdiocese without taking much account of him. Fr. De Magistris says that when Ros (the first Jesuit archbishop of the Serra) became archbishop, the power of the archdeacon began to dwindle, "because he did not need the archdeacon either as interpreter or as intermediary to gain the good will of the people, since he himself knew well Syriac and Malayalam, and since he was tenderly loved and respected by all".[6] But this attempt to degrade the archdiaconate met with strong resistance not only from the archdeacons but also from Cattanars and the people. Archdeacon George of the Cross rose up against Archbishop Ros and was really pacified only when Ros nominated him the administrator of the archdiocese during the vacancy of the see. From Archbishop Britto the Archdeacon managed after some fight to obtain a document which granted him all what he wanted. As for what happened under Archbishop Garcia, we have seen it in detail. The archdeacons were able to make so much resistance because not only they but also very large sections of the Cattanars and the Christians considered the maintenance of the power and the prestige of the archdiaconate necessary for the maintenance of the privileges and the enviable status that the community as a whole enjoyed in the kingdoms of Malabar. The words of some Cattanars who submitted to Sebastiani in 1657 will illustrate my point. The Cattanars told Sebastiani and his companions that, even apart from the episcopal dignity usurped by Archdeacon Thomas, the archdeacon had always been the natural head of their community. All or at least the majority of the people realised the necessity of abandoning him, but at the same time no one wanted to ruin him. Without him their community would be nothing but a body without a head. In a very short time it would disintegrate. The archdeacon was the symbol that kept them united, and it was their union that forced the infidels among whom they lived,

---

[6] *Goa 68-II*, f. 741.

to respect them. All the Christians were aware of this fact, and it was for this reason that they wanted to maintain the Archdeacon in his place of pre-eminence.[7]

The two most fundamental causes of the rebellion are the ones that I have mentioned so far, viz the general dissatisfaction of the St. Thomas Christians with the Jesuits for several of the decisions taken at the synod of Diamper and the fight over the position of the archdeacon. But several other factors also contributed their share in bringing about the rebellion. The role that they played was however, secondary.

The most important of these secondary causes was the persistence with which the Jesuit archbishops excluded all the other religious families from the Serra. Thus Archbishop Britto expelled Fr. Francis Donati O.P. and his companions who had established at Kaduthuruthy a successful school for the teaching of Syriac. This caused very much ill feeling, and many complaints were sent to the Holy See. Similar complaints must have been made also from elsewhere. So on 22 Frebruary 1633 Pope Urban VIII issued a brief prohibiting all religious orders, under pain of excommunication to be incurred ipso facto, to reserve any region to themselves, and ordering that every region in Japan and India should be open to all those who wanted to work there. On 14 April 1636 the Propaganda followed it up with a letter, allowing all religious to work in the Serra, provided they had the permission of their major superiors. The Archdeacon was told that the Jesuits would not be able to make any further difficulty regarding the admission of the other religious in the Serra, since the papal brief contained the excommunication to be incurred ipso facto. But apparently the Jesuits circumvented the difficulty by obtaining an order from the king of Portugal (Spain) to the contrary! At least, so we are told by Bishop Rangel O. P. of Cochin. In his letter of 6 December 1643 to the Propaganda he wrote that together with the papal brief he received also "a letter of King Philip who then ruled us, obtained, as it appears, by the

---

[7] VINCENZO MARIA, *Il Viaggio* ..., p. 211.

Jesuit fathers who had from Rome news of the brief". The
letter of the king asked him to see that no Dominicans or
other religious entered the Serra which was reserved to
the Jesuits, and to see that no others communicated with the
Archdeacon either through letters or through third persons!
The king said that he was also writing to the viceroy to
suspend the allowances of those religious who entered the
Serra in contravention of his order.[8]   In chapter 2 we
saw how Garcia continued the same policy and foiled the
attempts of the Dominicans and of the Carmelites to obtain
a foothold in the Serra.   It is to be pointed out that the
argument brought forward by the Jesuits to justify their
policy, is not very convincing.   Their argument was that
the Christians of the Serra were by nature restless and inclined to schisms, and hence the presence of the various religious
orders would only help their rebellious and schismatic tend-
encies.[9]   On the contrary, it was the rigorous execution of
this policy that drove Archdeacon Thomas to look for help
beyond the pale of the Catholic Church, and brought about
the general rebellion of 1653.   Thomas was convinced, and
rightly too, that there was no real possibility in the fore-
seeable future, of the Jesuits being dislodged from the
government of the Serra, since in spite of all the complaints
and petitions to the higher authorities, no other religious
family was allowed to establish itself in the Serra.   It was
this conviction that drove him, restless and unscrupulous
as he was, to take the fatal step which in the end left the
Church of Malabar divided, a division which unfortunately
lasts to this day.   As Charles Ferrarini (a Theatine missionary in Goa) rightly remarked in his letter to the Propaganda on 2 January 1654, this disaster would surely not
have happened, had there been also the other religious orders
present in the Serra.   As ministers of the Supreme Pontiff,

----

[8] APF, *SOCG 109*, ff. 116, 127: letter of Bishop Rangel to the
Propaganda on 6 December 1643. — *Ibid.*, f. 118: copy of the letter
of Bishop Rangel to King Philip in 1638. — APF, *Acta 12*, f. 67; *Acta 13*,
f. 28. — AHEI, *LM 25*, f. 118: letter of Bishop Rangel to the Portuguese
King on 28 January 1646.

[9] ARSI, *Goa 18*, f. 110v: letter of Britto to the Propaganda on
28 January 1629, seeking to justifv the expulsion of Donati from
the Serra. — Cf. also *Goa 68-II*, f. 508v.

they could have made the Christians some promise, and the situation could have been saved.[10]

In the third section of the second chapter I made mention of several charges that were brought forward against Garcia and the Jesuits. The difficulty about many of these accusations is that the historian is unable to come to any firm conclusion about them. If there are many witnesses that make these accusations, there are also as many or more that deny them, and often there is no valid reason why the testimony of one group should be preferred to that of the other. Nevertheless there are some accusations which, though accepted as true by some historians (e.g. Werth, Bufalini), can be shown to be unfounded. Both Werth and Bufalini make special mention of the charge contained in some of the documents of the Propaganda Archives, according to which Garcia ordained very few natives, so that he could confide the larger parishes to the Jesuits.[11] Now the Jesuits working in the archdiocese were altogether too few for this. In the third section of the second chapter I have shown from contemporary documents that, besides the rector of the seminary of Vaipicotta and Fr. De Magistris (the Archbishop's secretary), there were only two or three other Jesuits that worked in the Serra at the time of Garcia. There was also little likelihood of Garcia being able to obtain more Jesuit priests from the other parts of the Malabar Province, since it had only about 90 priests at that time, and the territory which it had to look after included the coast of Travancore, Ceylon, the Fishery Coast, Madurai, the Coromandal Coast, Bengal and Malacca.[12] According to a contemporary Jesuit account of the history of the seminary of Vaipicotta, the reason for ordaining less priests from 1627 onwards was that an agreement was reached on 27 January of that year at a meeting

---

[10] APF, *SOCG 191*, f. 372v.

[11] WERTH, *Das Schisma der Thomaschristen...*, pp. 58-59. Incidentally it may be noted that Werth is mistaken when he says on p. 58 that the two priests, Christopher Miranda and Manuel Vas, who furnished this information to Sebastiani, were Portuguese. They were both Indians. Manuel Vas was by birth a St. Thomas Christian. (Cf. *SOCG 234*, f. 329v; *Goa 49*, ff. 116, 188). Werth was probably misled by the names! BUFALINI, *L'opera Pacificatrice...*, pp. 176-177.

[12] APF, *SOCG 191*, f. 157.

held at Edapally, and attended by Archbishop Britto, Arch-deacon George of the Cross and the Jesuit fathers. They all agreed that thereafter fewer priests should be ordained, since there were already 300 priests and clerics in the Serra. The number was too high and it was becoming difficult to maintain them.[13] In the third section of the first chapter I have shown that also some other accusations against Garcia (e.g. the neglect of the duty of visitation, remissness regarding the administration of the sacrament of confirmation), found in the Propaganda Archives and accepted as true by Werth [14] and Bufalini,[15] are false.

A word has to be said about a proof often brought forward by Garcia and his friends to show that the charge of harshness levelled at Garcia, was false. They argued that Garcia could not molest or oppress the Christians since he had no prisons. The Christians lived in the territories of Hindu kings, and if the Archbishop were to imprison anyone, his king would immediately demand his release. If the Archbishop were to disregard the demand, it would be impossible for him to go to that kingdom any more. Garcia and his friends pointed out also that even spiritual weapons were wielded by him very rarely. During the first 13 or 14 years of his government as archibishop he excommunicated only two priests.[16] Now, this line of argument seems to forget that one can be harsh with others even without throwing them into prison and without excommunicating them! I think that the accusation was not without a certain foundation, in as much as Garcia despised and distrusted the Cattanars and the Christians. In fact, even from the writings of Garcia and of the Jesuits it can be shown that, though they worked among the Christians of the Serra with zeal and sought to benefit them also materially by using their influence with the Portuguese authorities and the local

---

[13] ARSI, *Goa 50*, f. 242.

[14] *Das Schisma der Thomaschristen ...*, p. 62.

[15] *L'Opera Pacificatrice ...*, p. 424.

[16] ARSI, *Goa 68-I*, ff. 69v-70: copy of a memorandum to the king of Portugal. (An Italian copy to be found in *Goa 68-II*, f. 605). *Goa 68-I*, ff. 39-40, 41v-42, 84v. — *Goa 50*, f. 96v: refutation of a letter of the viceroy. — AHEI, *LM 23-B*, f. 398v: substance of the testimonies sent to Goa and to Lisbon by Garcia and the Jesuit Provincial of Cochin.

rajahs,[17] their general attitude towards the Cattanars and the Christians was not one of esteem or trust. Thus in an account which Garcia sent to the Jesuit authorities in Rome in 1645 regarding the behaviour of the Recollects of Edapally, he reminded them that Britto had to write to the General and to the Portuguese Assistant in 1634, requesting that they should not consent to the approbation of the Recollects as a religious order, nor allow the Basilians to go and instruct them. According to Garcia, the Assistant (Fr. Nuno Mascarenhas) replied Britto in these words: "Your Grace will remember how often *we told you not to trust the Cattanars*, and how we warned you that a congregation made up of the Cattanars would give you and that Church all the difficulties that you are now suffering. We shall do the needful with the Pope to settle this problem".[18] Frequently Garcia and the Jesuits use such expressions as "false", "liars", "deceivers" and the like, to indicate in general the Cattanars and the Christians or even all the people of Malabar.[19] Now it is obvious that a person or persons who entertain such ideas about a group, will not be able to treat that group with respect or esteem.

Finally it has to be said that the character of Arch-

---

[17] ARSI, *Goa 68-I*, f. 42: declaration by the Portuguese officials of Cochin. — *Ibid.*, f. 155: sworn statement of Canon Rebello Palhares of Cochin. — *Ibid.*, ff. 217-218: Statement of the Chapter of Cochin. — *Goa 68-II*, f. 549v: sworn statement of Diego d'Amaral, a former captain of Cranganore. (ff. 551, 559-560, 561-562 contain more statements).

[18] ARSI, *Goa 68-I*, f. 22. (See also ff. 10v-11).

[19] "... cum *omni dolo et fallacia* huius Asiae Provinciae gens abunde sit referta". From a letter of Garcia. (ARSI, *Goa 68-I*, f. 234). "Circa experientiam istorum sacerdotum et Christianorum cum quibus Archiepiscopus abhinc viginti annis ... agit, et tamen *tam fallaces et ficti sunt* generaliter loquendo, ut nondum omnino eorum fraudes agnoscere potuerit". Garcia to Sebastiani. *Goa 68-II*, ff. 439v, 719). "Nao estou tão escandalizado e magoado do meu Arcediago, *que por ser malavar* (as though Malayalees are universally known to be deceivers and rogues!), moço e idiotta, pode ter alguma desculpa, nem dos Cassanares que o seguem *que em fim são malavares*..." (from a writing of Garcia: *Goa 68-I*, f. 29).

"*His Malabaricis fallaciis* nimium credulus..." (From a writing of Fr. Francis Barretto S.J.: *Goa 68-I*, f. 93v).

"*Propter innatam superbiam et elationem*..." (From Fr. Barretto S.J.: *Goa 68-I*, f. 120v).

For more examples see *Goa 68-II*, ff. 381, 514v, 520v; *Goa 21*, f. 18v.

bishop Garcia and of Archdeacon Thomas played a very important role in bringing about the rebellion of 1653. If Garcia had been less intransigent, he would have been able to find a reasonable compromise between his claims and those of the Archdeacon, and thus the latter would not have been driven to desperation. If Thomas had been less un-scrupulous, he would not have pushed things so far.

Till now I have been enumerating the most important of the factors that prepared the way for the rebellion. But it can be asserted with a fair amount of certainty that, in spite of all the above mentioned factors, a rebellion of the proportions of that of 1653 would not have occurred but for the arrival of Mar Atallah. We have seen in the first section of this chapter that it was the unconscionable acti-on of Archdeacon Thomas and of a few of his close collabora-tors like Cattanar Ittithommen, that was responsible for Atallah's arrival in India. They were also the ones that whipped up the emotions of the simple folk. The unwise handling of the situation by Garcia completed the work of the Archdeacon. The great majority of the Cattanars and the Christians were but the unfortunate victims of the crimes and the follies of their ecclesiastical rulers.

3. A BRIEF ENQUIRY
ABOUT ATALLAH'S LIFE AND ORTHODOXY

No one has so far studied this subject in detail. Most of what has been written on it till now is the fruit of shrewd guessing, based on a few known facts, and not the result of a study of the contemporary documents. Hence there is little to be surprised if many writers have given us theories that are quite far from the truth.[1] The following data may be gathered from a careful comparison of the information available at the Propaganda Archives, the Roman Archives of the Society of Jesus and the Historical Archives of Goa.

Atallah (= Adeodatus or Diodato) was born in the year 1590. He was a Jacobite, a native of Aleppo in Syria.[2] We

---

[1] Cf. WERTH, *Das Schisma der Thomaschristen...*, pp. 47-50 for some theories.

[2] ARSI,*Goa 21*, f. 23: letter of Fr. Marçal de Leiva S.J., the rector of the Jesuit college of San Thomé, to Archbishop Garcia on 1

do not know exactly when he became the (Jacobite) archbishop of Damascus, Ems (=Homs) and Nicomedia. But it
was certainly before the years 1632, since on 15 March of
that year the cardinals of the Propaganda listened to a letter
of Fr. John Firmus, the guardian of the Franciscans in Aleppo, which spoke of the conversion of Archbishop Cyril
(that was his other name) of the Jacobite nation and of his
journey to Rome.[3] It fact, he made his profession of faith
in Aleppo (most probably in 1631), and once again in Rome
before the Holy Office in 1632. His entry into the Catholic
Church was brought about by the Latin missionaries of
Aleppo.[4]

Archbishop Cyril Atallah arrived in Rome most probably around the middle of the year 1632. There is a petition
of his to the cardinals of the Propaganda, dated 30 August
1632, in which he declared that he came to Rome to render
the Pope that obedience which every good pastor of the
Catholic Church should give. His patriarch was called
Hadaith Ellah (= Hidayath-Allah) who resided at Diar-
bechir.[5] During his stay in Rome which lasted more than
an year, Atallah asked for several favours from the Pope
and the Propaganda. Thus in August 1632 he requested that
also his nation be given a special lodging in Rome, since all
the other nations already had theirs. Another request was
that the Jacobite missal which he had brought with him, be
corrected and printed for the use of his nation. He asked
that in the meantime he be permitted to say mass in his
rite, using the printed missal of the Maronites.[6] This last

---

September 1652. Fr. Marçal had ample chance to obtain reliable
information about Atallah, both from personal observation and from
his talks with the latter, since Atallah was staying at the college
from 25 August onwards. Fr. Marçal says in his letter that Atallah
was then 62 years old. So we can fix the year 1590 as the year of
his birth.

[3] APF, *Acta 8*, f. 45. *Ibid.*, f. 65 speaks of him as archbishop of
Damascus, Ems and Nicomedia.

[4] *Ibid.*, f. 107. — *SOCG 393*, ff. 305, 315.

[5] *Ibid.*, f. 325-326.

Fr. gInazio da Seggiano O.F.M. Cap., as cited by Fr. Hambye S.J.
on p. 5 of his short article on Atallah in *Indian Church History
Review* 2 (1968) 1-5, asserts that Atallah was the brother of Patriarch
Hidavath-Allah who died in 1639.

[6] APF, *SOCG 393*, ff. 325-330.

request was repeated on 12 April 1633. He pointed out
that he had not been able to say Mass for so many months
in Rome. The petition was endorsed by some one who
described Atallah as a person very devoted to the Holy See.[7]
In February of the same year he asked for papal briefs, so
that on his return to Syria he could present them to his
patriarch and urge him to unite with Rome.[8] On 29 August
1633 he asked for money to return to his country where he
would try to induce his patriarch to submit to the Holy See.
The petition was granted on the same day and the Propaganda granted him 50 scudi for the journey.[9]

Even after his return to Syria, he kept himself in touch
with the Propaganda by means of letters, at least up to
1646. In general these letters described the persecutions
that he had to suffer from the Turks and even from his own
people, because of his submission to the Holy See. Every
one of these letters contained also a request for financial
help.[10] The Propaganda granted him the requested help
now and then, after making independent enquiries regarding
the firmness of his Catholic faith, the genuineness of his
need and the sincerity with which he worked for the reunion
of the Jacobite Patriarch.[11]

Atallah's letter of 22 January 1638 from Aleppo gives
us a number of details about his work in Syria and the persecutions that he had to suffer after his return from Rome.
The letter says that when he reached Aleppo after his return
from Rome, he was accused before the Turkish authorities
for having become a Catholic. In the space of two years he
was fined three times for this. (From the Acts of the Sacred
Congregation of the Propaganda we know that the guardian
of the Reformed Franciscans in Aleppo testified to the truth
of this statement).[12] So he decided to leave Aleppo and to

---

[7] *Ibid.*, f. 305, 315.

[8] APF, *Acta 8*, f. 194v.

[9] *SOCG 393*, f. 90. — *Acta 8*, f. 296.

[10] *SOCG 59*, ff. 140-141: letter of Atallah from Aleppo on 12 July
1634. — *Acta 12*, f. 18: reference to another letter of Atallah. — *SOCG
107*, ff. 151, 164: letter of Atallah from Aleppo on 22 January 1638. —
SOCG 122, ff. 219-220, 224: letter of Atallah from Asphahan in Persia
in 1643 (?). — *Acta 16*, f. 32v. — *SOCG 128*, ff. 98-99: letter of Atallah
from Egypt on 16 January 1646.

[11] APF, *Acta 10*, f. 187. — *Acta 13*, f. 124v. — *Acta 15*, f. 315. —
Acta 16, f. 32v. — *Acta 17*, f. 7. — *SOCG 107*, f. 151. (See also f. 164).

[12] *Acta 12*, f. 18.

return to his see in Damascus. But the Jacobites of Damascus refused to admit him because he had submitted to the Pope. Once again, therefore, he set out for Aleppo, hoping to receive the 50 scudi which the Propaganda used to send him through its agent. On the way he was attacked by some Arabs who beat him and robbed him of everything including his clothes. When he recovered from his wounds, he went to see his patriarch who received him with great kindness and kept him with him for about two months. Atallah claims that during this time he persuaded the Patriarch to submit to the Pope. The Patriarch would have immediately sent to Rome the letter of his submission, but for the fear of being prosecuted by the Turks if it should fall into their hands. So he asked Mar Atallah to go to Rome as his proxy and to make submission in his name. Atallah would have already set out for Rome for this purpose, but for the advice given by the guardian of the Franciscans to wait for the permission of the Sacred Congregation.[13] On 19 July 1638 the Propaganda decided that the Archbishop of Damascus and Homs could come to Rome if he brought with him the letter of obedience of the patriarch and if he came with a special mandate from the latter to make the profession of faith in his name.[14] Things did not go any further since Patriarch Hidayath-Allah died in 1639.

From two other letters of Archbishop Atallah (written in 1643 [?] and 1646) to Mgr. Ingoli, the secretary of the Propaganda, we learn that he left Syria some time after 1639. The reason he gave was that at that time there were two patriarchs who were fighting each other. He proceeded to Babylon where he converted some Jacobites and handed them over to the care of a Capuchin missionary called Michael Angelo. The new patriarch now appointed him to rule the Church of Persia, and so he went to Aspahan (=Ispahan). There also he had to face much opposition. But the Augustinian missionaries of the place received him into their house. They advised him to go once again to Rome to plead that he be given an annual subsidy and the administration of the church built up at Ispahan by the Latin bishop of Persia.

---

[13] APF, *SOCG, 107*, f. 151. See also f. 164.
[14] *Acta 13*, f. 124v.

There was at that time no one to administer that church.
The second letter of Atallah was written in 1646 from Egypt
where, he said, he was awaiting the reply of the Propaganda.[15]
Also a certain Fr. Joseph de Rosario of the Augustinian
monastery of Ispahan wrote in 1643 to the Propaganda
regarding the work of Atallah in Persia. The Augustinian
reported that in Persia Atallah always showed himself a
Catholic in word and deed. He added, however, that the
Christians of Babylon held the contrary. The letter went
on to say that the Jacobites of Ispahan were too poor to
maintain Atallah. If he were to be given an annual subsidy
from Rome, he would work among them and bring them
to the Catholic faith.[16]

Atallah waited for a long time in Egypt for the reply of
the Propaganda. Since this time he asked not merely for
a subsidy but also for the administration of the Latin
churches in Persia, the Sacred Congregation decided to
write first to the missionaries of Egypt to find out how
firm he was in the Catholic faith and whether he was
really persecuted by the Jacobites because of the Catholic
faith.[17] It does not seem that after 1646 Atallah received any
reply from the Propaganda.

It was during Atallah's long years of waiting in Cairo
that the letter of Archdeacon Thomas reached the Coptic
Patriarch of Alexandria. Since it must have been well
known to everyone in the ecclesiastical circles of Cairo
that Atallah was waiting to have a church to govern, the
Patriarch invited Atallah to answer the call from Malabar.
He accepted the offer and went over to India. His adventures in India have already been described in the first
section of this chapter.

There is no doubt at all that the Atallah who reached
India in 1652 was the same as the one whose activities in
Rome and in the Middle East we have been seeing till now.
In fact, Sebastiani wrote to the Propaganda from Aleppo on
28 June 1656 that the Jacobite bishop who seduced the Chris-
tians of Malabar and who was imprisoned and taken to
Europe by the Portuguese, had previously spent some time
in Rome and hence was no longer persona grata in Jacobite

---

[15] APF, *SOCG 122*, ff. 219-220. See also f. 224. — *SOCG 128*, ff. 98-99.
[16] APF, Acta 15, f. 442. — *Acta 16*, f. 32v.
[17] *Acta 17*, f. 7.

circles when he returned to his native land. Sebastiani
added that it was because of this that he went to Malabar.
Sebastiani received this information from the Jacobite
Patriarch.[18] Besides, there is no contradiction at all to be
found between the detailed information that Atallah gave
regarding himself to Fr. Marçal de Leiva at San Thomé and
what we know of him from elsewhere. Thus he told Fr.
Marçal that he was Adeodatus, a Syrian national, a native of
Aleppo and archbishop of Damascus. He had been to Rome
at the time of Pope Urban VIII. On his return to his
country, he was attacked and wounded by thieves who took
away everything from him. Fr. Marçal adds that Atallah
still bore the marks of the wounds.[19] According to what
Fr. Marçal says elsewhere in the same letter, Atallah knew
Italian well. This, too, is in perfect agreement with what
we know from the Propaganda Archives.[20] It is true that at
San Thomé Atallah furnished more details than we know
from the documents of the Propaganda. But this should not
create any difficulty for our question.

The additional information that Atallah gave to Fr.
Marçal amounted to this: When he was in Damascus, a
crafty rival of his made use of a stratagem to deprive him
of his see. He proposed that Atallah should hand over to
him the archdiocese of Damascus, in return for his being
made patriarch. In fact, the bishops elected Atallah patriarch and gave him the name Ignatius, a name which all
the patriarchs of Antioch bear in honour of St. Ignatius the
martyr. But his successor in Damascus, wishing to make
sure of his position, bribed the Turk in order to drive Atallah
out. Accordingly, the Turkish captain ordered him to leave
the place soon, unless he wanted to be killed. The bishops
who had elected him patriarch, now made him patriarch
of all the Syrians spread over the world.[21]

We shall now follow up the fortunes of Atallah after he
was taken to Goa early in 1653. When his ship reached Goa,

---

[18] APF, *SOCG 191*, f. 491v.

[19] ARSI, *Goa 21*, f. 23: letter of Fr. Marçal to Garcia on 1 September 1652.

[20] APF, *Acta 8*, f. 194v.

[21] ARSI, *Goa 21*, f. 23. — *Goa 68-I*, ff. 82v-83: Relação da Christandade da Serra . . . — *Ibid.*, f. 62: Sommaria Relatione della Christianità della Serra . . .

he was handed over to the Inquisition, which ordered that he be kept under close custody in the Professed House of the Jesuits. No one was allowed to speak to him. Even the Archbishop of Myra (Francesco Antonio Frascella O.F.M. Conv.) had to obtain the permission of the Inquisitors when he wanted to meet him. Even so, he could speak only in the presence of the Jesuit superior.[22]

From Goa the viceroy (Dom Vasco Mascarenhas, the Count of Obidos) sent him to Portugal without much delay. When Garcia wrote to the Viceroy on 5 June 1653, he could already speak of "the Armenian whom Your Excellency *sent* to Portugal".[23] On 18 September of the same year the viceroy mentioned in a meeting which was held in Goa to discuss the situation in Malabar, that Atallah had been sent to Portugal in the ship "Nossa Senhora da Graça".[24] There are numerous other statements or references made by qualified persons regarding the removal of Atallah from Goa to Portugal.[25] Hence what Werth and others say about Atallah being burned at the stake in Goa, has to be rejected as absolutely untrue.

The Jesuit author of the "Relação da Christandade da Serra ... ate o anno 1656" says that in Portugal Atallah found many to favour him, "either because reliable information was lacking or because he knew well how to dissimulate". In 1654 he was sent from Portugal to Rome in the company of the Archbishop of Myra. Probably both of them died in Paris.[26]

---

[22] *Ibid.*, f. 182: letter of Garcia to Fr. Hyacinth O.C.D. in 1658. Regarding Archbishop Frascella cf. MEERSMAN, *A few Notes...*, in *Miscellanea Francescana* 59 (1959) 346-351.

[23] AHEI, *LM 23-B*, f. 379.

[24] PISSURLENCAR, *Assentos do Conselho do Estado*, vol. 3, pp. 274-275.

[25] AHEI, *LM 25*, f. 108v: An account of the rebellion of the Serra, written by the Goan Inquisitors in 1656. — *Ibid.*, *LM 23-B*, ff. 376, 398: Letter of Dom Brás de Castro (governor) to the king of Portugal on 25 January 1654. — APF, *SOCG 191*, f. 391: Letter of the Theatine father, Ardizone, to the Propaganda from Lisbon on 28 December 1655. — ARSI, *Goa 50*, f. 192v: letter of Garcia to the Jesuit General on 8 December 1654.

For more statements cf. *Goa 68-I*, ff. 56, 84, 40v, 42v, 62v-63.

[26] ARSI, *Goa 68-I*, f. 84: Relação da Christandade da Serra ... — *Ibid.*, f. 182: letter of Garcia to Fr. Hyacinth of St. Vincent O.C.D. on 22 August 1658. — *Ibid.*, ff. 62v-63: Sommaria Relatione della

Let us now briefly examine the question of the orthodoxy of Atallah. We have seen that also after his return from Rome to the Middle East, the Propaganda continued to receive satisfactory reports about him from the Latin missionaries of those regions. The last such report that we know of, was from Persia in the year 1643. Some time after that he went to Egypt, hoping to receive fresh instructions from the Propaganda. The fact that during his stay at Cairo he accepted to go to Malabar at the instance of the Coptic Patriarch, does not necessarily show that he had apostatised in the meantime. The patriarch in question was quite friendly with Catholic missionaries like Elzeario di Sansay O.F.M. Cap., as may be seen from some of the letters of the latter to the Propaganda. Besides, the intention of Atallah might have been to work as a Catholic archbishop in Malabar, just as he had worked earlier as a Catholic archbishop in Persia, even though the commission to go to Persia had been given him by his own Jacobite Patriarch of Antioch.

The accusations of heresy made against him in India seem to be contradictory and unreliable. Since Atallah had originally been a Jacobite and since he received the commission to go to Malabar from the Coptic Patriarch of Alexandria, the heresy of which he could, if at all, be suspected, would be some type of monophysitism. Yet what his opponents in India accused him of, was Nestorianism! He is accused of having said to some simple people that Jesus is not God but a mere man and Mary should not be called the Mother of God.[27] Now it must be noted that the persons who made these accusations, did so merely on the authority of the supposed statements of Fr. Marçal S.J. (rector of San Thomé) and Fr. Ephrem de Nevers O.F.M. Cap. But it is rather strange that the only two letters of these two persons that I could find, far from saying anything of the kind, say exactly the opposite! Fr. Marçal's letter of 1 September 1652, addressed to Archbishop Garcia, says that

---

Christianità della Serra... — APF, *SOCG 191*, f. 391: letter of Fr. Ardizone from Lisbon to the Propaganda on 28 December 1655.

The last two authorities are not so sure about Atallah's death in Paris.

[27] ARSI, *Goa 68-I*, f. 182: Garcia's letter to Fr. Hyacinth O.C.D. in 1658. — *Ibid.*, f. 62: Sommaria Relatione della Christianità della Serra... — *Ibid.*, f. 91: narration by Garcia. (See also *Goa 50*, f. 219v).

he found Atallah well instructed in matters pertaining to the Catholic faith, and *that he did not notice in his conduct anything against faith or morals.* He heard mass daily with great devotion. He fasted often and on Wednesdays he observed a rigorous abstinence. Among the seven or eight Syrian books found in his baggage, there was also a Maronite (Catholic) missal printed in Rome at the time of Pope Clement VIII. Fr. Marçal concluded the letter with the remark that if Atallah was a heretic, he knew well how to pretend, seeing that he spoke so often of the things of God.[28] Fr. Ephrem de Nevers from Madras wrote to the Jesuits of Cochin on 27 August 1652 that *Atallah denied that he was a Nestorian, and to prove it he cursed Nestorius.* He showed Fr. Ephrem and his companion a Maronite missal printed in Rome. Fr. Ephrem added that it was possible that Atallah brought it in order to deceive the people.[29]

Another assertion which the opponents of Atallah made in order to prove that he was a Nestorian, was that he wrote to the Archdeacon that Mary should not be called the Mother of God, but merely the Mother of Christ.[30] I have shown in the first section of this chapter that Atallah sent only one letter to the Archdeacon and to the people of Malabar. This letter speaks of Mary clearly and unmistakably as the Mother of God![31] It is, therefore, not improbable that the accusations of heresy brought forward against Atallah by interested persons, were prompted by prejudice of the kind clearly to be seen in the following information sent in the name of Garcia to the king of Portugal by one of the collaborators of Garcia. The author of this memorandum admitted that it was being said that the Patriarch who sent Atallah to India was the Syrian Patriarch in union with the Holy See. But he added that no credit should be given to this assertion, "since *all* those who came to the Serra from the same place as this man were Nestorian heretics, as were Mar Joseph, Mar Abraham and their predecessors"(!).[32]

---

[28] *Goa 21*, f. 23.

[29] *Goa 18*, f. 163v.

[30] *Goa 68-I*, f. 91; *Goa 50*, f. 219v: narration by Garcia. — *Goa 68-II*, ff. 722v-723: memorandum to the king of Portugal.

[31] APF, *SOCG 232*, f. 2: "In nomine tamen *Dei Genitricis Mariae* ...".

[32] ARSI, *Goa 68-II*, f. 722v.

The only irregularity for which he could have been indicted, was that he went to Malabar without the authorisation of the Pope and on instructions from the Coptic Patriarch of Alexandria. This irregularity explains the words used by the Propaganda in its instructions to Bishop Sebastiani in 1660. Sebastiani is asked to read to the people of the Serra the papal brief "in which the false patriarch Ignatius who was arrested at Mylapore, is declared to be a schismatic, and not one sent from Rome".[33]

---

[33] APF, *SOCG 233*, f. 34v, no. 45.

(IV)

THE EXERTIONS OF THE VARIOUS AUTHORITIES
IN INDIA TO WIN BACK THE REBELS

1. THE RATHER FRUITLESS EFFORTS
OF GARCIA AND THE JESUITS

The rejection by the St. Thomas Christians of the government of Garcia and the Jesuits was so passionate and so thorough that for a long time the latter could not even think of any direct negotiations with them. Hence Garcia tried to induce the Portuguese authorities of Cochin to use force in order to compel the Christians to submit to his authority. But the captain of Cochin explained to Garcia that the City had already enough of enemies and could not afford to make more. Garcia then tried to win over the most important kings with bribes.[1] Thus he offered 6000 fanoms each to the queen of Cochin and to the king of Kaduthuruthy, 3000 to the king of Parur (=Paravur) and 1500 to that of Mangat. But also this proved useless since the Christians rioted when one or two of the kings spoke to them of obeying the Archbishop.[2] Besides, they offered the kings larger bribes than those offered by Garcia. The kings therefore came to the conclusion that their interest would be best served by keeping the whole problem in suspense and by trying to get what they could from both sides. The only one among the kings that supported Garcia with any constancy was the king of Parur. He upheld the vicar of Parur who had remained faithful to Garcia, and forbade the Christians of his realm to recognise Thomas Parampil as archbishop. The Queen

---

[1] ARSI, *Goa 49*, f. 180v: narration by Fr. Bras de Azevedo S.J.

[2] AHEI, *LM 25*, f. 112(?): a paper written by Fr. Bras de Azevedo in Goa on 2 February 1656. — ARSI, *Goa 9-I*, f. 216: letter of Fr. Bras de Azevedo to the Jesuit General on 13 February 1656.

of Cochin on the other hand, turned a deaf ear to all the pleas of the Portuguese authorities of Cochin to favour Garcia.[3]

Seeing that ever since his "consecration" Archdeacon Thomas found himself obliged to remain within the boundaries of the kingdom of Mangat, because none of the other kings had as yet recognised him as bishop, Garcia made a special effort to win over the king of that place. The king therefore ordered Thomas to produce before him the papal letters which he claimed to have with him, or else to leave his territory. Thomas was now forced to confess before the king and before a number of other persons that he had no such letters. So the king decided to eject him from his kingdom. But Thomas fled to a church for asylum. In the meantime some of his partisans placated the king with a bribe, and thus Garcia's efforts failed once again to achieve their aim.[4]

Garcia now turned to the viceroy of Portuguese India. In his letters of 5 and 30 June 1653 he informed the viceroy that the queen of Cochin, though bound to the Portuguese by so many ties of friendship and gratitude, refused to do anything effective in his favour. She merely tried to deceive him by writing to the churches of her realm that they should obey him. But she did nothing to punish those who refused to obey. Garcia, therefore, suggested that the viceroy should order the suspension of the payment of customs to the queen until she agreed to support Garcia in earnest. There need be no fear for the possibility that she might invite the Dutch. If she did so, the Portuguese authorities of Cochin could recall the legitimate king whom she had expelled, and thus she could be driven out in her turn.[5]

Dom Vasco Mascarenhas, the viceroy, treated the whole question with all the seriousness that it deserved. The letters of Garcia as well as those of the captain of Cochin, etc. reached the viceroy on 17 September 1653. On the very

---

[3] ARSI, *Goa 68-I*, f. 107: Sommaria relação da Christandade da Serra. — *Ibid.*, f. 42: Testimony of the authorities of Cochin on 12 November 1653. — AHEI, *LM 23-B*, f. 384: letter of the captain of Cochin to the viceroy on 29 May 1653.

[4] ARSI, *Goa 68-II*, f. 402v: from a paper of Garcia, written in 1656. — *Ibid.*, f. 387: a copy of the document with which Garcia excommunicated and deposed Thomas in 1656.

[5] AHEI, *LM 23-B*, f. 377: Garcia's letter to the viceroy on 30 June 1653. — *Ibid.*, f. 379: Garcia's letter of 5 June 1653 to the viceroy.

next day he held a council of state presided over by himself.
The meeting was attended by the councillors of state and
other high officials, two canons representing the cathedral
chapter of Goa, the major superiors of the Dominicans, the
Augustinians, the Franciscans and the Capuchins, each of
whom was accompanied by a companion, Fr. Gregory
Domingues of the Society of Jesus and Fr. Manuel Duarte,
the procurator of the Jesuit province of Cochin.[6]

After the viceroy had acquainted those present with the
situation in Malabar, the vicar general of the Dominicans,
Fr. John of St. Hyacinth O.P., took the floor, pointing out
the evils that afflicted the Church of the Serra because of its
having Jesuit prelates all the time. To put a remedy to the
miserable situation in which the Serra then found itself, he
suggested that it should be given to the care of some other
religious family and that the Archbishop should be asked
to appoint a governor who was either a diocesan priest or
a religious who was not of the Society of Jesus. Also the
other religious who were present, fully agreed with him.
They pointed out also that since the state was then not in a
position to use force, they had to look for milder methods
to bring the St. Thomas Christians back to the unity of the
Church. The three councillors of state were also substan-
tially in agreement with the rest. They added that there
should be no supension of the customs rights of the queen
of Cochin, since such a step might bring about a breach
with her.[7]

Fr. Gregory Domingues S.J. opposed at great length
the proposals made by the other religious. He asserted
that the proposals were based on the false premise that the
Archbishop and the Jesuit fathers had treated the Christians
with great harshness. He claimed that the suggestions was
also impractical since the other religious did not know Syriac and since the Archbishop could not delegate to anyone
his powers to ordain and to dispense from matrimonial im-
pediments. The appointment of a governor would not serve
to bring about peace, but would only create greater trouble,
since the Archdeacon was not likely to give up his usurped
dignity just because a governor was appointed. He added
that the execution of the proposal would only serve to de-

---

[6] PANDURONGA, *Assentos do Conselho do Estado*, vol. 3, p. 274.
[7] *Ibid.*, pp. 274, 275, 278, 279.

fame unjustly an archbishop of great merits and learning, and a religious family which had worked there with great zeal for over 50 years. It would also encourage further rebellions on the part of the Archdeacon and his friends. The remedy that he suggested was that they should bide their time. The queen of Cochin was already old. On her death the rightful heir to the throne could be supported by the Portuguese authorities after imposing on him the condition that he should subject the Archdeacon to the Archbishop or expel him from his dominions. With that the whole situation would become normal once again. In the meantime both the ecclesiastical and the civil authorities of Goa could inform the citizens of Cochin and the Cattanars of the Serra that the Archdeacon was an intruder and that he had no episcopal jurisdiction.[8]

The viceroy concluded the meeting, saying that he would once again write in a very charitable way to both the Archbishop and the Archdeacon, exhorting the latter to submit to his prelate, and asking the Archbishop to use greater moderation.[9] Letters were accordingly prepared. But before Dom Vasco Mascarenhas could sign and dispatch them, a rebellion in Goa overthrew him from power. Hence it was his successor, Dom Bras de Castro, that sent the letter to Garcia on 21 October 1653. It expressed the sorrow of the viceroy for what had taken place in the Serra, particularly since it happened at a time when the state, because of its miserable conditions, could hardly do anything to help him. It strongly hinted, however, that things would never have reached such a pass if the people had not been pressed too hard. The council of state disapproved of the suggestion to suspend the customs rights of the queen of Cochin. Instead, many of those who took part in the meeting suggested, and the viceroy agreed with them, that Garcia should send some other religious to the Serra, to prevent the Christians from becoming thorough-going schismatics. The complaints of the Serra were, in fact, directed only against the Jesuits and their prelates. Hence the arrival of the other religious might calm them.[10]

---

[8] *Ibid.*, pp. 275-278.

[9] *Ibid.*, p. 279.

[10] ARSI, *Goa 50*, f. 95: a copy of the letter of the viceroy. Cf. also *Goa 68-I*, f. 69 and *Goa 68-II*, f. 605.

Needless to say, Garcia rejected in toto the viceroy's suggestions. He denied the charge of harshness, bringing forward the usual argument that he had no prisons, and citing the authority of a number of certificates given him by the Portuguese secular and ecclesiastical authorities of Cochin. He contended that the accusation of harshness was a calumny spread by certain unprincipled ecclesiastics of Cochin. If the Jesuits and their archbishop could not reduce the rebels, the other religious would succeed much less. Finally he asserted with more vehemence than objectivity that the Christians rebelled against the Jesuits, not because the latter oppressed them, nor because they wanted to have the other religious, but because they wanted to follow the Babylonian customs! [11] In a letter which he wrote to Dom Bras de Castro on 8 December 1653 he repeated these points and urged him to revoke the resolution taken in the meeting of 18 September, "since the reasons on which the resolution was based, were false." He told him also that he was sending Fr. De Magistris to Lisbon to explain to the king the whole situation.[12]

Towards the end of January 1654 Fr. De Magistris and Fr. Manoel Duarte appeared in Goa before Dom Bras de Castro, as procurators for Garcia and for the Jesuit provincial of Malabar. They had with them a number of certificates which sought to prove that the Archbishop and the Jesuit fathers, far from being the cause of the rebellion, worked with great edification for the good of the Serra. The rebellion arose from the bad will of the Archdeacon and the

---

[11] ARSI, *Goa 50*, ff. 96-98: a refutation made by Garcia or by one of his close associates, of the viceroy's letter of 21 October 1653.

Though Garcia speaks here only of Babylonian *customs*, Fr. Gregory Domingues had been more explicit at the meeting of the Council of State on 18 September 1653. He had said that the real cause of the rebellion was the "attachment of the ecclesiastics of Malabar to *the faith of Alexandria and to the errors of Nestorius* which they call the faith of St. Thomas". (PANDURONGA, op. cit., p. 276). Now one does not need to bring many proofs to show that this assertion is false. If this was really true, one does not understand how the majority of the rebels returned to the unity of the Church, even though it meant abandoning the Archdeacon who was the traditional head of their community.

[12] AHEI, *LM 23-B*, ff. 381-382: letter of Garcia to Dom Bras de Castro.

Cattanars who resented to see the schismatic bishop being sent away to Portugal.[13]

Garcia's energetic protests and action produced the desired result. At the request of the two Jesuit procurators from Cochin, Dom Bras de Castro held a new meeting on 27 January 1654. After hearing the substance of the papers and certificates brought by the two procurators, the governor questioned Manoel Mascarenhas d'Almada and Francis Telles de Menezes, two captains who had been in Cochin a short while before. They affirmed under oath that all what was contained in the papers presented by the Jesuits was true. On the following day, therefore, the governor (Dom Bras de Castro) prepared for his king a new report which was in complete agreement with the views of the Jesuits, and which contradicted on several points the report which he had prepared only three days earlier. The governor now requested the king to go through all the papers that he was sending, and to decide about the best course to be followed.[14] In practice this meant that at least for the time being the resolution of 18 September would not be executed and the Archdeacon would have more time to consolidate his position.

After this successful intervention in Goa, Fr. De Magistris proceeded to Lisbon as the procurator of Garcia and of the Jesuit province of Malabar, to convince the king that Garcia and the Jesuits were not to be blamed for the rebellion of the Serra and that therefore they should be allowed to carry on there as before, and that the other religious should once again be told not to busy themselves with the affairs of the Serra.[15] It is indeed a pity that even under

---

[13] AHEI, *LM 23-B*, f. 398v: The substance of the certificates sent by Garcia to Goa in January 1654. — *Ibid.*, f. 398r: letter of Dom Bras de Castro to the king of Portugal on 28 January 1654.

[14] *Ibid.*, f. 376: Dom Bras to the king on 25 January 1654. — *Ibid.*, f. 398r: Dom Bras to the king on 28 January 1654. — ARSI, *Goa 68-II*, f. 671: a copy of the minutes of the meeting held in Goa on 27 January 1654. — *Goa 68-I*, f. 87: Relação da Christandade da Serra...

[15] ARSI, *Goa 68-II*, ff. 605-610: a refutation of the decision of 18 September 1653, presented to the king of Portugal. (a Portuguese copy of it is found in *Goa 68-I*, ff. 69-72). — *Goa 18*, f. 165v: Garcia to Fr. Lud Brandão, the Portuguese Assistant to the Jesuit General, on 8 December 1653. — AHEI, *LM 23-B*, f. 382: letter of Garcia to Dom Bras de Castro on 8 December 1653.

such tragic circumstances Archbishop Garcia and his missionary helpers felt the need of insisting that the other religious should be prevented from going to the St. Thomas Christians.

After obtaining a favourabale decision from the Portuguese Court, Fr. De Magistris was to proceed to Rome. He was to inform the Pope of the situation in the Serra and to beg him to issue a declaration that he had not sent anyone to depose Garcia or to appoint the Archdeacon in his place.[16] Garcia hoped that most of the rebels would abandon the Archdeacon and return to him when this declaration of the Pope would become known in the Serra. We shall hear more about this in the next chapter.

The authorities of Goa were not idle while the decision of the Court of Lisbon was being awaited. Dom Bras de Castro wrote to the Archdeacon, exhorting him to retrace his steps and assuring him of his protection and favour in case he did so. But the letter produced no results.[17] Garcia now approached the Inquisition of Goa to see if it could do something to clear up the situation. Accordingly the Inquisition sent its commissary, Fr. John Rangel O.P., to the Serra some time in 1654, to treat with the Archdeacon.[18] Fr. Rangel's work in the Serra will be dealt with in detail in the next section of this chapter.

In the meantime the Jesuit missionaries began to contact some Cattanars through letters and intermediaries. Their arguments raised scruples in some of them. But the fear of insults from the people and the fear of losing all the income from their churches prevented them from taking the decisive step and submitting to Garcia. Cattanar George Bengur, however, did not allow these considerations to get the upper hand. He submitted to the Archbishop and his example was followed by some others. In some cases the Archbishop had to maintain them, since they were expelled from their churches. The same was the case with some

---

[16] *Goa 68-I*, f. 115 (also *Goa 68-II*, f. 516: Informatio P. Francisci Barretti de Statu Archiepiscopatus Serrae. — *Ibid.*, f. 152: a rough copy of Garcia's memorandum to Propaganda. — *Goa 68-II*, f. 742: Ecclesiae Cranganorensis... Calamitates et Remedia. — *Goa 18*, f. 165v: Garcia's letter to Lud. Brandão.

[17] *Goa 68-I*, f. 87v: Relação da Christandade da Serra...

[18] *Ibid.*, f. 92: letter of Fr. Barretto to the Jesuit General.

others who had received invalid orders from the Archdeacon, and who now out of scruples of conscience went to receive valid orders from Garcia. Those among them who did not know Syriac and moral theology, were lodged in the house of the Archbishop and were sent for classes to the college of Cranganore. Others were lodged in the seminary of Vaipicotta. Thus the seminary had as many students as it could maintain.[19]

The Southist parishes of Kaduthuruthy, Kottayam, Udayamperur and Turugure (Thodupuzha?) now definitely went over to the side of the Archbishop. Though these churches had never followed the Archdeacon in his rebellion, it was only now that they paid a visit to the Archbishop and thus openly and clearly declared themselves to be on his side.[20] The annual letter of 1654 (written on 15 December) of the Jesuit province of Malabar speaks of some people who were slowly returning to the obedience of Garcia, because they had been frightened by the mishaps which had overtaken some of the rebels, and which they regarded as chastisements from heaven for their rebellion.[21] In a description which Garcia wrote in 1656 regarding the state of his archdiocese, he claimed that at that time the churches of Kuravilangad, Elaur, Punnatra, Changanacherry, Chembu, Udayamperur, Marutholi, Parur, the larger church of Kottayam and the two churches of Kaduthuruthy recognised him as their prelate.[22] This statement has to be taken with a certain amount of caution. It is true that they recognised Garcia as their lawful prelate. They did it because they found the position of the Archdeacon to be absolutely unjustifiable. But their return to Garcia was by no means whole-hearted or unreserved. We shall see that in 1657 several of these parishes declared that they preferred to remain under the government of the Apostolic Commissary.

In March 1655 King John IV of Portugal, who was a great friend of the Jesuits, declared that he had carefully gone through all the papers he had received from India and

---

[19] *Goa 49*, f. 181: description by Fr. Bras de Azevedo S.J. — *Goa 9-I*, f. 219: letter of Fr. Barretto to the Jesuit General. — *Goa 68-II*, f. 509v: letter of Fr. Barretto to Fr. Matthew of St. Joseph O.C.D.

[20] ARSI, *Goa 49*, f. 181: description by Fr. Bras de Azevedo S.J.

[21] *Goa 56*, f. 554v.

[22] *Goa 68-II*, f. 403.

had also listened to what Fr. De Magistris had to tell him, and had reached the conclusion that the Jesuits had worked a great deal to reduce the rebels of the Serra. He was also convinced that the Archbishop had fully carried out all the obligations of a good pastor. Hence nothing should be changed with regard to the position of the Jesuits in the Serra. The king issued orders to the Count of Sarzedas who was setting out for India as viceroy, to interest himself in this question after his arrival in Goa. He was to hold a meeting in which the councillors of state, some nobles of his choice and the Jesuit fathers were to take part. Together with them he should see what could be done to bring about peace between the Archbishop and the Archdeacon.[23]

Soon after his arrival in India, the Count of Sarzedas wrote to Garcia to send him someone who could give him the necessary information regarding the state of affairs in Malabar and the remedy that should be applied to bring about the reduction of the St. Thomas Christians. Accordingly, Fr. Francis Barretto and Fr. Bras de Azevedo were dispatched to Goa. But before they could do anything, the viceroy died on 3 January 1656.[24]

A month later (2 February) Fr. Bras de Azevedo placed before the authorities of Goa a number of proposals which would, according to him bring about the submission of the Serra. He said that since other methods like the use of mildness, bribes to the kings etc. had not produced the desired results, there remained nothing but the use of force. Hence armed boats should be placed in the backwaters and rivers around Cochin to capture the disobedient Christians or to impose a blockade on Mangat which was the headquarters of the rebels. The bazaar of Mangat would be ruined if all trade between it and the city of Cochin could be banned under pain of excommunication. The king of Mangat would expel the Archdeacon rather than suffer this.

---

[23] ARSI, *Goa 68-II*, f. 637: copy of a letter of the king to the viceroy on 21 March 1655. — *Ibid.*, f. 454: Refutation by a Jesuit of a letter of Fr. Vincent Mary. — *Ibid.*, ff. 461-463: selected parts from the letters of the king and the queen of Portugal. — *Goa 68-I*, ff. 51-52: letter of the king of Portugal to the Jesuit provincial of Cochin on 17 March 1655. — *Ibid.*, ff. 87v: Relação da Christandade da Serra.
[24] *Goa 9-I*, f. 204: letter of Fr. Barretto to Fr. General on 30.1.1656. — *Ibid.*, f. 217: letter of Fr. Barretto to Fr. General on 8.9.1656.

Fr. Bras de Azevedo suggested also that a ban should be placed on the sale of wine and wheat flour to the Serra, to prevent the Cattanars from saying mass.[25]   It is surprising to see that he could not think of anything better than these crude methods of coercion.   It merely showed that the great majority of the St. Thomas Christians continued to maintain such a hostile attitude towards Archbishop Garcia and the Jesuits that the latter could not hope to bring them under their authority without the use of violence.

2. THE FAILURE OF THE ATTEMPTS OF THE GOAN INQUISITION

It has been mentioned that Archbishop Garcia requested the Goan Inquisition to see if it could do something to help him.   In accordance with this request, the Inquisition sent its commissary, Fr. John Rangel, to Malabar in 1654 to negotiate with the Archdeacon.[1]   The Commissary carried with him the letters of the Governor of Portuguese India addressed to the kings of Malabar.   He had with him also the letters of the Chief Inquisitors, in which the Archdeacon and the Cattanars were promised full pardon if they returned to the Church.   They were told also that their complaints would be fully considered.[2]

Some of the kings accepted the letters of the governor, but did not go any further.   The Archdeacon and the Cattanars refused even to accept the letters of the Inquisition,

---

[25] AHEI, *LM 25*, ff. 112-113 (?) (There are no numbers given on the folios.   But the probable numbers are the ones I have given).

[1] ARSI, *Goa 68-I*, f. 92: letter of Fr. Barretto to Fr. General on 10 September 1656. — AHEI, *LM 25*, f. (?) (The folio is between 114 and 118, but its exact number is not seen).   It says that when he was commissary to the Serra, Fr. Rangel O.P. copied certain notes in July 1654. — APF, *SOCG 232*; ff. 12-15: copy of the letter which the Archdeacon wrote to the Goan Inquisition on 30 June 1656.   Inter alia he says that Fr. Rangel went to the Serra in 1654.   (Another copy to be found in *SOCG 233*, ff. 285-288). — Fr. Bufalini is mistaken when he says on p. 159 of his dissertation that the Archdeacon wrote this letter to the Propaganda.

[2] AHEI, *LM 25*, f. 109: an account of the events in the Serra, written by the Goan Inquisitors in the first months of 1656.   It says nothing about the work of Fr. de Lisboa in the Serra.   Hence it must have been written before he went to the Serra as commissary.

because they suspected Fr. Rangel of being partial to Garcia and the Jesuits. Though Fr. Rangel went to Mangat and tried for about 10 days to meet the Archdeacon and to speak to him, the latter refused to give him an audience, and Fr. Rangel had to return to Cochin in disappointment. He tried to obtain the aid of the queen of Cochin, but that did not bring him any better luck. He now published in the churches of Cochin and Cranganore a notice which said that Atallah had not been sent by the Pope to be the prelate of the Serra, that the Archdeacon was not a bishop because his consecration was invalid, and that he was a schismatic because he was refusing obedience to his legitimate prelate. But these declarations did not produce any result. The Christians were convinced that Mar Atallah had been sent by the Pope. Hence they regarded all these declarations as manoeuvres on the part of the Jesuits to deceive them.[3]

Fr. Rangel was so annoyed with the behaviour of the Archdeacon and the Cattanars that on 4 March 1655 he issued an order which was to be read out in all the churches of Cochin and its vicinity, forbidding under pain of major excommunication to be incurred ipso facto, the sale of wine, balsam, wheat, wheat flour and hosts to the Archdeacon and his followers. To make sure that there would no loophole, he directed that only with his permission or with that of the Archbishop should these objects be sold or given even to those who were loyal to Garcia.[4] But the Chief Inquisitors of Goa reversed this decision of their commissary and declared it unjust, since it would deprive many people in good faith, of the mass and of the sacraments. Besides, they feared that it might drive the Cattanars to their old practice of saying mass with toddy.[5]

The complete failure of the mission of Fr. Rangel convinced the Goan Inquisitors that the work of reunion would be impossible if the Jesuits insisted on ruling the Serra.

---

[3] *Ibid.* — ARSI, *Goa 68-II*, f. 366: a short description by Garcia. — *Ibid.*, f. 403: description by Garcia. — *Goa 68-I*, f. 56. — *Ibid.*, ff. 87v-88: Relação da Christandade da Serra. — *Ibid.*, f. 92: letter of Fr. Barretto to Fr. General on 10.9.1656.

[4] *Goa 68-I*, f. 57.

[5] AHEI, *LM 25*, f. 110: an account written by the Goan Inquisitors in 1656. — ARSI, *Goa 68-I*, f. 92: letter of Fr. Barretto to Fr. General on 10 September 1656.

This is clear from a paper which the Chief Inquisitors, Paulo Castelino Freitas and Lucas da Cruz O.P., wrote in the first months of 1656 for the perusal of the governor of Portuguese India.   After dismissing as altogether impractical and imprudent the means suggested by Fr. Bras de Azevedo S.J. (enumerated in the last paragraph of the first section of this chapter), the Inquisitors went on to suggest what, according to them, might bring about good results. They suggested that religious belonging to all the other orders should be allowed to enter the Serra to teach the Christians and to tell them that the Archdeacon was not a bishop and that those ordained by him were not priests. Seeing that so many religious belonging to so many different orders and congregations asserted the same thing, and did not say anything about submitting to the Jesuits, the people might believe them, and not say that also that was a trick of the Jesuits.   If ever the other religious were needed in the Serra, it was now . The people needed instruction.   Their own Cattanars were too ignorant and the Jesuits were not admitted.   Hence that was the only remedy.   The Archbishop should retire to Goa after delegating his powers to a governor who was not a member of the Society of Jesus.   If need be, His Holiness could be asked to appoint a prefect or vicar.   The Inquisitors concluded their paper with the remark that it would indeed be a pity if it should ever have to be said that the Serra was lost because the other religious could not go there.[6]

Shortly after this, the Inquisition decided to send a a second commissary to Malabar.   The new commissary, Fr. John de Lisboa O.P., was instructed to avoid contacts with the Archbishop and the Jesuits, lest he too should be suspected of partiality.   Some 15 or 20 days after his arrival in Cochin, Fr. de Lisboa heard that Garcia was preparing to excommunicate solemnly Archdeacon Thomas and to deprive him of all offices and dignities and to appoint Cattanar Kunnel Mathai of Kaduthuruthy to take his place as archdeacon.   Cattanar Mathai was a nephew of Archdeacon George of the Cross and had a better claim than Thomas Parampil to succeed his uncle.   But at the time of the death of his uncle he was mad and hence Thomas de

---

[6] AHEI, *LM 25*, ff. 109-111.

Campo was appointed. Now he was once again in normal health and so the kings of Cochin and Kaduthuruthy requested Garcia to consider his claims.[7]

Realising that any such action against Archdeacon Thomas at this moment would spoil all chances of a settlement, Fr. de Lisboa wrote to Garcia informing him that he was authorized by the Inquisitors to deal with the schism of the Serra and that, "salvo meliori iudicio", he was of the opinion that Garcia should for the time being abstain from appointing another archdeacon, lest Thomas should become more exasperated. Garcia replied that the negotiations had reached such a point that he could no longer draw back. The newly elected was already on his way to Garcia's residence. Besides, the kings of Cochin and Kaduthuruthy might turn against him if he did not take their recommendation into account. He said also that he was convinced that this step would prove very useful to break the contumacy and arrogance of Thomas Parampil![8] It may be remarked by the way, that none of the difficulties raised by Garcia was insuperable. The new situation arising from the advent of the Commissary of the Inquisition could have been easily explained to Cattanar Mathai. This explanation accompanied by a present would have certainly satisfied the kings. As for the third reason given by Garcia, it is enough to say that anyone not blinded by passion and interest could have easily seen that the problem of pacification and reunion would become only more complicated and not in any way rendered easier by declaring at that moment Archdeacon Thomas excommunicated and deposed! One suspects that the real reason was some other. It is not improbable that Garcia had come to know from his agents in Goa of the change of mind of the Inquisitors. As we have seen, they were now openly advocating that all religious should be allowed to enter the Serra and that Garcia should retire to Goa after nominating a governor. Hence it is not illogical to think that with this move against Thomas, Garcia sought to make it impossible for the commissary of the Inquisition to negotiate.

---

[7] ARSI, *Goa 68-I*, f. 93: Barretto to Fr. General on 10.9.1656. — *Goa 68-II*, f. 371: letter of Garcia to the Goan Inquisitors.

[8] *Goa 68-II*, f. 393: narration by Garcia. — *Ibid.*, f. 371: letter of Garcia to the Goan Inquisitors.

Whether this be true or not, on 26 April 1656 Garcia solemnly declared Thomas Parampil excommunicated and deposed from his office, on the charge of usurpation of Garcia's jurisdiction.[9] When the Archbishop wanted to have the sentence published in Cochin, the Commissary forbade the Chapter of Cochin to do so, on the ground that Garcia had acted ultra vires. Garcia now proceeded to appoint Cattanar Kunnel Mathai as archdeacon. In his letter to Fr. de Lisboa, Garcia had claimed that with this step he hoped to divide the rebels and thus break their resistance. How unrealistic these calculations were, was demonstrated by the subsequent experience of Archdeacon Mathai. He had so few followers in the Serra that he had to remain all the time in Garcia's house in Cochin! [10]

Archdeacon Thomas heard of the efforts made by Fr. de Lisboa to prevent the publication of the sentence against him. Hence he was given a very warm welcome when he went to Alangad to negotiate with Thomas. The ember days of the octave of Whitsunday came when the Commissary was in Alangad. He sent word to Thomas that he should abstain from giving orders since he was not a bishop. The latter agreed and actually kept his promise also during the ember days of September. In return he asked that the Commissary should write to the Inquisition of Goa to procure his appointment as archbishop of the St. Thomas Christians. He said that he was living in the territories of Hindu kings, all of whom had already recognized him as archbishop. If he now told them something else, they were likely to molest him. The Commissary replied that Thomas should first cease to act as a bishop and write to the Holy Office expressing his regret for what had happened. In the same letter he could also express his desire. The Commissary himself would then write to Goa, requesting the Inquisitors to recommend the Archdeacon's case to Rome. He promised also to obtain from the governor of Portuguese India the allowances of the Archdeacon and the Cattanars.[11]

---

[9] *Goa 68-II*, ff. 386-387: authenticated copy of the sentence of excommunication and deposition. (Two years later, when writing to Fr. Hyacinth of St. Vincent, Garcia gave the date of the excommunication and deposition as 27 April. Cf. *Goa 68-I*, ff. 139, 233).

[10] ARSI, *Goa 68-II*, ff. 371v, 393. — APF, *SOCG 232*, ff. 88-91: Racconto dell'operato da doi Commissari del S. Officio nella Serra.

[11] APF, *SOCG 232*, ff. 88-91. — ARSI, *Goa 68-I*, f. 93v.

Accordingly on 30 June 1656 Archdeacon Thomas sent to the Inquisitors of Goa a letter that was certainly humble enough, but at the same time also very crafty. He declared that since the letters dispatched from Mylapore by Mar Atallah stated that he (the Archdeacon) was appointed bishop of the St. Thomas Christians, the people proclaimed him as such. He was also recognized as a bishop by the kings and by the religious who spoke to him. He therefore began to exercise all episcopal functions! The Christians and he did all that out of obedience to the letter of the patriarch sent by the pope. They did not have the slightest intention to be disobedient or to break away from Rome. If they had unwittingly made any mistakes, they now humbly asked for pardon and mercy. If they did anything wrong, it was out of ignorance, and this ignorance was due to the fault of the Jesuits who failed to teach them! The letter concluded with the request for the appointment of a governor for the Serra, and with the warning that worse disorders would follow if the Jesuits would be sent back there.[12] Fr. Barretto S. J. and others point out that the Archdeacon signed the letter to the Inquisitors in Syriac, using the title "Gate of the East", a title that used to be employed by the Syrian archbishops of Malabar, thus showing that he was really not sorry for his usurpation.[13]

The Archdeacon's letter to the Inquisition was accompanied by a letter of Fr. de Lisboa, which recommended that Garcia should be sent to Goa and a governor appointed to take his place in Malabar. To discuss these problems, the Inquisitors with the permission of the governor (Manoel Mascarenhas) organized a meeting to which, besides the governor and his councillors, also the first two dignitaries of the Chapter of Goa and all the superiors of the religious orders were invited. The Jesuit superiors as well as the procurator of Garcia were excluded on the ground that they were a party to the case. The governor, however, considered this unfair, and so Fr. Bras de Azevedo S.J. was allowed to present the views of the Jesuits before the

---

[12] APF, *SOCG 232*, ff. 12-15: Italian copy. (Another copy of it is found in *SOCG 233*, ff. 285-288).

[13] ARSI, *Goa 9-I*, f. 220: Fr. Barretto's letter to the Jesuit General on 10 September 1656. — *Goa 49*, f. 199: narration by Fr. Bras de Azevedo S.J.

assembly. In the meantime Fr. Barretto S.J. spoke privately to the governor and to some of the councilors, seeking to influence them in favour of his religious family. When the meeting finally took place, the majority of those present decided that the Archbishop be asked to appoint a governor for the Serra. This good news was communicated to the Archdeacon by the Inquisitors.[14] On 7 September 1656 they wrote also to the Archbishop, requesting him to appoint a governor to rule the archdiocese until the situation would change for the better. They pointed out that the schism would continue if that drastic remedy were not to be applied. Then they went on to express their surprise at Garcia proceeding all of a sudden with censures against the Archdeacon, after they had taken cognizance of his case, and just at the moment when their commissary was in Malabar to negotiate with him. They solemnly forbade him to proceed any further against the Archdeacon, remarking that the steps taken by Garcia, far from procuring the submission of the Archdeacon, would only ruin the whole business.[15]

The Archbishop now informed Fr. John de Lisboa that he was willing to appoint a governor, provided Thomas would first carry out what he had promised to the Holy Office. But he added that he could not restore Thomas to the archdiaconate, since the new archdeacon appointed by him had already taken possession of his benefice and acquired "jus in re". Garcia was evidently taking shelter behind a legal position. It should have been obvious to any person that Thomas would never give up his usurped episcopal dignity if subsequently he would have to remain without even his former archdiaconal office. It was this common sense view that Fr. de Lisboa expressed in his reply of 5 November. In the meantime Garcia had written once again to the Commissary, stating that in his eagerness to see the question settled he would be ready to allow Thomas to choose as governor any one of the five dignitaries of the Chapter of Cochin or its vicar general. The Commissary,

---

[14] *Goa 9-I*, ff. 220v-221: Fr. Barretto to Fr. General on 10.9.1656. *Goa 68-II*, f. 366: description by Garcia. — APF, *SOCG 232*, f. 88-91: an account of the work of the commissaries of the Goan Inquisition.

[15] ARSI, *Goa 68-II*, f. 379. (a copy is found in APF, *SOCG 232*, f. 87).

however, was quick to retort that Garcia was exhibiting not generosity but hypocrisy, since when he made the new offer, he already knew that Thomas had broken his promises to the Inquisition.[16]

In fact Thomas began all of a sudden to give minor orders to some clerics. The Commissary was utterly taken aback when he heard of it, since it meant the total failure of all his efforts. He wanted to find out the reason for this sudden change. Therefore he sent the four vicars of Cochin who had helped him during the negotiations,[17] to Kaduthuruthy and Kuravilangad to make enquiries. They returned to the Commissary with the somewhat questionable information that a certain Fr. Michael de Lemos, "the vicar of the island of the Jesuits" (Vallarpadam), had paid a visit to Archdeacon Thomas and promised that Garcia would pay him 5000 serafins and make him his coadjutor bishop, provided he ceased to negotiate with the Commissary. Thomas was told that the intention of the Commissary was to ruin both Garcia and Thomas and then to make himself the archbishop of the Serra.[18]

On the other hand, the letters exchanged between the Archbishop and the Commissary in the first days of November 1656 suggest that the reason which prompted the Archdeacon to break his word to the Commissary, was the calumny that was spread against the Inquisition that it never forgave anyone except with fire. Garcia himself admitted that this calumnious rumour was going round Malabar. In his reply, the Commissary strongly hinted that Garcia was responsible for spreading it.[19]

Before the end of the year 1656, Garcia replied at great length to the letter which the Goan Inquisitors had sent him on 7 September of that year. He complained bitterly

---

[16] *Goa 68-II*, f. 381: Garcia to Fr. de Lisboa on 4 November 1656. — *Ibid.*, ff. 381v-382: Reply of Fr. de Lisboa on 5 November 1656. — *Ibid.*, f. 366v: narration by Garcia. — *Ibid.*, f. 373: Garcia's reply to the Goan Inquisitors.

[17] The four vicars were: Fr. Christopher de Miranda, Fr. Emmanuel Vaz, Fr. Andrew de Pinho and Fr. Dominic Mendez.

[18] APF, *SOCG 232*, ff. 88-91: Racconto dell'operato da doi Commissari del S. Officio nella Serra. See especially the last part. — *Ibid.*, ff. 134v, 139, 143: sworn statements of three priests of Cochin.

[19] ARSI, *Goa 68-II*, f. 381: Garcia to Fr. de Lisboa on 4.11.1656. — *Ibid.*, ff. 381v-382: the reply of Fr. de Lisboa on 5.11.1656.

of the way in which they and their Commissary treated him. The whole of the letter is a vigorous, though not always convincing, defence of himself and his actions against the accusations and imputations of the Inquisitors and their Commissary, and a refutation of their claim to be authorized to tell him what he should do.[20]

The total failure of the efforts of the Goan Inquisitors to pacify the Serra convinced them that the only hope of remedy lay in a direct intervention by Rome. Hence they decided to give their whole-hearted support to the Apostolic Commissary, Fr. Joseph of St. Mary O.C.D. (Sebastiani), who reached India at about this time.

---

[20] *Ajuda 50-V-38*, ff. 240-244: the original letter. — ARSI, *Goa 68-II*, ff. 371-377: a copy of the same.

THE INTERVENTION OF ROME AND THE MISSION OF THE PAPAL COMMISSARIES

1. ROME'S DECISION TO INTERVENE

The news of the rebellion of the St. Thomas Christians was brought to the Eternal City by Fr. De Magistris S.J. when he came over here as Garcia's procurator. The news must have reached here at least in August 1655 since we see that the Propaganda discussed the report of Fr. De Magistris in the "General Congregation" of 16 August. At about the same time there arrived in Rome also some letters sent from the Serra to the prior of the Carmelite monastery of Santa Maria della Scala, and through him to the Holy See.[1]

Some authors (e.g. Werth, Bufalini) hold that these letters were sent by the "400 Christians" who had remained faithful to Garcia.[2] This view seems to be untenable because of the following reasons. To begin with, no such letter from the few who had remained faithful to Garcia, is found in the Propaganda Archives. Werth bases his assertion not on any contemporary document but on the statements of two Carmelite historians who wrote more than a century after the events. Bufalini's proofs are even less acceptable. He cites a part of the letter which the Archdeacon had written to the Holy Father and to the Propaganda in 1647! On the other hand, there are good reasons that

---

[1] APF, *Acta 24*, f. 52. — *Ibid., SOCG 233*, f. 456. — ARSI, *Goa 49*, f. 142: a paper written by Fr. De Magistris S.J. — *Goa 68-I*, f. 115: Informatio P. Francisci Barretti de Statu Archiepiscopatus Serrae. — *Goa 68-II*, f. 742: Ecclesiae Cranganorensis ... Calamitates et Remedia. (a very long paper written by Fr. De Magistris in 1659 or 1660.

[2] WERTH, *Das Schisma der Thomaschristen*, p. 75. — BUFALINI, *L'Opera Pacificatrice*, pp. 221-223; 234.

authorize one to say that the letters which reached Rome at this time were written by the Archdeacon. In the "Ecclesiae Cranganorensis. . . . Calamitates et Remedia" Fr. De Magistris says that at the same time that he was in Rome to inform the Holy See about the rebellion of the Serra, there arrived in Rome a letter from *the Archdeacon*, written at the time of the rebellion, in which he asked the Holy See for other missionaries, pretending that the Jesuits had made themselves too odious to the people. The letter was, he says, forwarded to Rome most probably by Fr. Joseph of St. Alexis, a discalced Carmelite, who had gone to Malabar at about that time.[3] Also Sebastiani speaks of the Pope and the Sacred Congregation receiving letters *of the Archdeacon*, the Cattanars and the other heads of the Serra, through the prior of the Carmelite monastery of S. Maria della Scala.[4] The question of the year in which the letters were written, still remains. Since no such letters of the Archdeacon written after the rebellion is to be found in the Propaganda Archives, and since it seems very unlikely that the Archdeacon would think of writing to the Holy Father and to the Propaganda after he had made himself a "bishop" by means of forged papal bulls, I am inclined to agree with Kollaparampil[5] who holds that the letters in question were the ones that the Archdeacon wrote in 1647 and 1649.[6] For some reason not known to us they reached Rome only in 1655.

No matter who wrote these letters from the Serra, the important point is that the Holy See could now take a decision based not merely on the report of one of the parties concerned, but after hearing what both parties to the dispute had to say. Fr. De Magistris requested in the name of Garcia that the Holy See should issue an authentic declaration that no one had been sent from Rome to depose Garcia or to substitute him with the Archdeacon. A papal brief should be sent to the rebels exhorting them to submit to Garcia. Those who remained faithful should be encouraged

---

[3] ARSI, *Goa 68-II*, f. 742.

[4] *Prima Speditione*, p. 6.

[5] *The Archdeacon of All-India*, pp. 169-170; 174-175. The author merely states his views without giving any reasons.

[6] Cf. APF, *SOCG 233*, ff. 455v and 456v. A comparison of what is said on these pages confirms my contention.

with an apostolic blessing. The Archdeacon should be excommunicated if he continued to show himself obstinate.
The viceroy of Portuguese India and the cathedral chapter
of Cochin could be exhorted to help the Archbishop in his
efforts to reduce the rebels.[7] It is to be carefully noted
that Garcia and his proxy asked merely for papal briefs and
not for any papal commissaries to be sent from Rome. In
another paper addressed to Mgr. Massari (the secretary of
the Propaganda) Fr. De Magistris rejected more explicitly
the idea of sending someone from Europe, saying that a
newcomer would not know the language and the customs of
the people, and hence would be at the mercy of interpreters
whose impartiality could not be guaranteed. If the Holy
See sent a religious from Europe, it would rouse the jealousy
of the other religious. Fr. De Magistris rejected also the
idea of committing this affair to someone in Goa. His conclusion was that the solution of the problem should be
committed to the chapter of Cochin or to any of its
dignitaries. According to him, the choice of the chapter
of Cochin would be satisfactory to both parties! Yet one
of the reasons which Fr. De Magistris had brought forward
to reject those of Goa, was that the Archdeacon was not
likely to agree to appoint any Portuguese to be his procurator for the trial in Goa, since in this affair he and the
Christians considered *all the Portuguese* as their enemies.[8]
Also the members of the chapter of Cochin were Portuguese!
Hence the intention of Fr. De Magistris and of Archbishop
Garcia, in whose name the petition was forwarded to the
Propaganda, becomes obvious. They wanted indeed to have
the question settled by papal authority, but by people within
their immediate sphere of influence. They did not relish
the idea of someone being sent from Rome to make awkward
and perhaps compromising enquiries. Above all, they did
not want that other religious should be sent to settle the
problem since it might break the monopoly of the Jesuits
in the Serra.

After mature reflection the Propaganda decided on
22 November 1655 to accept the recommendations of a special committee of cardinals which had earlier (16 August)

---

[7] APF, *SOCG 191*, f. 569 (also f. 577). Cf. also ARSI, *Goa 68-I*,
f. 152.

[8] APF, *SOCG 191*, ff. 583-584.

been deputed to study the question. Since the Archdeacon's letters had expressed special esteem for the discalced Carmelites, the Propaganda decided that the task of pacifying Malabar should be entrusted to them. Accordingly Fr. Hyacinth of St. Vincent O.C.D.[9] was chosen as papal commissary for the Serra. He was to take with him two or three companions of his choice. On reaching Malabar he was to find out the true reasons of the rebellion so that a remedy could be applied which would destroy the evil at its very root. He was given ample faculties to treat with the Archdeacon and his followers and to absolve them and to receive them back into the Church. In the same meeting the cardinals of the Propaganda decided to send papal briefs to the Archbishop, to the Archdeacon, to the faithful Christians, to those following the Archdeacon and finally to the chapter of Cochin.[10]

When Fr. De Magistris learned that the Holy See had decided to send an apostolic commissary with him to Malabar, he immediately petitioned the Pope, giving a host of reasons why he should be allowed to return to Malabar immediately, and not in the company of the commissary. One of the reasons he gave was that the commissary would be suspect to the Archdeacon if he went to Malabar in his company.[11] It is rather strange to hear this argument from Fr. De Magistris, seeing that the Jesuits always complained of the aloofness of the commissaries from them!

The Propaganda gave Fr. Hyacinth of St. Vincent very detailed instructions regarding his journey and his work. In case any of his companions for any reason whatsoever could not accompany him, he was given powers to take anyone else whom he liked, without the local superiors hav-

---

[9] Fr. Hyacinth of St. Vincent (Hyacinth Catini) was born in 1597 at Rapagnano, near Fermo in Central Italy. As a young man he studied law. At the age of 25 he made his profession as a discalced Carmelite in the Roman province of that order. After he became a priest, his chief activity was preaching. We shall see later in detail his work in Malabar. (Cf. BUFALINI, *L'Opera Pacificatrice*, p. 235; WERTH, *Das Schisma der Thomaschristen*, p. 76).

[10] APF, *Acta 24*, ff. 52, 80-81. — *SOCG 191*, ff. 561, 562v, 563v: letter of the Propaganda to the Archdeacon, dated 8 December 1655. — ARSI, *Goa 68-I*, f. 290: a copy of the Propaganda's instructions to Fr. Hyacinth of St. Vincent O.C.D.

[11] APF, *SOCG, 191*, f. 575.

ing any say in the matter. Together with his companions he was to proceed to Genoa and from there by boat to Lisbon. He should be friendly with Fr. De Magistris, but without contracting any obligation. Before leaving Rome he was to meet Cardinal Orsini who would give him letters of recommendation. These would be very useful to him since Cardinal Orsini's letters carried great weight at the Court of Lisbon. In Lisbon he was to make the royal ministers and councillors realise that the purpose of his mission was totally spiritual and that it had nothing to do with politics. He should try to obtain from the king, the queen and the principal ministers letters of recommendation, so that he would find help and assistance in all the dominions of Portugal. On reaching Goa he should try to gain the good will of the viceroy and of his ministers, and make them understand that his mission had only a spiritual aim. In every place he was to show himself friendly to the Jesuits, but with the due precautions already mentioned.[12]

The companions chosen by Fr. Hyacinth were the following: Fr. Marcel of St. Ives (Caspar Ignatius Marquart),[13] Fr. Joseph of St. Mary (Sebastiani)[14] and Fr. Vincent Mary of St. Catherine of Siena (Anthony Murchio).[15] Since Pope

---

[12] ARSI, *Goa 68-I*, ff. 290-293.

[13] Fr. Marcel was a German (Cf. *SOCG 233*, f. 415), born in Prague in 1626. He belonged to the Carmelite province of Cologne. He died in Goa in 1664. (Cf. BUFALINI, *L'Opera Pacificatrice*, p. 236).

[14] Fr. Joseph of St. Mary (Jerome Sebastiani) was born on 21 February 1623 at Caprarola in the province of Viterbo in Central Italy. He studied the humanities and rhetoric with the Jesuits in Rome. On 3 March 1641 he made his religious profession as a discalced Carmelite at the monastery of S. Maria della Scala. After that he studied philosophy and theology at Graz (Austria). From 1651 to 1653 he taught philosophy at the Carmelite monastery of Caprarola. During the two years that followed he was professor of theology at the monastery of S. Maria della Vittoria in Rome. Between the years 1656 and 1665 he made two journeys to Malabar as apostolic commissary. In 1666-1667 he was Visitor Apostolic to the islands of the Aegean Sea. On 22 August 1667 Pope Clement IX appointed him bishop of Bisignano in South Italy. In 1672 he was made bishop of Città di Castello in Umbria (Central Italy). He died there on 15 October 1689. (Cf. BUFALINI, *L'Opera Pacificatrice*, pp. 524-551).

[15] Fr. Vincent Mary of St. Catherine of Siena (Anthony Murchio) was born in the year 1626 at Bormio (Lombardy) in Northern Italy. He became a Carmelite in the Lombard province of that order in 1644. He accompanied Sebastiani on his first journey to Malabar.

Alexander VII was eager to settle quickly the problem of the Serra, and since he feared that Portugal in her anxiety to maintain intact the "padroado" might delay, if not altogether hinder, the voyage of the Apostolic Commissary, he decided to alter the plans somewhat and to send two apostolic commissaries by two different routes to Malabar. Fr. Hyacinth of St. Vincent accompanied by Fr. Marcel of St. Ives was to proceed to Malabar via Lisbon, as had been previously planned. With equal powers, Fr. Joseph of St. Mary accompanied by Fr. Vincent of St. Catherine and Fr. Raphael of St. Alexis [16] was to make his way to Malabar via Syria and Iraq.[17]

The two apostolic commissaries were given a number of papal briefs and other letters of recommendation. Some of the more important papal briefs were the following:

1. The brief "Cum sicut non" dated 19 January 1656 and adressed to Fr. Hyacinth of St. Vincent, in which he is told what he has to do and what powers are conferred on him for that purpose.[18]

2. Another brief with the same words, but adressed to Fr. Joseph of St. Mary and bearing the date 24 January 1656.[19]

3. "Ad aures" of 1 February 1656, addressed to Archdeacon Thomas, exhorting him to come to a better frame of mind.[20]

4. Two briefs, "Quae de istius" and "Relatum est nobis", addressed to Garcia and dated 18 and 19 February 1656, in which Garcia is asked to receive Fr. Joseph of St. Mary kindly and to help him in his work.[21]

From 1670 he occupied important offices in his province and in the General Curia of his order in Rome, where he died on 5 November 1679. (Cf. WICKI, *O Homem*, p. XIX, note 3; BUFALINI, *L'Opera Pacificatrice*, p. 236.

[16] Fr. Raphael of St. Alexis did not reach Malabar. He was too exhausted by the time the expedition reached Mt. Carmel. (Cf. SEBASTIANI, *Prima Speditione*, p. 22) Later Fr. Matthew of St. Joseph took his place. (Cf. ARSI, *Goa 68-I*, f. 115).

[17] SEBASTIANI, *op. cit.*, p. 9.

[18] ARSI, *Goa 68-II*, f. 421: an authenticated copy.

[19] *Jus Pontificium de Prop. Fide*, vol. VII, pp. 32-33.

[20] *Ibid.*, pp. 33-34.

[21] ARSI, *Goa 68-II*, ff. 419-420: authenticated copies. — *Jus Pontificium*, VII, pp. 35-36.

5. The brief "Percrebuit vos", dated 19 February 1656, in which the rebellious Christians are exhorted to return to the obedience of Garcia.[22]

6. "In gravissimo" bearing the same date, but addressed to the Christians who were obedient to Garcia. They are praised for their fidelity and exhorted to persevere and to help in the conversion of their brethren.[23]

7. Finally the brief "Cum pro componendis" of the same date, addressed to the chapter of Cochin. The chapter is asked to help Fr. Joseph of St. Mary in his work.[24]

The two groups of Carmelites led by the two commissaries left Rome in February 1656.[25]

2. The Rather Successful Activity of Fr. Joseph of St. Mary (Sebastiani)

In the second half of October 1656 Sebastiani and his companions reached Surat (on the West Coast of India), after a long and at times perilous jouney through the Mediterranean Sea, Syria, Iraq and the Arabian Sea. On their way from Surat to Malabar they stopped at Banda (near Goa) in the first days of January 1657, in order to meet Bishop Matthew de Castro.[1] In the same place Sebastiani was joined by Fr. Matthew of St. Joseph O.C.D. It was also at Banda that he had a visit from his confrere, Fr. Joseph of St. Alexis, who knew Malabar fairly well, since he had, as we have seen in chapter 2, spent some time with the St. Thomas Christians. From him Sebastiani came to know that though the Inquisition of Goa was ready to support him, the government was likely to impede his journey to Malabar, since it had received orders from Portugal to detain in Goa all those who reached India without passing through Lisbon.

---

[22] *Ibid.*, p. 34.
[23] *Ibid.*, p. 35.
[24] *Ibid.*, p. 36.
[25] SEBASTIANI, *Prima Speditione*, pp. 9-10.

[1] Matthew de Castro was the first Indian bishop (vicar apostolic) appointed by the Propaganda. For an account of his troubled life. see GHESQUIÈRE, TH., O.S.B. — *Matthieu de Castro, premier vicaire apostolique aux Indes.*

Sebastiani therefore decided to avoid Goa. At the same time he wrote a letter to Manoel Mascarenhas, the governor of Portuguese India, requesting his favour and protection and asking to be excused if he could not go to Goa because of the blockade by the Dutch. He wrote also to the Inquisitors of Goa, telling them that he relied on their powerful protection.[2]

After more adventures Sebastiani and his little band finally reached Palur, one of the northern-most churches of the St. Thomas Christians. On being informed by the vicar of Palur that the Archdeacon was than staying at Edapally, they proceeded to that place, where they reached at midday on 5 February 1657.[3]

They now wrote to the Archdeacon to inform him of their arrival and to tell him that they were there to help him and to favour him in every way within the limits of justice. Their letter was accompanied by that of some Cattanars to whom they had shown the papal briefs. The Archdeacon, however, showed no eagerness to meet them. So they made use of the good offices of some Cattanars to tell him that they had undertaken that long and perilous journey solely for the sake of his salvation and that of his people, since his position as an intruder into the ranks of the episcopate was unlawful and dangerous both for himself and for the people. But they took care to add that they would always keep in mind his honour and reputation. Besides, they sent him the letter which the Propaganda had written to him, as also a letter from Fr. Joseph of St. Alexis O.C.D., whom he had in 1647 and 1649 appointed as his procurator and who was a great friend of his. The Archdeacon thanked the Carmelites for these letters, but they were allowed to meet him only after seven days of waiting. It seems, he was waiting for the arrival of Cattanar Ittithommen. When the Archdeacon finally granted them an audience, he de-

---

[2] SEBASTIANI, *Prima Speditione*, pp. 77-79. — APF, *SOCG 191*, ff. 486, 487, 488, 491, 495: letters of Sebastiani to the Propaganda; *Acta 26*, pp. 236-237. — *SOCG 232*, f. 203: Sebastiani's letter to the Propaganda from Banda. — *SOCG 233*, ff. 455 et sq.: Breve racconto di tutto l'operato dal P.F. Gioseppe di S. Maria...

[3] VINCENZO MARIA, *Il Viaggio*, p. 138. — SEBASTIANI, *Prima Speditione*, pp. 88-89.

clared that he was receiving them not as papal commissaries but as simple discalced Carmelites! [4]

The meeting was short. Hence the Commissary and his companions had no chance to enter into any meaningful discussion with the Archdeacon. At the end of the meeting the latter suggested that the Carmelites could retire to Cochin and await there the decision of the meeting of Cattanars which he would convene to discuss the proposals of Sebastiani. He requested that the briefs of His Holiness be given over to him for safe custody! But Fr. Joseph of St. Mary replied that they could consign the brief only when the priests and the people would assemble in a largely attended meeting. As for their retiring to Cochin, he replied that they preferred to remain in those parts, so that they could be of service to him. Before they withdrew, the Archdeacon insisted once more about the briefs. But He was told that he would have to provide the attestation of three witnesses with the legal certification of a notary public. He did not want to do this and hence made no further mention of the briefs. [5]

Sebastiani now saw clearly that his work would be long and difficult. Hence he decided to send Fr. Vincent Mary to Cochin and to Cranganore to present the papal briefs to the chapter of Cochin and to Archbishop Garcia, and also to gain the good will of the Portuguese authorities of Cochin, so that his work would not be hindered by them. Fr. Vincent Mary found Fr. John de Lisboa, the commissary of the Inquisition, eager to help him in every way. Also the political and the military situation on the Malabar Coast worked in favour of the papal Commissary. Two of the three governors of Portuguese India, viz Francisco de Melo e Castro and Antonio de Sousa Coutinho, happened to be in Cochin just at that time. They were on their way to Goa after losing Colombo (Ceylon) to the Dutch. In such circumstances they

---

[4] ARSI, *Goa 68-II*, f. 447: letter of Fr. Vincent Mary to the Prefect of the Propaganda on 2.4.1657. — *Goa 68-I*, f. 115v: Informatio P. Barretti de Statu ... Serrae. — APF, *SOCG 233*, f. 458: Breve racconto di tutto l'operato dal P.F. Gioseppe di S. Maria. — *Goa 49*, ff. 181v-182: narration by Fr. Bras de Azevedo S.J. in 1666. — Copies of the letter which the Propaganda wrote to the Archdeacon on 8.12.1655 are found in *SOCG 191*, ff. 560-563.

[5] ARSI, *Goa 68-II*, f. 447: letter of Fr. Vincent Mary to the Propaganda. — SEBASTIANI, *Prima Speditione*, pp. 92-93.

could realise even more clearly how necessary it was to pacify the martial St. Thomas Christians and to bind them closely to the Portuguese in Cochin. They were, therefore, ready to welcome the efforts of anyone, even of a non-Portuguese commissary, provided the commissary promised not to do anything that would injure the rights of the Portuguese Crown. Fr. Vincent Mary was willing to give this assurance and hence they decided to support the work of the Apostolic Commissary. Also Archbishop Garcia promised to promote the work of the Carmelites in every way.[6]

During the night after his meeting with the Carmelites, the Archdeacon left Edapally in secret and went to Pallipuram. From there he sent to all the churches of the archdiocese a letter calculated to discredit the Commissary and his companions before the people. He told them that they were Jesuits disguised as Carmelites who had gone there with the intention of murdering him. The briefs which they had with them were nothing but forgeries made in Goa. They had with them much money to bribe the local rajahs. They did not answer to the point when they were asked whether Atallah had been sent by the Pope or not. Besides, they stole from the church of Edapally several valuables and the alms-box.[7]

Soon the Carmelites had all the people against them and they did not know what to do. It was at this moment that Cattanar Chandy Parampil,[8] a relative of the Archdeacon and one of the most prominent priests of the archdiocese, went to their rescue. He was a great friend and admirer of the Carmelites. Hearing of their arrival in the northern parts, he sent two of his clerics to conduct them to his church at Kuravilangad. He then wrote to several of the neighbouring churches, inviting them to go and meet the papal Commissary. Many people thus came to recognize the trickery of the Archdeacon. He wrote several letters also to the

---

[6] VINCENZO MARIA, *Il Viaggio*, pp. 168-169.

[7] ARSI, *Goa 68-II*, f. 447v: letter of Fr. Vincent Mary to the Propaganda. — *Goa 68-I*, f. 115v: narration by Fr. Barretto S.J. — *Goa 49*, ff. 181v-182: narration by Fr. Bras de Azevedo S.J. — SEBASTIANI, *Prima Speditione*, p. 97.

[8] Both Bufalini (p. 292) and Werth (p. 82) mistakenly make him the head of the Southists. But it is certain that he was not a Southist. (Cf. APF, *SOCG 233*, f. 197).

Archdeacon, urging him to surrender to truth and to make his submission to the Pope. The Archdeacon replied him only once. He told him that if the papal briefs were in his favour he would accept them; otherwise he would not.[9]

When the Commissary and his companions were staying at Kuravilangad, the two governors of Portuguese India who were then at Cochin, realised that an effort to raise the prestige of the papal Commissary would be useful for the conversion of the rebels. They therefore asked Dom Antonio da Silva, the outgoing captain of Cochin, to betake himself to Kuravilangad with a suitable retinue, in order to pay his respects to the Apostolic Commissary. Antonio da Silva did it at the beginning of March 1657. Following this, the whole chapter of Cochin and the vicar general went in solemn procession to Kuravilangad to honour Sebastiani and his companions as the representatives of the Pope. Some time later, also the Commissary of the Holy Office (Fr. John de Lisboa O.P.), accompanied by some knights of the Order of Christ, did the same.[10]

These manifestations of respect and veneration enormously increased the prestige of the Apostolic Commissary. Seeing that many more Cattanars and Christians from the churches of the southern parts were now going to see Sebastiani and thus becoming convinced of the truth, the Archdeacon sent a circular to all the churches, forbidding everyone under threat of severe penalties to make these visits. This letter, however, produced exactly the opposite result. Several of the Cattanars threw the Archdeacon's letter into the fire and went to pay their respects to the papal Commissary and to promise their obedience to the Roman Pontiff even if that should mean death for them. On the advice of the vicar of Kuravilangad, a number of Cattanars went in a group to the Archdeacon, asking him whether he wished to live according to truth and justice or merely according to his whims. He replied that he intended to live well. But he refused to give it in writing, giving a thousand excuses to cover up his real intention. Finally the people of Pallipuram held a meeting and demanded that the Archdeacon should either write to the Commissary promising him obedience

---

[9] *Goa 68-II*, f. 447v: letter of Fr. Vincent Mary to the Propaganda.
[10] VINCENZO MARIA, *Il Viaggio*, pp. 177-180. — SEBASTIANI, *Prima Speditione*, p. 97.

or send some of his priests to promise the same thing in his name. The Archdeacon chose the latter alternative. He sent some Cattanars to Kuravilangad. They promised in writing in the Archdeacon's name that he would convene on Low Sunday a general meeting of the Cattanars and the people, to hear the reading of the papal briefs. He would do all what the briefs ordered. He promised also not to confer orders and not to bless oils at the end of Lent.[11]

In the meantime Sebastiani had contacted Cattanar Chandy Kadavil (Caro),[12] the vicar of the church of Mangat, which was perhaps the most important church of the northern parts. The reply that he received was most encouraging and so on 20 March Sebastiani sent his two companions to Mangat. In a meeting held there on 22 March and attended by the Cattanars from the important northern parishes like Angamaly, Chenota (Vaipicotta), Parur and Kanjoor, the participants declared their readiness to submit to the papal Commissary, but did not even want to hear of submission to Garcia.[13]

At about this time an order reached Cochin from Manoel Mascarenhas Homem, the governor of Portuguese India, who

---

[11] *Goa 68-II*, f. 447v: letter of Fr. Vincent Mary to the Propaganda.

[12] The Jesuit accounts give a rather uncomplimentary picture of Cattanar Chandy Kadavil. He was a native of Kaduthuruthy. During the time of Archbishop Britto he was under excommunication for several years. Nevertheless he continued to say mass and administer the sacraments. In 1645 he turned against Garcia and warmly supported the Archdeacon because Garcia had refused to ordain the son of a servant of his. (*Goa 68-I*, ff. 23, 21v). He had him later "ordained" by the Archdeacon. (Cf. *Goa 68-II*, f. 440v). At the time of the general rebellion of 1653 he was one of the closest friends and supporters of the Archdeacon. According to Fr. Barretto S.J., Cattanar Chandy Kadavil was responsible for the veto which Sebastiani imposed on the exercise of jurisdiction by Garcia and on the re-entry of the Jesuits in the Serra. (*Goa 68-II*, f. 510).

In the Carmelite accounts, on the other hand, he is depicted as quite a respectable Cattanar. He was perhaps the most learned among the Cattanars of the time and was a good preacher. He knew Syriac well. In 1663 (i.e. at the time of the consecration of Bishop Chandy Parampil) he was about 75 years old. His advanced age, humble origin, relative poverty, and certain defects like ambition and excessive love of money, stood in the way of his being made bishop in 1663. (Cf. SEBASTIANI, *Seconda Speditione*, pp. 138-139).

[13] VINCENZO MARIA, *Il Viaggio*, pp. 180-181.

was residing in Goa. He ordered that the work of the Carmelites should be absolutely impeded since they had come to India without the permission of the Portuguese Crown. Hearing of this, Fr. Matthew of St. Joseph and Fr. Vincent Mary went to see the other two governors who were still in Cochin. The Commissary of the Holy Office, too, pleaded for them. The Carmelites solemnly promised not to do anything injurious to the patronage of the Portuguese king. So the governors once again assured them that they would not be disturbed by the Portuguese.[14]

It was also at this time that Sebastiani was forced, because of the insistence of Garcia, to write to the latter that he would do his best to lead the Christians back to Garcia's obedience. Sebastiani wrote so, because he was afraid that otherwise he would be accused before the Portuguese authorities of not respecting the patronal rights of the Portuguese king who had nominated Garcia as archbishop of the Serra. Perhaps in an effort to oblige Sebastiani to stick to his promise, Garcia decided to publish in Malayalam and Portuguese the contents of this letter as also certain parts of the papal briefs that favoured him. Sebastiani complains that this imprudent action of the Archbishop prejudiced his (Sebastiani's) work very much, in as much as it made him appear as an agent of Garcia, whose intention was to re-establish Garcia's authority. The Archdeacon made use of this news to discredit the Carmelites before the people. But Sebastiani's supporters among the Cattanars were able to a certain extent to counteract this damaging propaganda.[15]

Since the Archdeacon failed to keep his promise of convening a general meeting of the Cattanars and the people on Low Sunday and of not holding ordinations and the blessing of oils at the end of Lent, Sebastiani began with the help of some of the more important southern churches like Kuravilangad, Muttuchira and Kaduthuruthy to organise a meeting of the churches, to be held under his own presidency. The Archdeacon realised how dangerous this move of Sebastiani would be to his position. Besides, the

---

[14] ARSI, *Goa 68-II*, f. 449: letter of Vincent Mary to the Propaganda. — VINCENZO MARIA, *Il Viaggio*, p. 182.

[15] APF, *SOCG 233*, f. 460: Breve racconto di tutto l'operato dal P.F. Gioseppe ... nella Serra. — VINCENZO MARIA, *Il Viaggio*, pp. 188-190.

Cattanars of the northern churches of Mangat, Angamaly, Vaipicotta and Parur threatened to abandon him if he refused to convoke the promised meeting. Faced with this double threat, the Archdeacon communicated to Sebastiani his willingness to hold the general meeting of the churches at Edapally on the fourth Sunday after Easter. But due to the delaying tactics of the Archdeacon, the meeting actually took place only on 19 May, the eve of Whit Sunday. Thomas manoeuvred in such a way that the great majority of those who took part in the meeting were his firm supporters.[16]

At the meeting, Sebastiani was subjected to strong attacks because he had sent some clerics who had been invalidly ordained by the Archdeacon, to Garcia so that they might receive valid orders from him. The people saw in it the secret intention of Sebastiani to re-establish the government of Garcia. Sebastiani now plainly told the assembly that the Archdeacon was not a bishop. He was then asked if he had faculties from the Pope to make the Archdeacon a bishop. He replied that neither he nor any of his companions had episcopal orders, and that before the Archdeacon's case could be recommended to the Holy See for consideration, he would have to make satisfaction for the scandal which he had caused. There was now pandemonium in the assembly, and the Commissary and his companions were expelled from the meeting with contumelious words. They retired to a castle near Cochin to carry on their work from the safety of that castle.[17]

The meeting of Edapally thus ended apparently without any fruit. But in reality it was not so. When it was known that the Commissary was approached by the Archdeacon and his friends with the request that the Archdeacon should be consecrated a bishop, it became evident to all that not even the Archdeacon believed in the validity of the episcopal consecration he had received at Alangad in May 1653. If Thomas was not a bishop, then those ordained by him were not priests. Hence several of those who had been

---

[16] *SOCG 233*, f. 255: Racconto di quanto passò nella ... Agionta ... di Rapolim alli 19 Maggio del 1657.

[17] *Ibid.*, ff. 255-256. — SEBASTIANI, *Prima Speditione*, p. 101. — VINCENZO MARIA, *Il Viaggio*, pp. 198 sq. — ARSI, *Goa 68-I*, f. 115v: Informatio P. Barretti de Statu Serrae. — *Goa 49*, f. 182: narration by Fr. Bras de Azevedo.

invalidly ordained by Thomas went to Sebastiani, who sent them to Garcia for valid orders. Garcia received them all with great gentleness. Some of them were even lodged and maintained for some time in his house, so that they could learn a little more Syriac and some moral theology. Several churches now invited Sebastiani to go and receive solemnly their submission and obedience.[18]

In this way the authority and following of the Archdeacon diminished and the Commissary was able to announce for 15 August 1657 a meeting of the churches to be held at Muttam. Due to various circumstances, however, the meeting began only on 8 September. It was attended by the most important Cattanars and laymen of 23 or 24 churches, that is to say, about a third of the whole archdiocese. In the first session the assembly declared that the Archdeacon was not a bishop and that the orders conferred by him were in consequence invalid. The second session recognized the authority of Sebastiani as the commissary of the Holy Father. After this there came up the question as to what was to be done regarding the letter of the Archdeacon and of the two important northern churches of Mangat and Vaipicotta which had suggested that the meeting should take place at Mangat. The four "Southist" churches that were on Garcia's side, demanded that everything should be settled in that same assembly. But the others who were far more numerous, not wishing to create a division among the Thomas Christians, which would necessarily follow if the Archdeacon were not to submit, proposed that the assembly should write immediately to the Archdeacon and the two churches that they should all meet at Mattancherry which was about half way between Muttam and Alangad. The council then voted for its transfer to Mattancherry. The Archdeacon now sent the vicars of Mangat and Vaipicotta to Mattancherry to insist that the assembly should be transferred to Mangat, since he could not go to Mattancherry which was too close to Cochin. The two vicars assured the Commissary that the Archdeacon would make his submission at the meeting of Mangat, but if he did not, all

---

[18] SEBASTIANI, *Prima Speditione*, pp. 102, 110 sq. — ARSI, *Goa 68-I*, f. 116: Informatio P. Barretti de Statu Serrae. — APF, *SOCG 233*, ff. 256-257: Racconto di quanto passò nella ... Agionta ... di Rapolim. — *Goa 49*, f. 182: narration by Fr. Bras de Azevedo S.J.

would abandon him. In spite of the accusations of insincerity which the Jesuits bring forward against these two vicars and more especially against Cattanar Chandy Kadavil (vicar of Mangat), it must be said that the vicars were sincere in what they said. In fact, we see that later they abandoned the Archdeacon, even though their hope that all would abandon him did not materialize. On the other hand, it is equally certain that the Archdeacon had no intention at all of keeping his word.[19]

The experience of the meeting of Edapally was still too fresh in the minds of all. Hence the assembly refused to move to Mangat where there were still a number of powerful and fervent supporters of the Archdeacon. It was decided, instead, that the meetings should take place in the church of St. Thomas which was close to the walls of Cochin. The partisans of Garcia were impatient at seeing that time was passing. They therefore demanded that the council should on the following day (23 September) read the papal briefs. The question of the reading of the papal briefs caused a veritable storm in the assembly. Some of the fervent supporters of the Archbishop wanted that the briefs should be read immediately and that all the participants should be asked to submit to Garcia. Others (including some supporters of Garcia), instead, feared that the reading of the briefs on that occasion would only disturb the work of pacification and reunion. According to Sebastiani, it was a very respectable Christian called Kadavil Thommachar belonging to the party of the Archbishop, that went to meet Sebastiani very early in the morning of 23 September, to warn him that it would be a serious mistake to read the briefs on that day. Since the briefs were very favourable to the Archbishop, their reading would create a great disturbance in the assembly itself and all hope of reuniting the rest of the churches would be irremediably lost. The partisans of the Archbishop, he continued, were determined to proclaim

---

[19] APF, *SOCG 233*, ff. 463-464: Breve racconto di tutto l'operato. — *Ibid.*, ff. 257v-258: Racconto di quanto passò nella giunta di Mutano e S. Thomé. (it is a narration by Fr. Vincent Mary). — ARSI, *Goa 49*, f. 182v: narration by Fr. Bras de Azevedo S.J. — *Goa 68-I*, f. 116: narration by Fr. Barretto S.J. — For the accusations of Garcia and Fr. Barretto against Cattanar Chandy Kadavil see *Goa 68-I*, ff. 116-117; *Goa 68-II*, ff. 510, 717, 719, 720v.

their submission to him immediately after the reading of the briefs. But the majority of those present would never agree to that. Several Cattanars and other respectable persons, too, gave Sebastiani the same warning. The vicars of Mangat and Chenota (= Vaipicotta) were the foremost among these. It was for this reason that Sebastiani decided to leave it to the assembly itself to decide whether to read the briefs that day or not.[20]

In his eagerness to show everyone that he was in no way an agent of the Archbishop, Sebastiani yielded to the demands of those who wanted to exclude from the assembly Cattanar George Bengur,[21] the procurator of Garcia, on the ground that his presence would disturb the peace of the meeting. This Cattanar was a fervent partisan of Garcia and hence was intensely disliked by all those who disliked Garcia. For the same reason he was respected and obeyed by those of Garcia's party. The latter now threatened to leave the assembly, but were persuaded by Bengur himself to remain.[22]

When the meeting commenced, Sebastiani showed the assembled the papal briefs and left it to their choice to read them or not. According to the sworn statement of the four priests of Cochin, who acted as Sebastiani's interpreters,

---

[20] APF, *SOCG 233*, f. 464: Breve racconto di tutto l'operato dal P. Gioseppe... — VINCENZO MARIA, *Il Viaggio*, pp. 219-220.

[21] Cattanar Bengur Kotteckel George was a native of Agaparambu. He was certainly one of the most prominent priests of the Serra, both because of the social position of his family and because of his learning. At the outbreak of the general rebellion of 1653 he too was on the side of the Archdeacon. In fact he was appointed one of his four councillors. At Mangat he was among the 12 priests chosen to "consecrate" the Archdeacon. But as soon as he came to know the truth, he abandoned Thomas and made his submission to Garcia. Ever since that time he worked hard to get others to follow in his footsteps. He succeeded in persuading even some of those who had been invalidly ordained by the Archdeacon. For these reasons he received letters of congratulation from the viceroy and from the Goan Inquisitors. (Cf. *Goa 68-II*, ff. 719v-720: statement by Garcia; *Ibid.*, f. 743: narration by Fr. De Magistris; *Ibid.*, ff. 496-499; *Goa 49*, f. 181; *Goa 68-I*, f. 116v). He became the most respected leader of the party of the Archbishop. For this very reason, however, he was intensely disliked by those who were opposed to Garcia. The Carmelite accounts describe him as imprudent and tactless. (APF, *SOCG 233*, f. 258v-259). In June 1662 we find him vicar of the church of Kanjoor. (Cf. *SOCG 234*, ff. 336v-340v).

the assembly unanimously decided to postpone the reading
to the meeting of Mangat. On the same day several Christians and Cattanars approached the Commissary and advised him not to make any mention of the Archbishop in the
meeting, lest the conversion of the absent be impeded and
lest many of those present at the meeting should turn back.
It was, therefore, decided that it would be enough for the
time being if the assembly promised to obey the Roman
Church, to accept the Commissary as the legate of the Pope,
to submit for the time being to his government alone, and
to reject that of the Archdeacon. All those present at the
meeting did so. Sebastiani adds that many of those who
suggested that on that day it was enough to have seen the
briefs to give credence to the Commissary, and that it would
be better to read the briefs in the presence also of the churches of Mangat and Chenota, belonged to the party of the
Archbishop. The meeting ended with the solemn imparting
of absolution from censures.[23]

Archbishop Garcia and his confreres accuse Sebastiani
of having committed an enormous blunder in not reading
the papal briefs at the meeting of Mattancherry. They accuse him also of having acted in bad faith. According to
Fr. Bras de Azevedo S.J., the Commissary refused to read
the briefs, because if he had read them, he would not have
been able to carry out his plan of depriving the Archbishop
of his see and the Jesuits of their mission. Fr. Barretto S.J.
adds that Sebastiani had to make use of some kind of stratagem in order to make himself the pastor of the Serra. He
says that the Commissary asked the assembled Cattanars
and Christians whether they recognized him as their pastor.
Since those present could make no distinction between
pastor and delegate, they willingly agreed! Garcia states
further that Sebastiani failed to declare at the meeting that
the Archdeacon was not a bishop.[24]

---

[22] ARSI, *Goa 68-II*, f. 743: Ecclesiae Cranganorensis ... Calamitates. *Goa 68-I*, f. 116: Fr. Barretto's "Informatio de Statu ... Serrae". — SOCG 233, f. 258v: Fr. Vincent Mary's narration.

[23] APF, *SOCG 232*, f. 157: sworn statement of the four interpreters. — SOCG 233, f. 464v: Breve racconto di tutto l'operato del P.
Gioseppe. — SEBASTIANI, *Prima Speditione*, p. 123. — ARSI, *Goa 68-I*,
f. 129: Sebastiani to Garcia on 24 September 1657.

[24] *Goa 49*, ff. 182v-183: narration by Fr. Bras de Azevedo S.J. —

These accusations seem to spring from the prejudice
of Garcia and his friends and from their understandable
eagerness to be once again rulers of the Serra, rather than
from a calm and objective judgement of the real situation.
If Sebastiani had insisted on reading the papal briefs in
spite of all the warnings he had received, a few more churches (besides the four already subject to Garcia) would probably have submitted to Garcia, though not without a certain
amount of reluctance. But it is certain that many others
would not have agreed. We have to remember that even
those churches like Kuravilangad which had in a certain
way submitted to Garcia before the arrival of the papal
Commissary, preferred to attach themselves to the Commissary as soon as the latter reached Malabar. The northern
churches led by Alangad were even more uncompromising
in their rejection of Garcia. We have, in fact, the statements
of a number of important witnesses like the captain of
Cochin, the president of the cathedral chapter of the same
city, twelve priests of that diocese, the vicars of the churches
of Kuravilangad and Palai, the captain of the castle near
Cochin and several others, which declare that it would be
impossible to bring all or the majority of the churches of
the Serra to obey Garcia, and that to insist on this would
impede their obedience and submission to the Roman
Church.[25] It is therefore clear that it was still too early to
think of re-establishing the government of Garcia and the
Jesuits. After all, the most important thing was to save

Goa 68-I, ff. 116-117: narration by Fr. Barretto S.J. — Goa 68-II,
f. 720v: a short treatise by Garcia. — Ibid., f. 743: a description by
Fr. De Magistris S.J.

[25] APF, SOCG 232, f. 171: 12 priests of Cochin and the vicar of
Kuravilangad on 5.1.1658. — Ibid., f. 173: Emmanuel Sanches Sarmento, cantor and president of the chapter of Cochin, on 5.12.1657.
— Ibid., f. 175: Simon Gomes da Silva, captain and governor of
Cochin, on 5.1.1658. — Ibid., f. 177: Emmanuel Netto Cortese, "genti-
luomo della casa di Sua Maestà" and a citizen of Cochin, on
26.12.1657. — Ibid., f. 178: Giovanni Pereira de Castro Soto Mayor,
on 11.12.1657. — Ibid., f. 179: Emmanuel Perera de Motta, captain
of the castle of Cochin, on 4.12.1657. — Ibid., f. 181: Fr. John of St.
Joseph O.F.M., guardian of the monastery of St. Antony in Cochin,
on 14.12.1657. — Ibid., f. 182: Fr. Paul of the Mother of God, superior
of the Monastery of St. John, of the Reformed Franciscans, on
1.1.1658. — Ibid., f. 188: The vicars of Kuravilangad and Palai, 12
priests of the diocese of Cochin and 3 laymen from the same city.

the Serra for the Church. The re-establishment of the government of Garcia was far less important than this. Hence one has to admit that the Commissary did what was best under the circumstances. As for Garcia's accusation that Sebastiani failed to declare that the Archdeacon was not a bishop, it may be pointed out that the Jesuits themselves admit that Sebastiani had made this declaration at the meeting of Edapally in May.[26] If he did not repeat it, it must have been due to some tactical reason. But we shall see that the declaration was emphatically made once again at the meeting of Alangad.

On 28 September Sebastiani sent his two companions together with the two interpreters, Fr. Emmanuel Vaz and Fr. Christopher Miranda, to Chenota and Alangad to treat with those two churches and with the Archdeacon, and to organise the general meeting of the churches which the Archdeacon had promised to convoke at Alangad.[27] But very little was achieved even though the two Carmelites remained at Alangad for nearly a month. The Archdeacon invited some people, but sent them away almost immediately, saying that the meeting was postponed to a more opportune time.[28] Nevertheless Fr. Matthew of St. Joseph and Fr. Vincent Mary were able to hold a meeting with the participation of some churches. In the name of Sebastiani they placed before the assembly four demands: first, that the participants declare themselves obedient to the Roman Church; second, that they accept Sebastiani as the commissary of the Pope; third, that they recognize Garcia as their true prelate, given them by the Pope; fourth, that they no longer recognize Thomas as bishop, since he was not consecrated by order of Rome and since the consecration was performed by 12 simple priests.[29] The assembly made no difficulty regarding the first two points. But they stubbornly refused to entertain the idea of a return to the obedience of Garcia.

---

[26] Cf. ARSI, *Goa 68-I*, f. 115v: statement of Fr. Barretto. — *Goa 49*, f. 182: narration by Fr. Bras de Azevedo.

[27] APF, *SOCG 233*, f. 259v: Racconto di quanto passò ne trattati che si fecero in Mangati...

[28] *Goa 68-I*, ff. 117v-118: Fr. Barretto's "Informatio de Statu Serrae".

[29] *SOCG 232*, f. 189: sworn statement of Fr. Matthew of St. Joseph O.C.D., Fr. Vincent Mary O.C.D., Fr. Emmanuel Vaz, Fr. Christopher Miranda and Fr. Chandy Kadavil. (Cf. also *SOCG 233*, f. 1).

The Carmelites in the end agreed to drop this demand. Regarding the fourth point, the Archdeacon's partisans demanded that his deposition from the episcopal dignity should be done in private and that he should be allowed to retain the title and the dress of a bishop until the Pope would actually appoint him one. Sebastiani, however, refused to yield on this point. He insisted that Thomas should be satisfied with the title and the dress of an archdeacon until Rome would decide his case. But Thomas retorted that he was not interested in further negotiations unless the Commissary agreed to make him a bishop immediately. The talks therefore broke down and the two Carmelites and their interpreters returned to Sebastiani.[30]

We have now to go back a little to examine the disputes between Sebastiani and the Archbishop. The day after the conclusion of the meeting at the church of St. Thomas, near Cochin, Sebastiani wrote to Garcia to inform him how those present at the meeting had placed themselves under his (Sebastiani's) immediate government, until some other definitive arrangement would be made. They renounced obedience to the Archdeacon. At the same time, for the sake of avoiding divisions, they did not also want to accept the government of Garcia. Sebastiani added that he hoped for the best at the meeting of Mangat. Since the situation was like this and since any premature exercise of authority by Garcia might ruin all prospects of reunion, Sebastiani requested him in the name of the Pope that he should not without Sebastiani's consent exercise acts of jurisdiction nor confer orders. At the same time he told him that it was not his intention to include in this prohibition the Southists who had always remained faithful to Garcia, though even in their case he expected him to act with circumspection.[31]

Sebastiani informs us that he did all this because the chief Cattanars of the meeting had told him that this was necessary to allay the fears and the suspicions caused by the largeness of the number of clerics ordained by Garcia during the ember days of September. Sebastiani himself

---

[30] SEBASTIANI, *Prima Speditione*, pp. 125-127. — VINCENZO MARIA, *Il Viaggio*, p. 226.

[31] ARSI, *Goa 68-I*, f. 129: copy of Sebastiani's letter to Garcia on 24 September 1657. (another copy in *Goa 68-II*, f. 417). — APF, *SOCG 233*, f. 467: Breve racconto di tutto l'operato dal P. Gioseppe ...

might be taken for a Jesuit or an agent of the Jesuits, unless the people realised that the Archbishop conferred orders in dependance on the Commissary and that therefore these acts were not necessarily a prelude to the re-establishment of the government of Garcia.[32]

The Archbishop did not reply to the letter of Sebastiani. So the latter secretly sent for Fr. Barretto (the Jesuit provincial of the province of Malabar) and convinced him of the reasonableness of his requests. Fr Barretto spoke with Garcia, and the latter wrote to Sebastiani, excusing himself for the delay. But when the news of the failure of the talks at Alangad reached him, Garcia informed the Commissary that he would no longer abstain from the exercise of his rights, since no good had resulted from his abstention. The Commissary, however, insisted that Garcia should abide by his earlier request, pointing out that this was necessary for reunion. He was, he said, actually engaged in the work and hence he knew best what measures would help him in his work and what would not. He could not give him all the reasons why he was forced to make such decisions. In order to make sure that his request would be heeded, he informed Garcia that anyone from the Serra who would dare to get himself ordained without his (Sebastiani's) written permission, would be suspended ipso facto. Garcia was asked to inform all those who approached him for orders, about this decision of Sebastiani.[33]

Garcia was of the opinion that the Commissary had clearly gone beyond his powers in issuing this order. He would have dealt severely with the Commissary for this, but for the fact that he realised that it would only land him in greater difficulties. The Commissary had a large following in Cochin, especially among the religious. So Garcia feared that if the Commissary in his turn fulminated censures against him, these people would applaud the action of the Commissary and would accept it as a decision of the Apostolic See. The Jesuit provincial, too, counselled patience.[34]

---

[32] *Ibid.*, ff. 467v-468.

[33] *Ibid.* — ARSI, *Goa 68-II*, ff. 716-717 (also ff. 437-438); a tract by Garcia. — *Goa 68-I*, f. 130v: Sebastiani to Garcia on 26 October 1657. — *Ibid.*, f. 113: Sebastiani to Garcia on 27 October 1657. — *Ibid.*, f. 114 (also f. 143v): Sebastiani to Garcia on 5 November 1657.

[34] *Goa 68-II*, ff. 716-717: a tract by Garcia. — *Goa 49*, f. 183v: narration by Fr. Bras de Azevedo S.J.

Garcia, therefore, tried milder methods. He sent Fr. Bras de Azevedo S.J. to Cochin, with letters to the cathedral chapter and to the other authorities, in an effort to win them over to his side. But the chapter refused to make any moves against Sebastiani. Instead they asked Garcia to accede to Sebastiani's requests. They then wrote to Sebastiani to inform him that they did not consider his demands unreasonable.[35]

The Archbishop now wrote to the chapter and to Sebastiani that by virtue of the papal briefs adressed to him, he had the same powers as the Commissary, and hence did not need to depend on him for anything! The authority of the Commissary was not privative but merely cumulative.[36] The chapter was surprised to see Garcia's pretensions. Fr. Anthony Carvalho Mesquitta, the vicar general of Cochin, composed a long juridical tract refuting the claims of Garcia.[37] The latter avenged himself by refusing to ordain anyone of the diocese of Cochin during the ember days of December.[38]

On 18 November 1657 Sebastiani wrote a sharp letter to Garcia, accusing him of trying to twist the sense of the papal briefs in an effort to make himself the equal of the Apostolic Commissary, though it was obvious that Garcia was by law his subject. He once again demanded from Garcia due submission to his directions.[39]

In an effort not to give any reasons for unnecessary suspicions, Sebastiani had in the past never entered Cochin. But now he went into the city to justify his actions before a number of people. He secretly met also Fr. Barretto S.J. and explained to him how necessary the things that he

---

[35] APF, *SOCG 233*, f. 468: Breve racconto di tutto l'operato dal P.F. Gioseppe... — *Goa 68-I*, f. 143: Sebastiani to the chapter of Cochin on 5.11.1657. — *SOCG 232*, f. 86: The reply of the Chapter to Sebastiani on 11.11.1657.

[36] Garcia relied on the following words of the papal brief to support his claim: "fraternitatem tuam monemus et hortamur ut oves tuas ad ovile Christi reducere coneris, et ad propria pascua redeuntes benigne suscipias, illis debitum per inobedientiam contractum remittas" etc. (*Goa 68-II*, ff. 252-253: letter of Garcia to Sebastiani).

[37] APF, *SOCG 233*, ff. 248v-253v.

[38] *Ibid.*, f. 468: Breve racconto di tutto l'operato dal P. Gioseppe.

[39] ARSI, *Goa 68-I*, f. 133: The original of the letter.

demanded from Garcia were. He told him that The Archbishop's claim that he too was an apostolic commissary, was
altogether unreasonable. The reduction of the Christians
could proceed only step by step. First they should be made
to recognize the authority of the Pope and to accept the Commissary as his delegate. Then they should be severed from
the Archdeacon. Finally there would come submission to
the Archbishop. After the deposition of the Archdeacon,
the return to the Archbishop could be usefully tried. But to
want to do it at the beginning, would be to ruin everything.
He told him also that he was in conscience bound to procure
the first two steps even if he could not obtain the last. After
the first two steps the last would become easier.[40]

A few days later Garcia went to Cochin for the solemn
exequies of King John IV of Portugal. On that occasion he
intimated to one of the companions of Sebastiani who was
sent to meet him, that he would for a short time stand by
the request of Sebastiani, but that after that he intended to
act independently. In fact, during the ember days of December, Garcia ordained not only those sent to him by Sebastiani
but also some others.[41]

In the meantime the news reached Malabar that the
other papal commissary, Fr. Hyacinth of St. Vincent, had
arrived in Goa via Lisbon. Sebastiani could now return to
Rome in order to report to the Pope and to the Propaganda
regarding the situation in Malabar and to suggest the rem-
edies that he considered suitable to end the rebellion. Before leaving Malabar, however, he wished to meet once again
the representatives of the churches that had abandoned the
rebellious Archdeacon. Accordingly invitations were sent to
the churches to assemble once again towards the middle of
December at the church of St. Thomas near Cochin. The impression that one gets from a confrontation of the Carmelite
and the Jesuit accounts of the meeting, is that the actual
attendance was rather small. But the few that took part in
the meeting, went there not only in the name of their own
churches but also as representatives of several others, so

---

[40] APF,*SOCG 233*, ff. 468v-469: Breve racconto di tutto l'operato
dal P. Gioseppe.
[41] *Ibid.*, ff. 469-470. — Cf. also *Goa 68-I*, f. 117v: narration by Fr.
Barretto S.J.

that Fr. Vincent Mary could write with a certain amount of truth that 44 churches were present at the meeting.[42]

The meetings lasted from 14 to 18 December. Sebastiani explained to the assembled Cattanars and the Christians the reasons why he deemed it necessary to return to Rome. They warmly approved of his journey, but requested him to leave behind one of his companions, to govern them until the arrival of the other papal commissary. They asked to be excused if they could not bring themselves to accept their old prelate, and in a separate document they exposed their reasons. After this, all those present made the profession of faith composed for the occasion by Sebastiani. Inter alia the formula explicitly stated that no one can be a true bishop unless consecrated by another bishop. The assembly did not fail to send two of its representatives to the Archdeacon who was then staying at Kayamkulam, to make one more effort to win him over. Sebastiani picturesquely describes the result of this meeting of the two representatives with the Archdeacon. They found him, he says, "more like an atheist than like a Christian, denying hell which they threatened and laughing at the very idea of sin!".[43]

---

[42] VINCENZO MARIA, *Il Viaggio*, p. 229.

In APF, *SOCG 232*, f. 111 there is to be found the sworn declaration of the Carmelite companions of Sebastiani and of his three interpreters, according to which the Cattanars from several churches like Palai, Kuravilangad, Muttam, Cananatu, Chattukulangara, and the smaller church of Kaduthuruthy were present at the meeting. Besides representing their own churches, they went as proxies of many more, a list of which is also given.

Fr. Barretto S.J. writes in his "Informatio de Statu Serrae" that "none went to the meeting except those obedient to the Archbishop. From the rest there were only the vicars of Kuravilangad and Muttam with two or three clerics from these churches. It also happened that six vicars from the south, who had gone to Cochin at this time to offer their submission to the Archbishop, spoke with the Commissary too, and promised him obedience." (*Goa 68-I*, f. 118). About two months after the meeting, Fr. Barretto could write to Fr. Matthew of St. Joseph O.C.D., without fear of being contradicted by the latter, that "the majority of the participants of *the thinly attended meeting* was there precisely to offer submission to the Archbishop". (*Goa 68-II*, f. 510). Fr. Bras de Azevedo too, says that very few attended the meeting. (Cf. *Goa 49*, f. 184).

[43] APF, *SOCG 232*, ff. 111-112: Ultimo concilio fatto dal P.F. Gioseppe nella Serra. — VINCENZO MARIA, *Il Viaggio*, p. 229. — SEBASTIANI, *Prima Speditione*, pp. 135-139. — *SOCG 233*, f. 470v: Breve racconto di tutto l'operato del P.F. Gioseppe.

Before the assembly dispersed, Sebastiani took the chief Cattanars with him to Cochin. In the name of their Christians they promised friendship and loyalty to the Portuguese king, their protector. The captain of Cochin, in his turn, promised them the favour and protection of his king.[44] This was a clever move on the part of Sebastiani. He thus wanted to prove that his work, far from undermining in any way the interests of the Portuguese Crown, had only safeguarded it.

Sebastiani decided to leave behind Fr. Matthew of St. Joseph as his delegate in the Serra. The latter was to take his place until the arrival of Fr. Hyacinth of St. Vincent. In order to make sure that the line of action, followed by him would be continued, Fr. Matthew was given clear and precise instructions as to how to act towards the Archbishop, the Jesuit fathers, the captain and the other authorities of Cochin, the Christians who had submitted, the rebellious Archdeacon and the rebellious Cattanars and Christians. Under no circumstances was he to allow the Jesuit fathers to enter the Serra. If necessary, he should inform the Archbishop and the Jesuit provincial that any Jesuit who dared to set foot in the Serra without the consent of the Commissary, would incur excommunication. In his letter of 6 January 1658 to Fr. Barretto (the Jesuit provincial) Sebastiani felt the need of informing him of this decision of his.[45]

On 7 January 1658 Sebastiani and Fr. Vincent Mary began their long journey to Rome via Goa, Basra, Aleppo and Venice. They reached the Eternal City on 22 February 1659.[46]

Fr. Matthew of St. Joseph acted as the delegate of Sebastiani for about two months. It was during this time that the Archdeacon contrived to get himself declared a patriarch. The occasion was the feast of "Munnu Noyambu" at the church of Edapally. On the last day of the feast the Archdeacon appeared in front of the crowds and produced before them a sealed letter which, he declared, he had received from

---

[44] SEBASTIANI, *Prima Speditione*, pp. 137-138. — VINCENZO MARIA, *Il Viaggio*, p. 229.

[45] Cf. APF, *SOCG 233*, ff. 245-246: the full text of the instructions given to Fr. Matthew of St. Joseph. — ARSI, *Goa 68-I*, f. 245: Sebastiani to Fr. Barretto on 6.1.1658.

[46] BUFALINI, *L'Opera Pacificatrice*, p. 356, note 7. — Cf. also APF, *SOCG 232*, f. 261; *Acta 28*, f. 26.

Mar Atallah. He had been told by Atallah, he said, not to open the letter until he heard of his death. The Archdeacon now knew for certain that Atallah was dead. Hence it was right that he should open the letter. It said that Atallah was authorized by the Pope to make the Archdeacon a patriarch, in case Atallah happened to die. The new patriarch could then elect and consecrate bishops. The Pope had also sent a pallium for the new patriarch. After the reading of the letters, something made of silk and resembling a pallium was shown to the crowds. Amidst thunderous applause the Archdeacon was forthwith declared a patriarch! [47]

Sebastiani's work had seriously damaged the position of the Archdeacon. The antics that the latter now resorted to, were but a crude attempt on his part to regain the ground that he had lost. But they did not produce any lasting results, though they served to rouse the enthusiasm of his fanatical followers for the moment.

3. THE LARGELY FRUITLESS WORK OF FR. HYACINTH OF ST. VINCENT O.C.D.

Though Fr. Hyacinth and his companion, Fr. Marcel of St. Ives, left the Eternal City in February 1656, it was only on 23 April that they could set out from Genoa for Lisbon where they reached in the first days of August.[1] King John IV of Portugal was not at all in favour of allowing the papal Commissary to proceed to India, in spite of the fact that at that time Portugal was straining every nerve to obtain from the Holy See the recognition of the new dynasty. The traditional suspicion of the Portuguese authorities against the missionaries sent by the Propaganda had lately increased because of the allegedly imprudent behaviour of some Italian Capuchin missionaries whom the Propaganda had sent to the kingdom of Benim on the coast of Africa. Fr. Hyacinth was

---

[47] *Goa 68-I*, f. 119: Fr. Barretto's Informatio de Statu ... Serrae. — *Goa 68-II*, f. 744: Ecclesiae Cranganorensis ... Calamitates. — *SOCG 234*, f. 239: Sebastiani to the Propaganda on 1.1.1662.

[1] Cf. APF, *SOCG 191*, f. 452: Fr. Hyacinth to the Propaganda on 22 April 1656. — *Ibid.*, f. 58: Fr. Anthony Ardizone (the procurator in Lisbon of the Theatine Missions) to the Propaganda on 16 August 1656.

almost on the point of giving up all hope of obtaining the permission of the government of Lisbon, when things suddenly changed for the better. The king died in November 1656 and Queen Luisa Gusmão became regent. She yielded to the entreaties of the chief chaplain who was all in favour of the Carmelites.[2] The queen not only helped to clear away the political difficulties, but also provided Fr. Hyacinth and his companion with money for their journey, so that they could set out for Goa on 28 March 1657.[3]

A number of circumstances held them up for several months in Goa. Finally on 10 March 1658 they landed in Cochin.[4] Since they went with the approval of the Court of Lisbon, they were received with all honours by the authorities of Cochin. The most important members of the clergy and the laity belonging to the four churches obeying Garcia went to pay the Commissary their respects. They described how grateful they were to the Jesuit missionaries for their work in the past and begged him to allow the fathers to visit their churches as before. Fr. Hyacinth gave them a sympathetic hearing and congratulated them for their fidelity to the Archbishop.[5] On 20 March he was visited also by a group of about eight or nine Cattanars led by Bengur George, and by the seminarians staying at the seminary of Vaipicotta and in the house of the Archbishop. It was on orders from Garcia that they went to meet the Commissary. Since Cattanar George Bengur was the oldest and the most res-

---

[2] ARSI, *Goa 68-I*, ff. 343v-344: letter of Fr. De Magistris to Garcia on 20 June 1659. — *SOCG 191*, f. 497: Fr. Hyacinth to the Propaganda on 5 October 1656.

[3] *Ibid.*, f. 533: Fr. Hyacinth to the Propaganda on 24 March 1657. — *Ibid., Acta 26*, pp. 41-44.

[4] *SOCG 233*, f. 234: "Brevis et succincta relatio eorum quae successerunt in Missione Angamalensi tempore R. di Patris Hyacinthi a S. Vincentio Commissarii Apostolici, eiusque successoris, usque ad Adventum Ill.mi et Rev.mi D.D. Josephi a S. Maria". This is a detailed account of the events in the Serra from the arrival of Fr. Hyacinth to that of Bishop Sebastiani. It was composed by Fr. Marcel of St. Ives. (*Cf. SOCG 233*, f. 182: statement of Bishop Sebastiani). The "Breve notitia delli successi alla Missione di Serra", dated 10 September 1659, says that Fr. Hyacinth reached the Serra on 8 March 1658. (*SOCG 232*, f. 343).

[5] ARSI, *Goa 68-II*, f. 744v: "Ecclesiae Cranganorensis ... Calamitates et Remedia" by Fr. De Magistris S.J. — *Goa 68-I*, f. 119v: Fr. Barretto's informatio de Statu ... Serrae.

pected member of the group, he replied in the name of the whole group to the questions put them by the Commissary. Two of the Cattanars who took part in this meeting, inform us that Cattanar Bengur mentioned only the good things done by the Jesuits and passed over the injuries inflicted by them on the Archdeacon, the Cattanars and the Christians. The two Cattanars were unhappy about what Fr. Bengur did. They refused to affix their signatures to a report that was prepared on the same day by Fr. De Magistris and Cattanar George Bengur, since they found it to be full of praises for the Jesuits.   Only those who were waiting for holy orders and for the faculties for confessions, signed the document. The two Cattanars concluded their sworn statement with the assertion that no one except Cattanar Bengur wanted the Jesuits in the Serra and that if the latter were to go back to the Serra, great disorders would happen again.[6]

We have it on the authority of Fr. Bras de Azevedo S.J. that Fr. Hyacinth was at first friendly to the Jesuits.[7]   Fr. Barretto S.J. adds that Fr. Hyacinth said at the beginning that he was sorry for the unfriendly behaviour of Fr. Joseph of St. Mary (Sebastiani) towards the Society of Jesus.[8]   In fact, a letter of Fr. Hyacinth, dated 25 March 1658 and addressed to the Propaganda, confirms this to a certain extent, while at the same time it shows clearly the enormous difficulties of his task.   Fr. Hyacinth wrote that he could not follow the method of Sebastiani since that was against the papal briefs which asked him to bring about a reconciliation between the Archbishop and the Archdeacon and to bring the people to the obedience of the Archbishop. But the Cattanars wanted that he should openly show himself to be an enemy of the Society of Jesus. The Jesuits on the other hand expected that he should work for their interests, no matter to whom such a policy caused disgust. If he refused to act according to their wishes, they would hinder his work in every possible way, in order to prove that if the reduction of the rebels could not be done by them, it could not be done

---

[6] APF, *SOCG 232*, f. 202: sworn statement of two Cattanars in the name of several others as well, dated 20 March 1658.

[7] ARSI, *Goa 49*, f. 188.

[8] *Goa 68-I*, f. 148v: Fr. Barretto to the Jesuit general on 12.11.1658.

by anyone else either. He concluded saying that he would try to work according to the papal briefs.[9]

Not long afterwards he had an opportunity to put into practice his heroic resolution. The Archdeacon was at that time visiting the churches of the southern parts. He was solemnly welcomed in many places. But when he reached the larger church of Kottayam which had always remained faithful to the Archbishop, the people shut the church in his face and appealed to the local king, telling him that a commissary of the Pope had arrived from Rome to show everyone that the Archdeacon was not a bishop. The king therefore wrote to the Commissary that if he went to see him and convinced him of the falseness of the Archdeacon's claim to be a bishop, he would see that all his subjects abandoned the Archdeacon. Some priests and more than a hundred laymen went to Cochin to accompany the Commissary to Kottayam. When Fr. Hyacinth, accompanied by Fr. John Baptist O.S.A. (Garcia's procurator) and Cattanar George Bengur, reached Kottayam on 26 April, the king happened to be away on some business in the neighbouring kingdom of Kaduthuruthy. So the Commissary sent word to the king to inform him of his arrival, and waited there for three days. But since the king did not return, the Commissary went back to Cochin, though he was requested by the king's minister and by the Christians to wait a little longer. Some time later, more than 200 Christians went to Cochin to invite the Commissary to go once again with them to Kottayam. But the Commissary did not oblige them, bringing forward a number of pretexts for not going.[10] The reason for this change of attitude on the part of Fr. Hyacinth of St. Vincent is furnished by the "Brevis et succincta relatio", an account written by Fr. Marcel of St. Ives. He says that the journey of Fr. Hyacinth to Kottayam at the request of the Archbishop and his partisans, caused diffidence and suspicion in the

---

[9] APF, *SOCG 232*, f. 203.

[10] ARSI, *Goa 68-I*, f. 120: Fr. Barretto's Informatio de Statu Serrae. — *Ibid.*, f. 178: sworn statement of Cattanar George Bengur on 3.7.1658. — *Ibid.*, f. 285: an official document regarding the visit, drawn up by the Commissary on 28 April 1658. — *Goa 68-II*, ff. 368v-369: a description by Garcia. — *Ibid.*, f. 479v: sworn statement of Fr. John Baptist O.S.A. on 2 June 1658. — *Ibid.*, ff. 744v-745: Ecclesiae Cranganorensis... Calamitates. — APF, *SOCG 233*, f. 234: Brevis et succincta relatio...

minds of those Christians that had abandoned the Archdeacon but had not accepted the government of Garcia. Since they saw that Fr. Hyacinth was busying himself with the interests of the party of the Archbishop, leaving aside the interests of those who had placed themselves under the direct government of the Apostolic Commissary, they began to suspect that he was becoming the tool of Garcia and the Jesuits.[11] Fr. Hyacinth now feared that if he allowed that suspicion to grow, instead of making any progress he might lose even the 28 churches that had abandoned the Archdeacon at the time of Sebastiani. So he made up his mind to work in the same way as Sebastiani.[12]

At about this time, in a meeting held at Kayamkulam some of the more important Cattanars belonging to the party of the Archdeacon urged him to enter into talks with the Commissary, so that the divisions and the quarrels existing among the St. Thomas Christians could be ended. Accordingly they approached Cattanar Chandy Parampil, the vicar of Kuravilangad, to use his influence with the Commissary to bring about the desired meeting. Fr. Hyacinth, needless to say, was very happy to oblige. The meeting between the Commissary and a delegation of important Cattanars from the Archdeacon's party was arranged for 25 June 1658 at Pallipuram. Subsequently the venue of the meeting was shifted by mutual agreement to Muttam. The delegation from the side of the Archdeacon was led by Cattanar Ittithommen. After an initial exchange of views, he presented to the Commissary a written statement which sought by means of sophisms to defend the validity and the legality of the "episcopal consecration" of Thomas Parampil. But it contained also a petition that if by chance the consecration was invalid, the Pope should be so good as to validate it by supplying what was lacking. The Commissary too decided to give a written reply in which he refuted point by point the false assumptions and assertions contained in the paper presented by Ittithommen. Since the latter declared that he had no powers to enter into any binding agreement, the meeting ended with this exchange of views. The Commissary however, handed over to Cattanar Ittithommen a con-

---

[11] *Ibid.*, f. 234v: Brevis et succincta relatio...
[12] *SOCG 232*, f. 343: Breve notitia delli successi alla missione di Serra.

ciliatory letter for the Archdeacon, in which he was told that
if he gave up the schism, things would go well with him.
On 10 July the Commissary returned to Cochin.[13]

From there the Commissary continued to negotiate with
the Archdeacon and his Cattanars. Everything seemed to
proceed well. Under pressure from his Cattanars, Archdeacon Thomas sent "olas" (palm leaf documents) to the Commissary, promising to make his submission. Just at this
moment an unfortunate event occurred which destroyed all
the hopes of Fr. Hyacinth.[14]

The event in question was the public and solemn entry
into Kaduthuruthy, of Cattanar Kunnel Mathai (the new
Archdeacon appointed by Garcia in 1656). It came about
like this. On 15 July 1658 Kadavil Thommachar, an uncle
and benefactor of Archdeacon Mathai, died a sudden death
at Kaduthuruthy. Since the latter owed very much to his
uncle, it would have created a scandal among the relatives,
if within 41 days he had not gone there to offer his condo-
lences to them. So he decided to go to Kaduthuruthy.[15] In
the meantime some Christian belonging to the party of
the Archbishop requested the king of Kaduthuruthy, when
the latter was setting out for Trichur, to bring Archdeacon
Mathai along with him on his return. But the king did not
touch Cochin during his return journey. When some Christians of Garcia's party noticed this, they put the new Archdeacon in all haste in a boat and thus Mathai entered Kaduthuruthy solemnly in the company of the king.[16] On the feast
of the Assumption, in the official robes of the archdeacon
he assisted at the First Mass of a newly ordained priest in
the smaller church of Kaduthuruthy. The dalmatics, the
silver thurible, the boat etc. which he used on the occasion
were sent by the Archbishop.[17]

---

[13] APF, SOCG 233, ff. 234v-235: Brevis et succincta relatio...

[14] Ibid. — ARSI, Goa 68-I, ff. 138, 141: Fr. Hyacinth to Garcia on
27 August 1658. (another copy on ff. 232, 236).

[15] APF, SOCG 232, ff. 241v-242: Fr. De Magistris to Fr. Hyacinth
of St. Vincent on 27 August 1658. — ARSI, Goa 68-II, ff. 631-632: statement of six Cattanars, including the vicar of the smaller church of
Kaduthuruthy on 9.5.1659.

[16] SOCG 232, f. 371: Statement of Fr. Chandy Parampil, vicar of
Kuravilangad, on 31 August 1658.

[17] SOCG 232, f. 373: Statement of Cattanar Chandy Kadavil before the Commissary and Fr. Antonio Carvalho de Mesquita, the
vicar general of Cochin, on 23 August 1658.

When the details of this visit began to reach the Commissary, he seriously feared that it might make Archdeacon Thomas and his friends withdraw all the promises of submission that they had made. In fact, the worst fears of the Commissary were realised. Fr. Hyacinth now strongly suspected that either Garcia or the Jesuits had purposely sent the new Archdeacon to Kaduthuruthy to spoil the negotiations between himself and Archdeacon Thomas. He therefore demanded from Garcia the immediate recall of his protégé to Cochin where he had been staying till then. He also accused Garcia of having gone directly against the papal briefs which required him to restore Thomas and his friends to their former dignities, if they would give up their schism. How could Thomas be restored, he asked, if another took his place? [18]

A number of letters, some of which were rather sharp, were exchanged between the Commissary and the Archbishop. The latter defended himself, saying that the new Archdeacon's visit to Kaduthuruthy was not in any way caused by him and that he was ready to swear that he did not even know of it. Fr. De Magistris too, wrote to the Commissary that he as well as the other Jesuit fathers would, if necessary, affirm under oath that neither the Archbishop nor they were responsible for the journey of the new archdeacon to Kaduthuruthy.[19] Fr. Hyacinth was pacified only when on 3 September and again on 15 September Garcia wrote to Archdeacon Mathai, not to officiate any more as archdeacon and to return to Cochin.[20] But the suspicions of Fr. Hyacinth were revived when he saw that Garcia's protégé continued to remain at Kaduthuruthy and that Garcia continued to pay him his allowance in spite of his disobedience.[21]

---

[18] Cf. ARSI, *Goa 68-I*, f. 145 (also f. 226): Fr. Hyacinth to Garcia on 22 August 1658. — *Ibid.*, ff. 138-141 (also ff. 232, 236): the Commissary to Garcia on 27 August 1658. — *Ibid.*, f. 136 (also *SOCG 232*, f. 243): Garcia to the new archdeacon on 3 September 1658.

[19] *Ibid.*, ff. 139-140 (also ff. 233-234): Garcia to the Commissary on 3 September 1658. — APF, *SOCG 232*, ff. 241v-242: Fr. De Magistris to the Commissary on 27 August 1658.

[20] *Goa 68-I*, f. 135: Fr. Hyacinth to Garcia on 5 September 1658. — *Ibid.*, f. 136: Garcia to Archdeacon Mathai on 3 September 1658. — *Ibid.*, f. 224: Garcia to Archdeacon Mathai on 15 September 1658.

[21] *SOCG 233*, f. 235: Brevis et succincta relatio...

In the course of this somewhat acrimonious correspondence between the Archbishop and the Apostolic Commissary,
there flared up once again the old quarrel over the question
whether Garcia was a party in the case or whether he was
a judge along with the Commissary. When the Commissary
wrote to Garcia that the latter had acted illegally in sending
the new archdeacon to Kaduthuruthy, since Garcia who was
a party to the case could not change anything pertaining to
the case as long as the case was sub judice,[22] Garcia replied
that he was not a party, but joint judge, and that, by virtue
of the papal briefs addressed to him.[23]   The Commissary
therefore sent him an authenticated copy of the letter of
Cardinal Orsini which showed clearly that the Propaganda
considered Garcia as a party to the case. Garcia was now
forced to admit that Cardinal Orsini's letter spoke of him
as a party. But he continued to insist that the papal briefs
addressed to him, did not say anything of the kind! [24]

When these quarrels subsided, Fr. Hyacinth with the
help of the captain of Cochin began to negotiate with the
king of Kaduthuruthy who happened to be then at Vadayar.
On 14 October 1658 he set out for that place. The king was
easily won over with some gifts and he granted the Apostolic Commissary full freedom to exercise his jurisdiction
throughout the principality.[25]

From Vadayar Fr. Hyacinth proceeded to Kaduthuruthy
where he intended to hold a general meeting of the Cattanars
at the larger church which had always remained faithful to
the Archbishop. The Commissary had informed the vicar of
the church of his intention, both before he set out from
Cochin and also from Vadayar. It does not seem, however,
that he gave him the exact date of his arrival.[26] But as soon

---

[22] *Goa 68-I*, f. 145: Fr. Hyacinth to Garcia on 22 August 1658.

[23] *Ibid.*, ff. 145v-146: reply of Garcia on 25 August 1658.

[24] *Ibid.*, f. 304: Fr. Hyacinth to Garcia on 1 September 1658. —
Ibid., reply of Garcia on 6 September 1658.

[25] APF, *SOCG 233*, f. 235: Brevis et succincta relatio ... — ARSI,
Goa 68-I, f. 159: Garcia to the Propaganda on 6.12.1658.

[26] In fact, his message from Vadayar said merely that he was
there negotiating with the king of Kaduthuruthy the affairs of the
churches of his kingdom, and that when these negotiations would
be over, he would at once set out for Kaduthuruthy: "e acabado se
vinha logo para Carturte". (*SOCG 232*, f. 244: official paper regarding this visit, drawn up by Fr. Hyacinth and his companions and
interpreters on 19 October 1658).

as his boat touched the jetty of Kaduthuruthy on 17 October, he sent a messenger to the church to inform the Cattanars. Although at the beginning the priests and the clerics present in the church were inclined to follow the suggestion of a certain Cattanar called Punnose who wanted to ignore the message, in the end all of them except Punnose followed the lead given by the old Cattanar Thommi and went to the jetty to meet the Commissary and to accompany him to the church. But when the Commissary reached the church, it was found closed! The explanation given was that the sacristan was sick and hence had gone away to his house after locking the church. The Commissary flew into a rage when he heard this and refused to wait until the key would be fetched from the town. He was convinced that the partisans of the Archbishop had done it purposely in order to offer him an affront. He went away to the smaller church of Kaduthuruthy, but did not want to tarry there either, because the new archdeacon was staying there. The latter wanted to meet Fr. Hyacinth, but was told that he would be received only if he went without his archdiaconal robes. Mathai did not want to do it and so Fr. Hyacinth refused to grant him an audience and went away soon to the church of the Holy Spirit at Muttuchira.[27]

A general meeting of the Cattanars who had abandoned the Archdeacon, was now held at Muttuchira. Fr. Hyacinth wanted to know their opinion as to whether Archdeacon Thomas was to be excommunicated or not. The Cattanars replied that one more chance should be offered him before proceeding to this ultimate step. A meeting of all the churches, attended also by the most important laymen, should soon be called. This meeting should write to Archdeacon Thomas, asking him to submit to the Commissary within a

---

[27] *Ibid.* — ARSI, *Goa 68-I*, f. 158: Garcia to the Propaganda on 6.12.1658.

Cf. also *Goa 49*, f. 189v: An account written in 1666 by Fr. Bras de Azevedo S.J. He denies that any slight was offered to Fr. Hyacinth. According to him, the vicar and *many Christians* went to welcome the Commissary at the jetty. But it is difficult to believe his version of the story, seeing that a few days after the incident Fr. De Magistris tried to excuse the *absence of the Christians* on the ground that the visit had taken place on a week-day. (*SOCG 232*, ff. 247-251).

definite time limit. If he refused to listen to this solemn
call, the Commissary could think of excommunicating him.[28]

Fr. Hyacinth now announced to the Cattanars that he
had received from Goa some money to be distributed among
the vicars. To his surprise he found that the vicars did not
want to accept the money from him. They told him that one
of the chief grounds for the rebellion against Garcia was the
withholding of their allowances. In future they did not want
that the payment of these allowances be left to the discre-
tion of their pastor. They would choose two persons to
whom the money was to be paid by the Portuguese authorities. These two would see to the distribution of the money
to the vicars. Since the Cattanars refused to yield on this
point, a final decision was put off to the next meeting.[29]

Another matter on which the Commissary could not
agree with the Cattanars was the suggestion of the latter
that a deputation consisting of either the companions of the
Commissary or other delegates, should proceed immediately
to Rome to inform the Pope and the Propaganda about
the conditions in Malabar. This deputation should be able
to counteract the machinations and the accusations of the
Jesuits against Sebastiani. It should say clearly that no
Jesuit should in future be made archbishop of Cranganore
and that without the fulfilment of this condition the return
of the schismatics would remain a mere dream. Fr. Hyacinth was not convinced that it was necessary to send a new
delegation to Rome at that moment. But since he could not
prevail upon the Cattanars to drop their suggestion, also
this question was postponed to the next meeting for a final
solution. The meeting ended on 28 October and Fr. Hyacinth returned to Cochin.[30]

Within a month another meeting of the churches was
held at the church of St. Thomas, near Cochin. About 20
priests and a number of laymen were present. Garcia says
that the meeting was held behind closed doors and that
guards were posted outside, lest he should get to know of
anything decided there. As a further precaution the participants were ordered not to meet Garcia or the Jesuits.
Nevertheless Garcia managed to obtain all the information

---

[28] *SOCG 233*, f. 235: Brevis et succincta relatio...
[29] *Ibid.*
[30] *Ibid.*, ff. 235v-236.

he wanted! The meeting decided that four of the most respected priests and four distinguished laymen should go to Archdeacon Thomas to ask him whether he intended to cut himself off definitely from the Roman Church or not. He was to be told that if he gave up his schism and the usurped episcopal dignity and humbly obeyed the Roman church for some time, things would go well with him. The meeting decided that if Thomas repented, the Pope should be requested to confer the episcopal dignity on him. For this purpose the two companions of the Commissary should be sent to Rome. Garcia was, needless to say, horrified at the prospect. Over the question of the distribution of the allowances of the vicars, a compromise was reached. The Cattanars agreed to accept the money from Fr. Hyacinth this time, provided it did not become a precedent.[31]

The year 1658 was now nearly ending. At the close of his first year of work in Malabar Fr. Hyacinth could not really point to any significant results achieved by him. The Jesuit sources accuse him of remissness in his work. According to them, he spent most of his time in Cochin, preaching in all the churches of the city on all important occasions, with the result that he had not much time left for what should have been his principal task. He visited only nine or ten churches of the Serra, and that too, very hurriedly.[32] The Jesuit s thus ascribe to Fr. Hyacinth's negligence his failure to make any headway. The Carmelite sources on the other hand, attribute Fr. Hyacinth's failure to the machinations and disturbances caused by the Jesuits.[33]

The relations between the Commissary and the Archbishop were now most unfriendly. The following incident which happened on 31 December 1658, shows how far things had gone. Some Christians from Kuravilangad wanted to enrol themselves as soldiers in Cochin and hence they requested the Commissary to speak with the authorities of

---

[31] ARSI, *Goa 68-I*, ff. 159-160: Garcia to the Propaganda on 6.12.1658. — APF, *SOCG 233*, f. 236: Brevis et succincta relatio...

[32] *Goa 68-II*, f. 593: sworn statement of two Portuguese priests, Antonio Alvares de Sande and Antonio Cardoso Masseira on 9.12.1658. Fr. de Sande was the vicar general of Garcia. — *Ibid.*, f. 538. — *Goa 68-I*, f. 157v: Garcia to the Propaganda on 6.12.1658.

[33] *SOCG 232*, f. 343: Breve notitia, delli successi alla Missione di Serra.

the city. The Commissary gladly agreed to do so. He went
to Cochin and spoke to the magistrates. He was told that
since the question concerned war, he would have to see
about it with Dom Garcia who was then acting captain and
acting governor of the city.[34] But the Commissary immediately left the place without meeting Garcia.[35]

The first months of 1659 did not bring any progress in
the work of reunion. Fr. Hyacinth was so discouraged at
this, that he went to Ignatius Sarmento de Carvalho
(the general who reached Cochin on 15 March to take over
the defence of the city against the Dutch) and asked him
for a passage to Europe. But the general persuaded him to
remain, offering him all the help that he could.[36]

It was some time in the first half of 1659 that Fr.
Hyacinth ordered to be affixed to the doors of all the
churches a document which declared that the work of
reunion was being impeded and retarded through the machinations of malevolent men. If in the future anyone did
any such thing or counselled or helped anyone to do so, he
would ipso facto incur major excommunication reserved
to the Holy See. The same would be incurred by those who
in spite of knowing for certain that someone did such
things, failed to report the matter to the Commissary within
12 days of receiving the news of his order.[37]

---

[34] Garcia became acting governor of Cochin towards the end of
1658, when a powerful Dutch fleet of 17 ships appeared off Cochin,
at the invitation of one of the local rajahs. The governor of Cochin
happened to get mad just about that time. So Garcia was requested
by the citizens to take over the command of the city. Out of a
sense of duty to his country he responded to the call, though he
was then nearly 80 years old! He pacified the local kings and
gathered men and arms for the defence of the city. Seeing that
the prince who had invited them had changed his mind, the Dutch
went away. (Cf. WICKI, O Homem, pp. 327-328: second appendix;
FRANCO, Imagem... de Évora, p. 437). Probably Garcia held the
office till 15 March 1659, when Ignatius Sarmento de Carvalho reached Cochin to take charge of the defence of the city. (Cf. SOCG 232,
f. 343).

[35] ARSI, Goa 68-I, ff. 153-154 (also Goa 68-II, f. 693); statement of
the magistrates of Cochin. — Ibid., f. 746: narration by Fr. De Magistris S.J.

[36] APF, SOCG 232, f. 343: Breve notitia delli successi alla Missione di Serra.

[37] ARSI, Goa 68-II, f. 691: authenticated copy of Fr. Hyacinth's
order.

Fr. Hyacinth now tried to see if he could obtain the submission of the Christians of the principality of Mangat-Angamaly by bribing the rajahs (there were four of them, each more or less independent of the other three) of the place. His attempt did not succeed since Archdeacon Thomas too did the same thing. Fr. Hyacinth therefore had to retire to Cochin.[38]

Seeing that the new rajah of Cochin was disposed to please Ignatius Sarmento de Carvalho in everything, since he had obtained the throne through the latter's intervention, Fr. Hyacinth requested the general to intercede for him. The king issued a safe conduct for Fr. Hyacinth, so that he could freely visit all the churches of his kingdom. A second document of the king ordered all the rebel Christians to submit to the Commissary. A third one asked all the royal officials to favour Fr. Hyacinth in every way and to punish the refractory Christians. The king also promised to give Fr. Hyacinth some of his soldiers as an escort.[39]

In the first days of June 1659 an interesting exchange of letters took place between the Commissary and a Jesuit father who was addressed as "the procurator and companion of the Archbishop". It must have been Fr. De Magistris. The Commissary did not write directly to the Archbishop, most probably because Garcia and he were no longer on speaking terms. In his letter of 1 June Fr. Hyacinth admits that the papal briefs commanded that as far as possible the Serra should be made to obey its legitimate pastor. But he goes on to say that the briefs do not forbid, nay they actually ordain, that those who leave the schism of the Archdeacon and return to the bosom of the Church be received, even though they refuse to subject themselves to the Archbishop until the Pope comes to know of their grievances and decides what they must do. In the mean time no one can deny that such conversion, not alien to the spirit of the briefs, is a good thing in itself and that it is an obligation of justice and charity to protect them and to help them, so that they will not have to go back to the Archdeacon and to his followers. The latter, contrary to what they claim, cannot be obedient to the Holy See as

---

[38] APF, *SOCG 233*, f. 236: Brevis et succincta relatio...
[39] *Ibid.* — *Goa 49*, f. 194: narration by Fr. Bras de Azevedo S.J.

long as they adhere to a false bishop who has intruded into that office against the authority of the same Apostolic See. The schism really lies in that. Instead, not to submit to the authority of their legitimate pastor, but to place themselves under the immediate authority of the Holy See, until their difficulties are considered and solved by the same Apostolic See, is not schism or heresy.[40]

On the following day Fr. Hyacinth wrote another letter to the same "procurator and companion of the Archbishop", telling him that he was eagerly awaiting the Archbishop's reply to the questions that he had asked in his earlier letter, so that he could with greater satisfaction take up once again the work of bringing back to the fold the wandering sheep of the Serra. The most important question was this. Should those Christians be received back or not into the Church, who wanted to leave the schism of the Arch-deacon and promised to place themselves under the immediate authority of the Apostolic See, but who did not want to submit to the government of the Archbishop? And if he received them, would it mean that he was separating them from the Archbishop from whom they had remained obstinately separated for so long, or rather would it not mean that he was separating them from the Archdeacon whom they had been following till then? The Commissary wanted to know whether such Christians would be schismatics or Catholics. Fr. Hyacinth wrote that he wanted the Archbishop's reply to these questions for his "greater justification before God, before the Supreme Pontiff and before the whole world".[41]

These two letters of Fr. Hyacinth were an indirect and yet clear and forceful refutation of many of the pretensions of Garcia. The latter could not deny the force of Fr. Hyacinth's arguments. Hence in his reply of 5 June he harked back to the *letter* of the papal briefs, disregarding their *spirit*, and told Fr. Hyacinth that the latter had been sent to the Serra in order to bring the rebels back to his obedience and for nothing else. The rebels, he continued, had at least outwardly never refused obedience to the Supreme

---

[40] ARSI, *Goa 68-I*, f. 324: the original letter in the difficult hand of Fr. Hyacinth.

[41] ARSI, *Goa 68-I*, f. 325: the original letter in Fr. Hyacinth's own hand.

Pontiff. Hence it was useless to work for the return of the rebels to the obedience of the Pope, at least in the external forum. One wonders whether Garcia failed to see or refused to see the point which Fr. Hyacinth had tried to drive home, viz that there was an immense difference between those who merely said that they wanted to obey the Pope while continuing to adhere to the schismatic Archdeacon, and those who abandoned the Archdeacon in order to show that they were in earnest about their protestations of obedience to the Holy See. Garcia concluded his letter with these disappointing words: "I know these things for certain. The other things which you ask, do not concern me. Hence you may continue to do as you think best, without in any way consulting me, as you have been doing in the past".[42] It may be remarked by the way, that one is not able to recognize these words as those of a pastor burning with zeal for the salvation of his flock. One sees rather an individual, eager to re-establish his authority at all costs.

All this time Fr. Hyacinth had been waiting for the rajah of Cochin to send him the promised escort. Seeing that the rajah was putting it off from day to day, the Commissary decided to go once again to the principality of Mangat to see if anything could be done there. Ignatius Sarmento de Carvalho gave him 100 serafins for his expenses. The Commissary set out from Cochin on 4 June. In Mangat he found the Archdeacon enjoying the full support of the kings and holding ordination services during the ember days following Whit Sunday (9, 11, 12 June). The Commissary was, however, able to bring about a change in the attitude of the kings. The Archdeacon noticed it and decided to leave the place rather than come to a confrontation with the Commissary before the kings regarding his legal title to be a bishop. He told the king that he had to leave Mangat on an urgent business in the church of Kuruppampadi, but that he would without fail return within 8 days to settle the question raised by the Commissary. As may be easily imagined, he did not keep his promise. In the meantime rumours reached the ears of the Commissary that the Archbishop and the Jesuits had brought about the

---

[42] *Goa 68-I*, f. 326: a copy of the letter.

flight of the Archdeacon from Mangat by means of the false information which they sent him through Cattanar George Bengur and others that Dom Ignatius Sarmento de Carvalho was getting ready to make him a prisoner while the Commissary tried to detain him with negotiations.[43] Most probably this was nothing but a lie spread by malevolent persons who wanted to cause further enmity between the Carmelites and the Jesuits.[44] But the Commissary took it really seriously. On 19 June he sent Fr. Marcel to Cochin to tell the general (Ignatius Sarmento) that he was thinking of declaring that Garcia and the Jesuit fathers had incurred the excommunication which he had threatened against those who would impede the work of re-union. The general, however, told the Commissary not to do any such thing, since it would only increase the tension which was already quite unbearable.[45]

It was also in those same days that Ignatius Sarmento de Carvalho reached the very reasonable conclusion that if in spite of every effort the Christians of the Serra refused to submit to Garcia, they should be asked to throw the Archdeacon out and to make their submission to the Sovereign Pontiff, as the Commissary was telling them to do. But Fr. De Magistris S.J. to whom the general revealed his plan, succeeded to change the general's mind by means of specious

---

[43] APF, *SOCG 233*, f. 236: Brevis et succincta relatio. — ARSI, *Goa 68-II*, f. 538: narration by a Jesuit.

[44] *Ibid.*, f. 629v: sworn statement of Cattanar George Bengur. He solemnly denies that he has ever heard or said any such thing to anyone. — *Ibid.*, f. 627v: testimony of the third prince of Mangat. He too says the same thing. But it is to be noted that the Jesuits themselves say elsewhere (see *Goa 68-II*, f. 538v) that the testimony of this prince was generally most unreliable. — *SOCG 232*, f. 536: Canon Joseph de Rego of Cochin asserts that he heard from the Prince of Mangat that Cattanar Bengur sent word to the Archdeacon through an intermediary.

[45] *Goa 68-II*, f. 538: narration by a Jesuit. — *Goa 68-I*, ff. 337-338: (original) letter of De Magistris to Garcia on 19 June 1659. — *Ibid.*, ff. 341-342: (original) letter of Fr. De Magistris to Garcia on 20 June 1659.

The following words of Fr. De Magistris (found in his letter of 20 June 1659 to Garcia) give one an idea of the amount of tension and ill feeling that there was between the Jesuits and the Carmelites at that time: "... que verdadeiramente nao sei, se os chame espiritos enfernais, vestidos de burel". (= "I really do not know whether I should call them infernal spirits dressed in friars' robes!").

arguments and outright threats. In his letter of 20 June he informed Garcia: "I decided to make the general realise the malice of the friar and I told him: all the work done to make these Christians obey the Pope is a waste of time. I have with me many sworn statements to show that they have never denied obedience to the Pope. It is the deceitfulness of the friar that wants to make things go in this direction. This desire of his arises from the little love he has for the Portuguese Crown. Taking advantage of this rebellion, *he wants to remove this archdiocese from our Portuguese government.* The Congregation of the Propaganda wants to send here its missionary bishops. It says that these Christians live in the lands of pagan kings and not in Portuguese territory... I told the general not to be deceived by the friar and his talk of making the Christians obey the Pope, leaving the king's claims aside. His Majesty would with reason be angry with you (the general) and *I would be the first to accuse you and to tell everything to the king.* His Majesty has already chosen a Capuchin friar of Serpa as archbishop for this see. It is not good to leave this affair to the Pope, since the cardinals of the Propaganda favour Spain and hence will surely elect an archbishop, without His Majesty having any say in the matter, basing themselves on the one-sided information of this friar and of others whom we have every reason to suspect. — The general thanked me very much for my long talk in which I did not at all mention the interests of the Societey (of Jesus), but merely those of the Portuguese Crown. *He told me that he would now proceed in a different way in this affair,* since he did not want to receive blame where he was hoping to be rewarded".[46]

A few days after this, at the instance of Ignatius Sarmento de Carvalho the king of Purakkad who was an ally of the Portuguese, ordered his Christian subjects to submit to Garcia. Consequently in the first days of July 1659 a group of three Cattanars and four clerics representing the churches of Kallurkadu and Kudamaloor went to see Fr. Hyacinth at Alangad. The latter made them abjure the schism and then absolved them from censures. After that

---

[46] ARSI, *Goa 68-I*, ff. 343-344: the original in the characteristic hand of Fr. De Magistris.

they were sent to Cranganore in the company of Fr. Marcel of St. Ives. At Cranganore they were expected to recognize Garcia as their pastor. On reaching the place, however, they still showed some reluctance. But Garcia received them with so much love and fatherliness that they gave up all resistance and gladly made their submission.[47]

It was also at the instance of Ignatius Sarmento de Carvalho that the king of Cochin summoned to his presence the Cattanars and the chief laymen of the church of Vaipicotta which was one of the most important churches of the Serra because of the many rich and influential Christians to be found there. The king ordered them to submit to the Archbishop. They raised some objection because of the oath which they had made to support the Archdeacon. Another objection which they had was regarding the honour of their caste. But the king insisted very much and even uttered threats. In the end they yielded. They went to Cranganore to make their submission to Garcia who was by then very sick. In fact he had already received the viaticum. All the same, Garcia showed them such paternal love that they were sincerely reconciled to him. Then they went to see the Jesuit fathers of the seminary and invited them to go to preach in their church on Sundays and feast days, as they used to do before the rebellion.[48]

Both Garcia and Fr. Bras de Azevedo tell us that also the Christians of the kingdom of Paravoor would have made their submission but for the unnecessary intervention of Fr. Hyacinth of St. Vincent. At the request of Ignatius Sarmento de Carvalho who sent her gifts and messengers, the queen of Paravoor had promised to bring all the Christians of her realm to the obedience of the Archbishop. But Fr. Hyacinth, says Garcia, in his eagerness to obtain for himself the glory of the success, wrote to the queen that he would soon be making a visit to that kingdom. The

---

[47] APF, *SOCG 233*, f. 236v: Brevis et succincta relatio ... — ARSI, *Goa 49*, ff. 194v-195: narration by Fr. Bras de Azevedo S.J. — *Goa 68-I*, f. 329: Fr. Hyacinth to Garcia on 4 July 1659. (original). — *Ibid.*, f. 329v: Garcia's reply on 6 July 1659. (a copy). — *Ibid.*, ff. 169v-170 (also *Goa 68-II*, ff. 553-554 and 653v): statement by the vicar, Cattanars and seminarians from Kaḷḷurkadu.

[48] *Goa 49*, f. 194: narration by Fr. Bras de Azevedo S.J. — *SOCG 232*, f. 343: Breve notitia delli successi alla Missione di Serra.

queen, hoping to receive some present also from him, stopped half way in her efforts.[49]

The only tangible result of nearly two months of work by Fr. Hyacinth in the kingdom of Mangat-Angamaly was the submission of the former cathedral church of Angamaly on 25 July 1659. Fr. Hyacinth managed to win over the third prince of the kingdom. The latter ordered his subjects of Angamaly to make their submission to Fr. Hyacinth. Many of them obeyed the royal order. 10 Cattanars and 18 of the chief men of the church swore in front of Fr. Hyacinth that they would never recognize the Archdeacon as bishop. The disobedient Christians were punished by the king who ordered their houses to be destroyed. It is to be noted, however, that even those who submitted to the Commissary, refused to accept the invitation of the Commissary to obey the Archbishop. They said that they would write to the Pope, explaining the reasons why they did not want to submit to Garcia. Until the Pope would decide the question, they would submit only to the government of the Commissary, since they had made an oath never again to obey Garcia. They did not want Fr. Hyacinth to dispense them from the oath.[50]

In the second half of the month of July Fr. Hyacinth sent his companion, Fr. Marcel of St. Ives, with the letters of the king of Cochin, to the two churches of Kanjoor and Chowara to see if he could get those two communities to submit to the authority of the Apostolic Commissary. But Fr. Marcel could achieve nothing, even though he stayed there a number of days and did his best. The rebels refused even to talk with him. The intervention of the royal official stationed at Kanjoor and the force that he employed, only made the rebels even more stubborn. Fr. Marcel had to withdraw to Cochin on 6 August in total disappointment.[51]

---

[49] APF, *SOCG 232*, f. 325: Garcia to the Propaganda on 25 July 1659. — *Goa 49*, ff. 194v-195: Narration by Fr. Bras de Azevedo S.J.

[50] *SOCG 232*, f. 343: Breve notitia delli successi alla Missione di Serra. — *SOCG 233*, f. 237: Brevis et succincta relatio... — See also *SOCG 232*, ff. 329 and 307v.

[51] *SOCG 233*, f. 238: Brevis et succincta relatio...

4. THE DEATH OF ARCHBISHOP GARCIA

Dom Garcia's health suffered a great deal as a result of the exertions of the period when he was acting governor of Cochin. During the months that followed his retirement, an indisposition of the stomach considerably reduced his appetite. With the onset of the rainy season he caught bronchitis. He was already bed-ridden by the beginning of August. Realising that the end was near, he began to prepare himself for death.[1]

A new fear, however, began to assail him, viz that the Carmelites might make use of the vacancy of the see to get one of their own number appointed to govern the Serra. He therefore decided to nominate, Fr. Francis Barretto S.J. (bishop elect of Cochin and ex-provincial of the Malabar province) as administrator of the archdiocese. Fr. Hyacinth of St. Vincent feared that this move of Garcia might seriously impede the work of reunion.[2] Hence on 23 August 1659 he wrote to Garcia that he had come to know from reliable sources that Garcia intended to appoint a governor to rule the archdiocese after his death. Fr. Hyacinth told him that this was clearly to overstep his authority and that the appointee would incur censures if he accepted.[3] In the reply that Garcia dictated from bed to Fr. De Magistris on 26 August, he repeated that the Commissary had been sent by the Pope to bring the Serra back to the obedience of its true pastor and that he (Garcia) could not leave his archdiocese without a head.[4] On the following day the Commissary wrote to Fr. De Magistris that the papal briefs empowered him to take other measures as circumstances might demand. The situation demanded that the Archbishop should not appoint an administrator to govern the Serra after his death, in the presence of an apostolic commissary, sent to remedy the situation. This was all the more

---

[1] *SOCG 233*, f. 378: letter of Fr. De Magistris to the chapter of Goa on 8 September 1659.

[2] APF, *SOCG 233*, f. 238: Brevis et succincta relatio... — ARSI, *Goa 68-I*, f. 331: Fr. Hyacinth to Ignatius Sarmento de Carvalho on 4 September 1659.

[3] *SOCG 232*, f. 335.

[4] *Ibid.*

so, since it was clear to all that the Serra would not obey the appointees of the Archbishop after his death, seeing that it refused to obey him when he was alive.[5] Garcia now had a letter sent to the Chapter of Goa, asking it to confirm his nominee.[6]

The quarrel, however, ended soon, since Fr. Barretto refused to accept the nomination of Garcia and since the latter died before he could think of any other nominee. In his letter of 4 September to Ignatius Sarmento de Carvalho, the Commissary praised the prudence and good sense shown by Fr. Barretto in refusing the nomination. He pointed out to the general that the Archbishop could not legally appoint Fr. Barretto to be the governor of the Serra, since it was against the mind of the king of Portugal who, because of the rebellion of the Serra, had nominated Fr. Barretto to the see of Cochin, though earlier he had been nominated to the see of Cranganore. Besides, canon law and the universal practice of the Roman Church did not authorize bishops to nominate governors at their death.[7]

Archbishop Garcia breathed his last in the early hours of 3 September 1659. Fr. De Magistris who was by the side of his dying leader and friend, tells us that death came at about an hour after midnight.[8] It is again Fr. De Magistris that tells us that on the very last day of Dom Garcia's life on earth, during some lucid interval he bade good-bye, by letter, to the viceroy, to the city of Cochin and to its cathedral chapter. He called to his bedside the clergy and the people of the fortress of Cranganore, to bless them and to recommend himself to their prayers. He was calm and serene, though all the others were weeping.[9]

---

[5] *Ibid.*

[6] APF, *SOCG 233*, f. 238: Brevis et succincta relatio ...

[7] ARSI, *Goa 68-I*, f. 331.

[8] *SOCG 233*, f. 378: letter of Fr. De Magistris to the Chapter of Goa on 8 September 1659.

The testimony of so qualified a witness as Fr. De Magistris should be sufficient to remove all the confusion regarding the date of Garcia's death, caused by the letters of Fr. Hyacinth of St. Vincent. The latter mentioned 2 September in some of his letters and 4 September in some others! (Cf. *SOCG 234*, ff. 228, 229; *SOCG 233*, f. 238; *SOCG 232*, ff. 385, 387, 343).

[9] ARSI, *Goa 68-II*, f. 746v: Ecclesiae Cranganorensis ... Calamitates.

At the moment of the death of Garcia nine churches of the St. Thomas Christians were obedient to him.[10] The Cattanars of all these churches must have gone to take part in the solemn exequies of the Archbishop, held on the thirtieth day after his death, for we are told that on that day about 40 Cattanars celebrated mass for Garcia and took part in the office of the dead. Not all the 40 Cattanars, of course, belonged to these nine churches. There were those that were remaining permanently at the house of the Archbishop because they had been driven out of their churches by the rebels. We are told also that during the thirty days that intervened between Garcia's death and the solemn exequies, the Cattanars sang mass daily for him.[11]

Fr. De Magistris did not want to yield so quickly over the question of the appointment of a governor for the Serra. Seeing that Fr. Barretto did not want to do anything against the Commissary, Fr. De Magistris wrote on 8 September to the chapter of Goa. After explaining that the Commissary could not be the ordinary of the Serra because he had not been presented by the king of Portugal, Fr. De Magistris urged the Chapter to do what it "judged best in the Lord".[12]

When it became known that quite a number of Cattanars would get together for the exequies of the Archbishop, Fr. Hyacinth of St. Vincent suspected that Fr. De Magistris

---

[10] APF, *SOCG 232*, f. 352: sworn statement of Deacon Varghese on 13 September 1659. He was the Malayalam secretary of Garcia.

By putting together various bits of information we can find out that the nine churches were the following: the larger church of Kaduthuruthy, the larger church of Kottayam, and the churches of Udayamperur, Turgolim, Chembu, Elaur, Vaipicotta, Kallurkadu and Kudamaloor. The last three submitted to Garcia because of the intervention of their kings at the instance of Ignatius Sarmento de Carvalho. The first four churches were Southist churches and they had practically never rejected Garcia. Also the church of Elaur belonged to the Southists. Chembu had a considerable number of Southists. (See *SOCG 232*, f. 250: letter of Fr. De Magistris to Fr. Hyacinth). These two churches followed the example of the other four in the 1658 or 1659. (Cf. *SOCG 234*, f. 118).

[11] ARSI, *Goa 68-I*, f. 357 (also ff. 359 and 176): sworn statement of Fr. Francisco Teixeira: "vigario da vara" of the fortress of Cranganore, and of several citizens on 6 October 1659. — *Goa 68-II*, ff. 745v-746: narration by Fr. De Magistris.

[12] APF, *SOCG 233*, f. 378: an attested copy of the letter of De Magistris.

might make use of the occasion to get the Cattanars to elect
a governor for the Serra. Hence on 1 October he issued an
official warning to the Cattanars and forbade them under
pain of excommunication to take part in any such election.[13]

A few days later when the Commissary himself wanted
to have a governor elected and for this purpose called together the religious, Ignatius Sarmento de Carvalho forbade
him in the name of the king of Portugal, saying that that
right belonged to the king, and the fact of Fr. Hyacinth
being a papal commissary did not authorize him to do that.[14]

In the meantime the Jesuit superiors of Malabar decided to send Fr. De Magistris to Rome to plead the cause
of the Society of Jesus before the Roman Curia.[15] This time
he did not go via Lisbon but via Aleppo.[16] But before Fr. De
Magistris could reach Rome, the Pope had already decided
to consecrate Sebastiani as bishop and to send him to India.
In fact, Sebastiani was well on his way to India before
Fr. De Magistris arrived in the Eternal City. All the same,
Fr. De Magistris presented to the Pope and to the Propaganda the Jesuit case as persuasively as he could.[17] But it was
the voice of Sebastiani that prevailed. In a letter, dated 18
december 1662, Fr. John Paul Oliva, the vicar general of
the Society of Jesus, promised the Pope and the Sacred
Congregation of the Propaganda that Fr. De Magistris would
not be sent to the East without the express permission of
the Holy Father and of the Propaganda.[18]

---

[13] *Goa 68-II*, f. 753: the original of the warning by the Commissary. — *Goa 68-I*, f. 357: Statement of Fr. Francisco Teixeira etc. —
Ibid., f. 319: "Eccettione di sospetto" prepared by the Jesuits against
the Commissaries.

[14] *Goa 68-I*, f. 357: Statement of Fr. Francisco Teixeira etc.

[15] *Ibid.*, f. 332: letter of Fr. Barretto to the Jesuit general on 15
May 1659.

[16] APF, *SOCG 234*, ff. 142-143: letter of M. Piquet, the French
consul at Aleppo, to the Propaganda on 2 July 1660.

[17] Cf. ARSI, *Goa 68-II*, ff. 738-752 (also APF, *SOCG 233*, ff. 333-358);
Goa 68-II, ff. 613-616; *Goa 68-I*, ff. 318-319; *Goa 68-II*, ff. 520-523; *Goa
50*, ff. 177-187.

[18] APF, *SOCG 231*, f. 111.

(VI)

A SUMMARY ACCOUNT OF THE CHIEF EVENTS FROM THE DEATH OF ARCHBISHOP GARCIA TO THE CONSECRATION OF BISHOP CHANDY PARAMPIL

The death of Archbishop Garcia removed from the scene one of the major obstacles to reunion. But Archdeacon Thomas and Cattanar Ittithommen devised a new trick to deceive the simple people and to prevent them from deserting the pseudo-bishop. An Armenian or Syrian merchant called Stephen had reached Cochin in June 1659 to buy pepper and spices. A little after the death of Garcia, Stephen was promised a large sum of money by the Archdeacon, provided he would pose as the nephew of "the newly elected Pope". Stephen was expected to declare that he had been sent by his uncle to deliver to Thomas Parampil a brief which confirmed Thomas as archbishop and patriarch of the St. Thomas Christians. In the months that followed, the fictitious brief was solemnly presented by Stephen to the Archdeacon and exhibited at some meetings held in those kingdoms that were then at war with the king of Cochin and his allies, the Portuguese. Because of this war, several of the kings did not allow Fr. Hyacinth of St. Vincent to enter their kingdoms and to refute the false brief by showing the true ones. The Archdeacon and Stephen despoiled the churches in order to pay huge bribes to the kings and to their officials, so that they might be hardened in their opposition to the Apostolic Commissary. Fr. Hyacinth thus found himself unable to help the faithful Cattanars and Christians. But he was happy to see that they resisted gallantly in spite of their inferiority in numbers. The impudence and audacity of Stephen and his friends went so far that they cited Fr. Hyacinth to appear before a council to be held at Edapally, to answer the charge of "usurping" the title of apostolic commissary and of unjustly persecuting the Christians and their lawful prelate, Thomas Parampil. The schismatics had the effrontery to write to the captain and to the senate of Cochin to bring Fr. Hyacinth under arrest to the council, in case he refused to appear of his own free will![1]

The whole affair ended rather comically. Since Thomas showed himself reluctant to pay the money that he had promised to Stephen, the latter in a fit of rage, tried to kill him with a sword. Thomas was lucky enough to escape with only a wound on his left shoulder. Soon some others intervened and pacified them. Thomas now wrote to the churches that were devoted to him, to provide Stephen with cinnamon and pepper to be taken to the Pope as a present, since the Pope found himself in need at that time. Stephen could thus leave for his homeland with great satisfaction.[2]

The relations between the Apostolic Commissary and the churches obedient to Garcia improved very much after Garcia's death. This may be seen from the letter which the churches of Kaduthuruthy, Udayamperur, Kottayam, Turgolim, Chembu and Elaur wrote to the Pope on 4 July 1660.[3] Still Fr. Hyacinth found himself faced with a number of difficulties. Interested persons had spread the rumour that his commission had ended with the death of Archbishop Garcia, since it had been given merely to bring the Christians to the obedience of the Archbishop. The vicars in the Portuguese dominions therefore pretended that they were independent of him. He was unable to visit the greater part of the other churches because of the wars of the local kings with the king of Cochin and because he had no money to maintain interpreters and notaries.[4]

At the beginning of 1660 the mother of the Archdeacon died at Kuravilangad. A very large number of Cattanars and Christians went to take part in the burial. With the

---

[1] APF, *SOCG 234*, f. 228: Fr. Hyacinth to the Propaganda on 3.4.1660. — *SOCG 232*, f. 385 (also f. 387): Fr. Hyacinth to the Propaganda on 15 October 1659. — SEBASTIANI, *Seconda Speditione*, pp. 55-56. — *SOCG 234*, f. 239: Sebastiani to the Propaganda on 1.1.1662. — *SOCG 233*, f. 238: Brevis et succincta relatio...

[2] *SOCG 234*, f. 239: Sebastiani to the Propaganda on 1.1.1662.

[3] *Ibid.*, f. 118.

[4] *SOCG 234*, f. 229: Fr. Hyacinth to the Propaganda on 29.3.1660.

help of the assembled multitudes the Archdeacon tried to evict the vicar (Fr. Chandy Parampil) and the lay administrators of the church of Kuravilangad. He won over the local chieftain with gifts, and persecuted the vicar and his family so much that they were forced to appeal to the Commissary to go to their rescue. In spite of serious physical ailments, Fr. Hyacinth went to Kaduthuruthy on 8 May 1660 to obtain for his Christians the protection of the king. The latter promised to oblige the Commissary, provided he would bring about a reconciliation between himself (the king) and the Portuguese general, Ignatius Sarmento de Carvalho. Fr. Hyacinth succeeded to achieve this in spite of serious difficulties, thanks to the great interest that Ignatius Sarmento showed in reuniting the rebel Christians. According to the terms of the treaty signed by the Portuguese general and the rajah of Kaduthuruthy at Chembu on 10 August 1660, the Archdeacon was to be expelled from the kingdom of Kaduthuruthy (Vadakkankur) and also from the kingdom of Thekkankur which was ruled by a nephew of the rajah.

While these negotiations were going on at a higher level, the vicar of Kuravilangad was imprisoned for a month by the local chieftain, on the charge of disobedience to the Archdeacon. The Commissary complained to the king about this, and the king in his turn, deprived the Archdeacon of his liberty. After the signing of the treaty of Chembu, the king forced the Archdeacon to quit his territory, in spite of the fact that he had taken asylum in a spot sacred to the idols. The local chief of Kuravilangad, however, sent an escort of 40 soldiers to conduct Thomas to safety in the kingdom of Thekkankur.[5]

Even before the happy end of these negotiations Fr. Hyacinth was forced to retire to Cochin, because his sickness became more serious. He died in Cochin on 10 February 1661 and was buried with great pomp in the cathedral of Cochin. Six days before his death he had appointed his companion, Fr. Marcel of St. Ives, as his delegate, giving him all his powers.[6]

Fr. Marcel did not need to exercise for long his powers

---

[5] *SOCG 233*, ff. 238v-239: Brevis et succincta relatio...

[6] *Ibid.*, ff. 69, 239. — *SOCG 234*, f. 177: Sebastiani to the Propaganda on 15.3.1661. — *Ibid.*, f. 239v: Sebastiani to the Propaganda on 1.1.1662.

as subdelegate, since Bishop Sebastiani reached Cochin on 14 May of the same year.[7]   Nevertheless during his short tenure of power he had to face the serious situation caused by the appointment of Canon Manoel Serrão de Nabais, the treasurer of the cathedral of Cochin and a friend of the Jesuits, as the administrator of the Serra.   The appointment was made by the minority group of the chapter of Goa.[8] (The Archbishopric of Goa was vacant at this time and the chapter had split into two irreconcilable factions, the majority group residing at the cathedral and the minority group staying at the convent of the Reformed Franciscans, outside the city).[9]

Though Fr. Bras de Azevedo S.J. would have us believe that the appointment of Canon Serrão came as a matter of course, it is rather hard to accept his interpretation of the event.   He says blandly that when the news reached Goa that there was no pastor in the Serra, the chapter appointed Canon Serrão as governor.   To begin with, the appointment was made nearly two years after the death of Garcia!   Besides, it seems almost certain that Bishop Sebastiani was already in Goa when the appointment was made.[10] In fact, Sebastiani says in so many words that the chapter of Goa appointed a governor for the Serra at the instance of the Jesuits.   They made this request, continues Sebastiani, because they learned of his coming and wanted to prevent in all possible ways his entry into the Serra.[11]   Sebastiani's accusation is fully confirmed by a certain Fr. Carlo Ferrari, a Theatine, working in Goa.[12]

---

[7] *SOCG 234*, f. 504.

[8] *SOCG 233*, f. 182v: Breve racconto di tutto l'operato da Mons. F. Gioseppe. — *SOCG 234*, f. 183: Statement of Fr. Carlo Ferrari, a Theatine, on 13.4.1661. — ARSI, *Goa 49*, f. 197: narration by Fr. Bras de Azevedo S.J.

[9] *SOCG 233*, ff. 208 sq.: Breve racconto di quanto in Goa è successo a Monsig. di Hierapoli ...

[10] Bishop Sebastiani reached Goa on 24 February 1661. (Cf. *SOCG 234*, f. 504), and the news of the appointment of Canon Serrão as governor, reached Cochin on 14 April of the same year. (Cf. *SOCG 233*, f. 239; *SOCG 234*, ff. 6 sq; SEBASTIANI, *Seconda Speditione*, p. 58).

[11] *SOCG 234*, f. 239: Sebastiani to the Propaganda on 1.1.1662. — *SOCG 233*, f. 182v: Breve racconto di tutto l'operato da Mons. F. Gioseppe ...

[12] *SOCG 234*, f. 183: Fr. Ferrari's statement on 13 April 1661.

Somehow or other Sebastiani came to know of this appointment when he was still in Goa. Hence he was able to speak with the Chief Inquisitor (Castellino de Freitas) and the governor of Portuguese India (Francisco de Melo e Castro). With their help he induced the same faction of the Goan chapter that had appointed Canon Serrão, to issue an order to him not to resist Sebastiani. The other faction of the chapter was only too happy to send a rigorous order to Serrão not to accept the nomination.[13]

When the news of the appointment of Canon Serrão as administrator of the Serra reached Cochin, Fr. Marcel of St. Ives threatened to excommunicate him if he accepted the nomination. But the canon was not very much impressed by Fr. Marcel's threats. It was only after Bishop Sebastiani entered Cochin that Canon Serrão came to the conclusion that further resistance would be useless and even ridiculous. Hence he submitted to Sebastiani.[14]

As has already been mentioned, Sebastiani and his companions reached Cochin on 14 May 1661. He had been secretly consecrated a bishop in Rome on 15 December 1659.[15] Very wide powers were given him in order to enable him to solve the problems as they arose. Thus the brief "Iniuncti nobis divinitus" of 17 December 1659 appointed him apostolic commissary and administrator of the whole of the Serra, "tam superstite quam defuncto praedicto Francisco Garcia Archiepiscopo".[16] The brief "Pro commissa nobis", dated 24 December 1659, authorized him to hand over the administration of the archdiocese of Angamaly to one or two native priests whom he would appoint as vicars apostolic, after giving them episcopal consecration.[17] A third brief ("Magna accensione"), issued on 20 January 1660, ordered Garcia (already dead!) to give up the government of his diocese and to abstain from all exercise of the power of episcopal orders and of jurisdiction within the diocese.[17a]

---

[13] *SOCG 233*, f. 182v: Breve racconto di tutto l'operato da Mons. F. Gioseppe ...

[14] ARSI, *Goa 49*, f. 197: narration by Fr. Bras de Azevedo. — *SOCG 233*, f. 239v: Brevis et succincta relatio ...

[15] *SOCG 232*, f. 420.

[16] *Jus Pontificium de Prop. Fide*, vol. I, pp. 314-317.

[17] *Ibid.*, pp. 317-318.

[17a] ASV, *Secr. Brev. 1362*, f. 297.

Since Sebastiani had with him the letters of recommendation from the governor and the Chief Inquisitor of Goa, Ignatius Sarmento de Carvallo was ready to offer him all possible help. This was a very fortunate circumstance for Sebastiani, since it is admitted by everyone (including Sebastiani and his companions) that without the powerful help of the general, Sebastiani would not have been able to achieve much. Fr. Marcel of St. Ives, for instance, writing to the Propaganda on 30 November 1661, reported that after the coming of Bishop Sebastiani nine churches of the kingdom of Cochin submitted, not of their own free will, but forced by the king because of the insistence of the general. But further progress was stopped for the time being, because of the threat of the Dutch. The general was busy with the defence arrangements and hence could not help the bishop, and without his help nothing could be achieved with the local kings. Sebastiani too says more or less the same thing in some of his letters.[18]

To admit the part played by Ignatius Sarmento de Carvalho is not the same as to deny the merit of Sebastiani. The latter worked hard with great zeal all the time. As soon as the rainy season was over, he was on the move, going from one church to another, receiving their submission, conferring the sacrament of Confirmation and appointing capable vicars. Thus he visited the churches of Muttam, Kallurkadu, Pallipuram and Udayamperur. When on his way to Udayamperur, Sebastiani agreed to a proposal made by the rebels of Kandanadu that the division among the St. Thomas Christians should be settled by an examination of the credentials of the two rival heads, viz Sebastiani and Archdeacon Thomas. The examination was to take place at Tripunittura, before the court of the aged queen of Cochin. The Archdeacon, needless to say, could not produce any

---

[18] APF, *SOCG 234*, f. 429: Fr. Marcel to the Propaganda on 30.11.1661. — *Ibid.*, f. 239v: Sebastiani to the Propaganda on 1.1.1662: "*con la forza e favore di questo Capitan Generale* di Coccino, chiamato Ignatio Sarmento di Carvaglio, molto stimato e temuto dai Re Malavari, *fui ricevendo l'obbedienza di molte chiese...*". — *Ibid.*, ff. 216v-219: Sebastiani to the Carmelite superiors on 30 October 1661: "gran fortuna però è la mia l'haver detto Capitan Generale, perché *senza lui si poteva operar poco o niente*". — *Ibid.*, ff. 242, 243. — Cf. also the letter sent to the Pope by the chapter of Cochin on 7 September 1661. (*SOCG 234*, ff. 202-203).

papal document in his favour. But his astute counsellor, Cattanar Ittithommen, managed to find out a thousand means to waste time and to get the final decision postponed from day to day. Sebastiani realised that the intention of the Archdeacon was to wear out his patience and to waste time, hoping that in the meantime the Dutch would attack and capture Cochin. With that, Sebastiani would be forced to return to Europe and Thomas could become complete master of the situation. Sebastiani therefore made an appeal to Ignatius Sarmento de Carvalho to make an effort to capture the Archdeacon and Cattanar Ittithommen. The attempt was made on 9 October 1661, but it failed. The two managed to escape, disguised as Hindu soldiers. But in their hurry they left behind a number of documents which offered further proof of their bad faith. Several of the churches of the kingdom of Cochin (Kandanadu, Malamthuruthy, southern Paravoor, Nadamè and Caringachira) now made their submission to Sebastiani.[19]

The antagonism between the Jesuits and the Apostolic Commissary was even now as pronounced as it had been in the past. Sebastiani asserts that the Jesuits of Goa sent a letter to Ignatius Sarmento de Carvalho at about this time (i.e. after the attempt of the general to capture the Archdeacon), blaming him for helping the Carmelites. They told him that his going to Udayamperur to help the foreign Carmelites, created a very bad impression at the viceregal court of Goa. It was sure to produce a much worse impression at the court of Lisbon, since the general was helping in an enterprise which seriously harmed the royal jurisdiction. The Jesuits reminded him of their power and influence at the courts of Lisbon and Goa and taxed him with ingratitude, in as much as he was helping their enemies, even though his father owed so much to the Society of Jesus. They told him that the Carmelites would take all the glory for themselves, in spite of the fact that he did all the work.[20]

Also in several letters which Sebastiani wrote to the Propaganda, he spoke of the many efforts made by the

---

[19] *SOCG 233*, ff. 183-185: Breve racconto di tutto l'operato da Mons. F. Gioseppe ... — SEBASTIANI, *Seconda Speditione*, pp. 69-91.

[20] *SOCG 234*, f. 241 (also 240): a copy. It is but fair to point out that the authenticity of this letter rests on the affirmation of Sebastiani alone. It is not authenticated by any notary or witness.

Jesuits with the governors and the ministers of Goa, in order to have him thrown out of India. In one of these letters he says that if he were to say more on the point, he would be regarded as a liar, even though he would be saying only less than what was actually taking place.[21]

From December 1661 onwards the danger of a Dutch attack on Cochin became imminent. Quilon fell to them in December and Cranganore on 15 January 1662. At the beginning of February Cochin itself was attacked. Sebastiani decided to retire to Muttam, so that he would not be cut off from his flock during the siege. When the first rains started in March, the Dutch were forced to raise the siege and to withdraw to Cranganore. But it was evident that they would return as soon as the rainy season would end. Hence Sebastiani decided to continue his pastoral visit in spite of the heavy rains. He visited the churches of Chowara, Kanjoor and Malayattur. Then through the recommendation of Ignatius Sarmento de Carvalho he obtained the permission of the kings of Mangat-Angamaly to enter their territory. Nearly three months were spent in that region. But in the end he obtained the submission of the important churches of Angamaly and Mangat and also of some other neighbouring churches.[22]

The Dutch began the siege of Cochin once again in the month of September 1662. In spite of the insistence of Ignatius Sarmento who would have liked Sebastiani, to remain in Cochin during the siege, the latter decided to go to Muttam and from there to Kaduthuruthy. But he left behind in Cochin two of his companions, viz Fr. Marcel of St. Ives (a German) and Fr. Godfrey of St. Andrew (a Fleming).[23]

Cochin was forced to surrender to the Dutch on 7 January 1663.[24] The conquerors decided that all the priests and the religious except four or five Franciscans should immediately leave the city. According to a signed testimony

----

[21] *SOCG 234*, f. 244v: Sebastiani to the Propaganda on 1.1.1662. — *Ibid.*, f. 246v: Sebastiani to the Propaganda in December 1661. — *Ibid.*, f. 247v: Sebastiani to the Propaganda on 4.1.1662. — *Ibid.*, f. 385: Sebastiani to the Propaganda on 30.8.1662.

[22] *SOCG 233*, ff. 186-189: Breve racconto di tutto l'operato da Mons. F. Gioseppe... — SEBASTIANI, *Seconda Speditione*, pp. 101-122.

of the three Carmelite companions of Sebastiani,[25] Fr. Godfrey of St. Andrew (a Fleming) who was then in Cochin, tried his best to convince Rijkloff van Goens, the Dutch commander, to leave Sebastiani and his companions in the Serra. But the reply which he received after a consultation of the general and his council was that, because of the strict orders of the Dutch East India Company not to leave any ecclesiastic in their conquests, the Carmelites would also have to leave Malabar. They would be sent away in a friendly way to Persia or to some other place. Fr. Godfrey was asked to see that Bishop Sebastiani reached Cochin within four days. For this purpose the general issued him a passport. Sebastiani was very sad to receive this news. He tried unsuccessfully several times, both by letter and in person, to obtain the permission to remain. But the general remained inflexible on this point. In the end Sebastiani decided to leave Malabar, because he realised that if he remained in some remote region of Malabar against the wish of the Dutch, the latter would bribe the kings to force the Christians to obey the Archdeacon, and that would ruin his work completely.[26]

Before leaving Malabar, Sebastiani decided to confer the episcopal consecration on one of the faithful Cattanars and to appoint him vicar apostolic of the archdiocese of Angamaly, in virtue of the provisions of the brief "Pro commissa nobis". His choice as well as that of the representatives of the churches that had been invited to meet him at Kaduthuruthy, fell on Fr. Chandy (Alexander) Parampil, the vicar of Kuravilangad and a cousin of Archdeacon Thomas.

---

[23] SEBASTIANI, *Seconda Speditione*, pp. 124-125. — Cf. *SOCG 233*, f. 415 for the nationality of Frs. Marcel and Godfrey.

[24] *SOCG 234*, f. 504.

[25] The three Carmelites were: Fr. Marcel of St. Ives, Fr. John Thaddeus of St. Brigit and Fr. Godfrey of St. Andrew.

[26] *SOCG 233*, ff. 415-416: the signed testimony of the 3 Carmelites. — Since this statement was made by Fr. Godfrey who actually negotiated with Rijkloff, I am inclined to reject as unfounded the assertion of Fr. Bras de Azevedo (Cf. *Goa 49*, ff. 200-201) and Fr. De Magistris (Cf. *Goa 21*, f. 41), that Sebastiani left Malabar only because he found that he could not lead a comfortable life there after the capture of Cochin by the Dutch. The statement of Fr. Bras de Azevedo is based on hearsay, and that of Fr. De Magistris is even more so, since he was in Europe at that time.

He was consecrated titular bishop of Megara on 1 February 1663. The Archdeacon and his adviser, Cattanar Ittithommen, were then solemnly excommunicated by Sebastiani.[27]

According to a sworn statement of the Carmelite companions of Sebastiani and of the five priests from the diocese of Cochin who served as interpreters etc., the new bishop was about fifty years old and was noted for his piety, prudence, seriousness, modesty and compassion for the poor. In short, he was a man of exemplary life.[28] Fr. Bras de Azevedo S.J. too, agrees that he was a man of good life. But he adds that he was without any learning. All what he knew was a bit of Syriac to say Mass.[29] In a letter to the Jesuit General on 18 September 1665, Fr. De Magistris S.J. wrote that as vicar of Kuravilangad, Bishop Chandy had been very hostile to the Jesuits and that he was one of those most responsible for the expulsion of the Jesuits from the Serra.[30]

Sebastiani left Malabar on 14 February 1663 after obtaining an assurance from General Rijkloff that the Dutch would favour Bishop Chandy and not the pseudo-bishop.[31] The Dutch kept their promise at least for some time and Bishop Chandy was able to continue the work of reunion.[32] But in spite of some modest success achieved by Bishop Chandy, the divisions among the St. Thomas Christians that began with the rebellion of 1653, have unfortunately never been fully healed.

[27] *SOCG 233*, ff. 194-197: Breve racconto di tutto l'operato da Mons. F. Gioseppe... — *SOCG 234*, f. 504. — APF, *Acta 32*, f. 257: summary of a letter of Sebastiani to the Propaganda on 7 March 1663.

[28] ARSI, *Goa 49*, f. 157v: a copy.

[29] ARSI, *Goa 49*, f. 200v.

[30] *Goa 21*, f. 41.

[31] *SOCG 233*, ff. 198-202: Breve racconto di tutto l'operato da Mons. F. Gioseppe... — *SOCG 234*, f. 504.

[32] APF, *Acta 34*, f. 70. — *SOCG 233*, f. 429: Fr. João de S. Diogo, superior of the Franciscans of Cochin, to Sebastiani on 29 July 1663. — ARSI, *Goa 49*, f. 204: narration by Fr. Brás de Azevedo S.J.

A CRITICAL ESTIMATE OF ARCHBISHOP GARCIA

There is no doubt that right from the days when Francis Garcia was only a scholastic, his superiors esteemed him much. The high offices that he held for several years in the Goan province of the Society of Jesus, show that he continued to enjoy the esteem of the highest superiors of his religious family.

The list of the Indian languages that he knew well, is impressive. We are told that he knew Concani, Marathi, Tamil, Malayalam and Sanscrit. To this must be added Sinhalese, Syriac, Hebrew, Greek, Latin, Portuguese and Spanish. He was able to read nine different oriental scripts: three of Concani, two of Malayalam, two of Syriac, one of Hebrew and one of Tamil.[1] He showed great interest in Indian literature and folklore and was the first European to translate a number of tales directly from the Indian languages.[2]

For several years Garcia taught with distinction philosophy, speculative and moral theology, canon and civil law. He must have been a specialist in law, since he was the author of a much praised dictionary of canon and civil law.[3] The numerous little tracts that he composed in his defence against the papal commissaries,[4] are full of citations

---

[1] WICKI, *O Homem*, p. 326 (2nd appendix: a description by Fr. De Magistris). — ARSI, *Goa 50*, f. 98: refutation of the letter of the viceroy, dated 21 October 1653. — *Goa 68-II*, ff. 441v-442: Garcia to Sebastiani. — *Ibid.*, f. 377: Garcia's reply to the Goan Inquisitors in 1656.

[2] WICKI, *O Homem*.

[3] *Ibid.*, pp. 323-324 (1st appendix): Garcia's reply to the Goan Inquisitors in 1656. — *Goa 68-II*, ff. 441-442: Garcia to Sebastiani. — *Ibid.*, f. 444: testimony of Canon Francis de Figueredo Cardoso of Goa.

[4] These tracts are to be found in ARSI, *Goa 68-I and II*.

from jurists. Fr. De Magistris, his constant companion and friend, tells us that he composed in various languages the lives of the saints, some meditations and dialogues.[5] It is again from Fr. De Magistris that we learn that Garcia had a talent for arithmetic and music. All this proves that his intellectual capacities were truly extraordinary.

Also in the practice of several virtues he easily surpassed the ordinary ecclesiastics and religious of his day. Fr. John of St. Joseph, the Franciscan rector of their college of Cranganore, says that Garcia was generally considered as an example of virtue to others in those parts.[6] His charity towards the poor was really exceptional. We are told that he sheltered and looked after the orphans until they were able to stand on their own. He established a "monte pio" (a sort of charitable bank) for the people of Cranganore. The poor could borrow from it, the only condition being that if they failed to pay back, they would be debarred from borrowing again. In his last years he was so liberal in almsgiving that he nearly ran the risk of remaining without anything for himself. In the Jesuit college of Cranganore he deposited enough money for distribution to the poor for two years after his death.[7]

His diligence in the faithful performance of the practices of piety was exemplary. His house was like a religious house. Every day he celebrated holy mass and applied it to the holy souls in Purgatory. Besides this, he heard another mass daily on his knees. For meditation and examination of conscience he used to follow the bell of the Jesuit college of Cranganore. During the last days of his life he said that all through the 63 years that he spent in the Society of Jesus he was never aware of having offended God mortally.[8]

There are also several witnesses that testify to Garcia's zeal in visiting his archdiocese, in the administration of the sacraments, in providing for the proper adornment of the churches etc. It is narrated by Fr. De Magistris that Garcia

---

[5] WICKI, O Homem, p. 326 (2nd appendix).

[6] Goa 68-II, f. 566: statement made on 19 June 1658.

[7] WICKI, O Homem, pp. 327-329 (2nd appendix). — Goa 68-I, f. 265: testimony of 27 citizens of Cochin on 2.6.1658. — Goa 49, f. 196v: narration by Fr. Bras de Azevedo S.J.

[8] WICKI, O Homem, pp. 327-329. — FRANCO, Ano Santo, p. 506.

trained children in various dances, so that with this as well as other attractions like games he could gather the people in the churches for instruction.[9]

Garcia was also a great patriot. He repaired at his own cost the fortifications of Cranganore. Several times he paid the salaries of the hard pressed soldiers of the garrison. In times of danger he himself with his clerics patrolled the fortress in the night. Many people asserted that it was due to his vigilance and care that the fortress of Cranganore stood till his death. It was because of all this that when the city of Cochin was threatened by the Dutch in 1658-1659, the citizens insisted on Garcia taking over the defence of the town, even though he was then nearly 80 years old.[10]

In spite of all these exceptional qualities of head and heart, and in spite of the success that he had earlier as a Jesuit superior, the fact remains that as archbishop of Cranganore he was a dismal failure. It would seem that the explanation of it is to be sought in certain defects of his character and in the objective difficulty of the task that was assigned to him. In the second chapter the testimonies of his adversaries as well as those of his friends were cited to show that he was by nature harsh and intransigent. As a superior in the Society of Jesus where the subjects were constantly encouraged to obey "blindly" their superiors, these unfortunate traits did not bring about the deleterious effects that they produced among the freedom-loving Cattanars and people of Malabar, who were far less accustomed and disposed to obey. Besides, in the Society he respected his subjects as his confreres and collaborators. In the Serra on the other hand, he generally distrusted and despised the Cattanars and the Christians as so many "liars and deceivers". (see section 2 of chapter 3, where a number of passages from Garcia's own writings have been cited). One cannot be surprised, then, if he failed to gain the hearts of his priests and of his flock. Hence the latter were ready

---

[9] *Goa 68-II*, f. 687: statement of 8 Cattanars and one deacon on 20 December 1658. — *Ibid.*, ff. 549, 580 etc. — WICKI, *O Homem*, pp. 326-328.

[10] *Ibid.* — *Goa 68-II*, f. 746: Ecclesiae Cranganorensis ... Calamitates. — *Ibid.*, f. 586: the statement of Dom Manoel de Menezes, a former captain of Cranganore, on 22 June 1658. — *Goa 68-I*, ff. 39-40: statement of the chapter of Cochin on 22.11.1653.

to give a willing ear to Archdeacon Thomas who felt ag-
grieved because of Garcia's efforts to deprive him of his
traditional privileges and prerogatives.

When going through the pages which Garcia wrote regarding the behaviour of the Archdeacon, one can easily
have an idea of Garcia's unyielding nature. With inflexible
logic Garcia tries to show that he had every right to deny
Thomas any share in the amount that he realised from
fines. He asks: "Am I bound to pay him when he, far from
helping me in anything, places all sorts of obstacles in my
way? Besides, he has shown not the least desire to give
back the 3,500 fanams which he took from my church.
(i.e. the old cathedral church of Angamaly). So even if I
owed him this money in strict justice, I would nevertheless
be allowed by the same justice to retain it as compensa-
tion".[11] What I would like to point out is that, while his
logic is quite unassailable, he seems to have forgotten that
he was alienating the Archdeacon for such petty reasons as
this. Yielding on minor points like this, he could have kept
peace with the Archdeacon. In fact, his predecessor whom
he is inclined to dismiss as too weak, succeeded to a very
large extent in maintaining peace with the Archdeacon. Garcia instead preferred to break him, forgetting that he was
ruling a foreign church which had a long tradition of its
own, which he was bound to respect.

Also the way in which Garcia handled the situation after
the outbreak of the general rebellion of 1653, was far from
satisfactory. His excessive desire to save his own honour
and that of the Jesuit missionaries, and to retain the Serra
as the close preserve of the Society of Jesus, made him
impervious to all the suggestions that were made by the
authorities of Goa to appoint a non-Jesuit governor for the
Serra and to allow the other religious to go there to explain
to the people that Atallah had not been sent from Rome.
The quick application of this drastic remedy would in all
probability have saved the situation. But the positions became hardened as time passed. Even after the arrival of
the papal commissaries, he created difficulties for them by
maintaining that those who agreed to abandon the rebellious
Archdeacon and to obey the Pope and the Commissary sent

---

[11] ARSI, *Goa 68-II*, ff. 525-528. (see especially f. 526v).

by him, but who did not promise obedience to himself, could not be said to be reunited to the Church. He refused to see that there was a possibility of ending the schism even without re-establishing his authority.[12]

A certain amount of subjective justification for several of his actions and attitudes may be found in his conviction that he was bound to defend his jurisdiction even at the cost of his life.[13] This also explains how he was able to write to the general of the Jesuits on 8 December 1654 that his conscience was quite tranquil, since he did not feel that he was at fault for the schism.[14]

It has to be admitted that Garcia had a very difficult archdiocese to govern. But his own rigid character did not make his task any easier.

---

[12] Cf. *Goa 68-II*, ff. 442, 452-453, 535 etc.
[13] Cf. *Goa 68-I*, ff. 29, 181v; *Goa 68-II*, f. 410.
[14] *Goa 50*, f. 192v.

INDEX